Athletic Equipment Managers Certification Manual

EDITOR-IN-CHIEF

Dale Strauf, E.M.,C.
Head Equipment Manager
Cornell University
AEMA Member 26 Years
Certified 1991
Current AEMA President
Glenn Sharp Equipment Manager of the Year 1992

CONTRIBUTORS

Brian Allis, E.M.,C.
Assistant Equipment Manager
Cornell University
AEMA Member 11 Years
Certified 1994
Past District I Director

Alan Ansell, E.M.,C.
Head Equipment Manager
Bishops University
AEMA Member 15 Years
Certified 1991
Current AEMA Examination Chair and District 10 CEU Representative
Glenn Sharp Equipment Manager of the Year 1996

Donald Barnes, E.M.,C.
Head Equipment Manager
University of Missouri
AEMA Member 7 Years
Certified 2000
Current District 6 Director and Internet Committee Chair

Dorothy Cutting, E.M.,C.
Cornell University (Assistant Equipment Manager, Retired)
AEMA Member 19 Years
Certified 1991
Current AEMA Office Manager
Glenn Sharp Equipment Manager of the Year 1999

Mary O'Leary, E.M.,C.
Head Equipment Manager
Miami University (Ohio)
AEMA Member 20 Years
Certified 1991
Past AEMA Office Manager and Associate Executive Director
Glenn Sharp Equipment Manager of the Year 1991

Mark Litsky
President, Knowledge In Sanitary Systems (KISS) Industries
Laundry Consultant

Athletic Equipment Managers Certification Manual

AEMA National Office
460 Hunt Hill Rd.
Freeville, NY 13068
Dorothy Cutting, Office Manager
e-mail: dec13@cornell.edu
Phone: (607) 539-6300
Fax: (607) 539-6340
Web: www.aema1.com
List: aema-disc@aema1.com

MomentumMedia, Inc.
Ithaca, NY

Printed in the USA.

Table of Contents

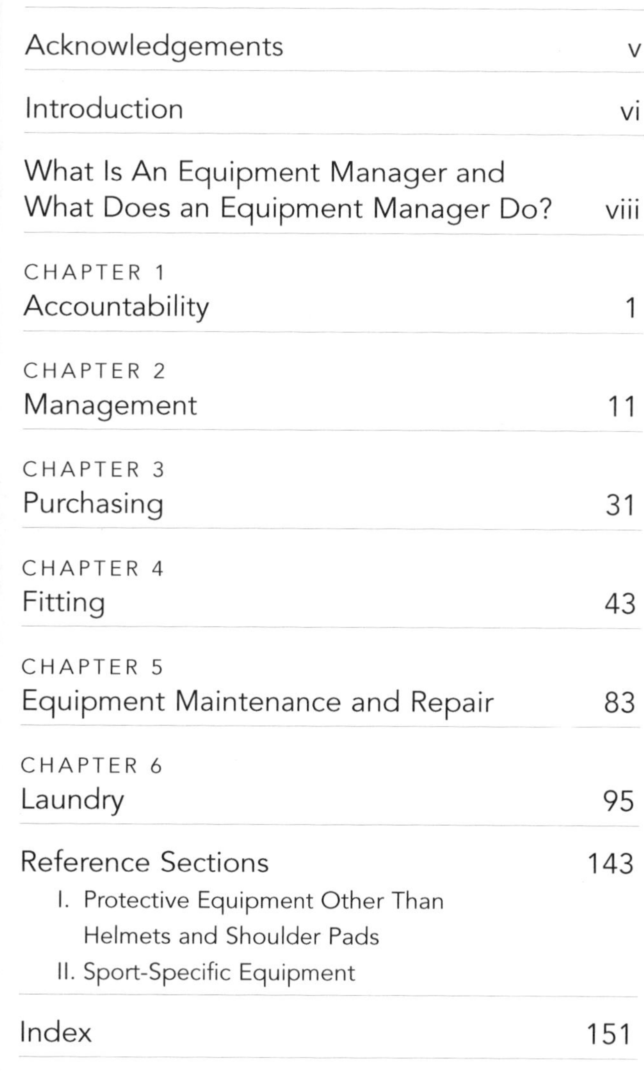

Jeff Boss:

A Tribute to a Devoted Member of the AEMA

On special occasions, I have taken a quote from Eleanor Roosevelt to describe my feelings toward very special people in my life. I think that I speak for the entire AEMA when I use this quote in reference to our feelings toward Jeff Boss. "Many people will walk in and out of your life, but only true friends will leave footprints in your heart." Jeff, you certainly left footprints in our hearts. We dedicate this Manual update to Jeff Boss because of his dedication to our profession and the AEMA.
— Dale Strauf, President, AEMA

Jeff Boss was at the heart of everything that LSU stands for. His positive attitude each and every day of the year was an inspiration to everyone who crossed his path. He made LSU a better place to be.
— Skip Bertman, LSU Director of Athletics

Jeff Boss was the best at what he did. More than that, he was without a doubt one of the absolute best people that you'd ever meet. You don't have many chances to meet someone who was as selfless as Jeff. He was always thinking of others and putting their feelings first. That quality above all others is something special that I wish everyone had, and I know it would make the world a better place because it certainly made LSU a better place. Jeff Boss was loved by everyone in our organization. We are going to miss him.
— Nick Saban, LSU Head Football Coach

Jeff Boss liked to do his work behind the scenes and with little fanfare. But there is no mistaking the mark he left on the equipment manager profession—and his impact will shine for years and years. Jeff played as great a role in the development of the profession and the AEMA as any member of the association. He was instrumental in the development of the Association Manual you hold in your hands. He raised the quality of the annual convention. He helped change the way equipment managers are viewed by athletic administrators at colleges and universities nationwide.

Jeff spent 24 years as an equipment manager at LSU. In 1990, he received the Glenn Sharp Award, which goes annually to the Equipment Manager of the Year as chosen by his peers. He had such a positive impact on the student managers who worked with him that 14 of them have gone on to enjoy successful careers in equipment management. Former proteges now work as full-time equipment managers at LSU, Oklahoma State, Tulane, Texas A&M, and Texas, while two are football operations directors at TCU and Clemson, respectively.

LSU honored Jeff by officially naming the football locker room in his honor. And the LSU football team dedicated the 2003 season to him. Jeff's spirit is a major reason the Tigers made it to the BCS National Championship Game that year. And his spirit is a major reason the AEMA will continue to flourish for many years to come.
— Mark Goldberg, Publisher, MomentumMedia

Acknowledgements

Certification in general terms still refers to the verification in writing of one's competence in a given profession. This Manual is designed to provide all the tools necessary to attain certification as an equipment manager. Many people came together to make this possible. Without the efforts of our original authors, this Manual update would be much less than it is. This is not a rewrite; much of the information was taken from the original Manual. Our original Manual was dedicated to Jim Roberts (the Father of Certification). The fact that we are dedicating this Manual to a different AEMA legend does not compromise the efforts displayed by Jim toward our Certification Program. Jim will always be AEMA Certification! We also acknowledge the tremendous efforts put forth by the other original contributors to this Manual: Gary Boevers, Jeff Boss, Charles Craig, Mike Davidson, Robert Jones, Dominic Morelli, Mary O'Leary, Sally Ross, Ron Salvemini, and Terry Schlatter.

Likewise, we thank the authors involved in our Manual update. Their dedication to the AEMA and the profession of athletic equipment management is above and beyond what is expected of our membership.

Introduction

AEMA AND ATHLETIC EQUIPMENT MANAGEMENT

Adapted from an article written by Dale Strauf for The NCAA News *(Vol. 39, No. 22, October 28, 2002).*

In 1974, a group of equipment managers met in Kansas City, Missouri, to form an organization that would work toward developing the profession of athletic equipment management. Ideas were discussed and goals and objectives were created. This original gathering of equipment managers marked the creation of the Athletic Equipment Managers Association. The goals that were established by these pioneers are still the very core of the association today:

- to promote a better working relationship among those persons interested in the problems of equipment management
- to further develop the professional ability of each member
- to better serve the common interest of membership by providing for free exchange of ideas within the profession
- to enable members to become better acquainted professionally through casual good fellowship
- to work as a group to bring equipment improvements for greater safety of participants

Today, the Athletic Equipment Managers Association is governed by an Executive Board consisting of 10 District Directors representing the United States and Canada, a President, Executive Director, Vice President, Associate Executive Director, Office Manager, and Treasurer. The membership consists of recreational and physical education, high school, college, and professional athletic equipment managers. The Executive Board meets twice a year at our National Convention.

Each year, the AEMA National Convention offers 20 educational workshops focusing on current issues in the profession. The National Convention serves as a perfect place for presenting annual AEMA awards, which include the following:

- The Membership Award (to the district with the most new members)
- The Newsletter Award (for the most informative district newsletters)
- Journal Articles (authors are awarded a cash prize)
- The Booker Kilgore Award (highest honor for a high school equipment manager)
- Scholarship Awards (six $500.00 scholarships are awarded to top students working in the field of athletic equipment management)
- Service Awards (presented for outstanding service to our association)
- The Glenn Sharp Equipment Manager of the Year Award (our most coveted award—voted on by the entire membership)
- The Lifetime Achievement Award (first awarded in 2003—voted on by committee)

At our National Convention, we also display a wall with photos of all Glenn Sharp Award and Lifetime Achievement Award winners.

A major goal of the Athletic Equipment Managers Association has always been to develop the professional ability of each member. At the onset, we needed to establish an educational program that would give equipment managers a certain level of proficiency in the performance of their jobs. To this end, Columbia Assessment Services (later renamed Castle Worldwide) was contracted to develop a Certification Standard for Athletic Equipment Management. Through a role delineation process, the following areas of job performance were identified for athletic equipment managers:

- Purchasing
- Fitting
- Equipment Maintenance and Repair
- Management
- Accountability

In 1991, certification in Athletic Equipment Management became a reality. Certification has never been a form of unionization to force recognition by the athletic community. Rather, it is an attempt to improve the profession of Athletic Equipment Management through education. We are confident that we will earn our recognition through a higher degree of job quality and efficiency. Certification candidates who meet the requirements are given the test at our National Convention. To be eligible to sit for the AEMA Certification Test, a candidate must:

- be a member in good standing;
- be 21 years of age; and
- be one of the following:
- a four-year college graduate with two years non-student employment in the profession,
- a high school graduate with five years non-student employment in the profession, or
- a four-year college graduate with 1800 hours documented student employment

The Association publishes a certification Manual, which you now hold in your hands. First put out in 1991, the Manual was completely revised in 2004 to meet the changing needs of equipment managers at all venues.

As of October 2002, there were 505 Certified Athletic Equipment Managers. The number of new members taking the Certification Test each year has consistently been above 60. Certification is bolstered by a host of other programs and initiatives. The Association has established a resource center, and has also developed the *AEMA Journal*, an annual publication written by professionals in the field of equipment management. Articles in the *Journal* are directed toward concerns within our role delineation areas. The AEMA publishes three national newsletters each year. The Association also has a Web site (www.aema1.com) that has a wealth of information. There is an on-line discussion group (mailto:aema-disc@aema1.com), which consists of equipment managers across the United States and Canada. And to coordinate it all, we opened our state-of-the-art National Office on January 7, 2002, in Freeville, New York.

The AEMA realizes that education fosters credibility. We want our profession to appreciate the highest level of credibility that we can achieve within the athletic community. The fact that we currently have two representatives on the National Operating Committee on Standards for Athletic Equipment (NOCSAE) and one representative on the NCAA Football Rules Committee are indicators of the progress that our profession has appreciated. Equipment managers also routinely occupy advisory committee positions for major manufacturers of athletic equipment.

Equipment managers will always issue towels, jocks, and socks, but our responsibilities have evolved into so much more. Equipment managers play a major role in the decision-making process for all aspects of equipment management. Our profession has earned the right to be responsible in professional sports, colleges, and high schools at all levels. We are confident that membership in the Athletic Equipment Managers Association and taking part in our certification program will greatly increase your job performance and efficiency while reducing the risk part of your equipment management operations.

We urge all equipment managers from all levels to get involved in our organization. Take the Certification Exam and maintain certification with Continuing Education. Attend our annual convention and our regional meetings. And make the most of this Manual, whether you're preparing to take the Certification Exam or looking into how best to upgrade part of your operations. We should strive to educate ourselves to the best of our abilities, because our athletes deserve the best.

What is an equipment manager and what does an equipment manager do?

The Athletic Equipment Managers Association's (AEMA) bylaws define an equipment manager as, "Any person who is actively engaged in the management and handling of athletic, physical education, and recreational equipment as a means of earning a living."

When beginning the first edition of this Manual, in the late 1980s, the hardest obstacle to overcome was answering the question, "What is an equipment manager and what does an equipment manager do?" An equipment manager can be a manager of one team; he or she can also be a manager of more than 30 teams. An equipment manager may be at the recreational level, such as health clubs, youth groups, or YMCAs. He or she may be at the high school level, or at any college level from community colleges up to Division I schools. He or she may be at the semi-pro or professional sports level. Some equipment managers are equipment managers/athletic directors/coaches/athletic trainers/grounds personnel. An equipment manager can be a combination of one or more—or even all—of the above.

Some equipment managers are in charge of only team laundry. Some issue equipment and secure the return of the equipment. Others purchase the equipment. Some equipment managers also are administrators within their organization. Others maintain all of the fields, grounds, and indoor and outdoor courts. The tasks of an equipment manager are hardly ever the same from one organization to another. But as defined in the AEMA bylaws as mentioned above, all equipment managers do have some things in common.

In the 1980s, in an attempt to answer the question, "What is an equipment manager and what does an equipment manager do?" the AEMA sent out a series of surveys to its members. These covered such areas as what venues equipment managers were employed in, their salaries, and the main responsibilities of their jobs. These surveys were compiled and used as the basis for a formal role delineation study, whose purpose was to determine the most appropriate content for the certification of entry-level athletic equipment managers.

This was the beginning of the AEMA's credentialing program. The major function of this program is to ensure competency and professionalism in the field of athletic equipment management. It provides assurance that the Certified Athletic Equipment Manager has met specific criteria and that he or she is competent in the provision of services.

The development of a quality credentialing or licensing program must follow certain logically sound and legally defensible procedures for creating a certification examination. These principles and procedures are outlined in federal regulation (Uniform Guidelines on Employee Selection Procedures) and manuals, such as Standards for Education and Psychological Testing (published by the American Education Research Association). In 1989, the AEMA contracted with Columbia Assessment Services, Inc. (CAS), later renamed Castle Worldwide, which adheres to all applicable standards in developing such examinations, to oversee its credentialing program.

Before a content-valid examination is developed, the knowledge and skills needed to be a competent professional in the field must be determined. The process for identifying these competency areas is a role delineation, or job analysis, which serves as a blueprint for developing the certification exam.

The job analysis study for the Athletic Equipment Managers Association consisted of the following three phases:

- *Initial Development and Validation.* The AEMA formed a Criterion-Referenced Testing Task Force, which identified the domains, tasks, knowledge, and skills essential to the performance of the duties of a Certified Athletic Equipment Manager.
- *Validation Study.* A study was mailed to 500 professionals in the field of athletic equipment management who then reviewed and validated the work of the job analysis panel.
- *Development of Test Specification.* Based on the ratings gathered from the representative sample of professionals, the test specifications for the certification examination were developed.

The results from the overall study showed that the certification exam should have five domains, each covered according to the following percentages:

1) Accountability 17.6%
2) Management..19.2%
3) Purchasing 17.6%
4) Fitting..22.2%
5) Maintenance & Repair
(including Laundry) 23.4%

The first edition of the AEMA Certification Manual was created to serve as an instructional tool for those wishing to become Certified Athletic Equipment Managers, as well as a reference for those in the field. Certain areas of this Manual go into more detail than is necessary for those preparing for the certification exam; yet, they are included because of this second function.

In 2002, the AEMA formed a diverse committee to review and upgrade the role delineation study. Based on its findings, the Certification Manual underwent a complete review; you now hold the revised and updated edition, which was published in 2004. The following report summarizes the domains, tasks, knowledge, and skill statements essential for anyone wishing to become a Certified Athletic Equipment Manager as delineated by the job analysis panel. Those studying for the exam should make sure they are proficient in each of these areas.

Accountability

1. Establish a system of distribution based on the characteristics and needs of the organization in order to ensure that the equipment/apparel is used by the appropriate end-user.

KNOWLEDGE OF:
a. accepted documentation methods
b. rules and regulations of applicable governing bodies
c. manufacturing specifications of each product
d. fitting specifications of each manufacturer
e. marking and/or identification systems
f. accurate record-keeping
g. computers

SKILL IN:
a. basic math
b. maintaining equipment database
c. legibly marking and identifying products
d. communicating importance of equipment/apparel distribution
e. communicating distribution knowledge with athletes and coaches

2. Establish a system of retrieval based on the characteristics and needs of the organization in order to ensure that all distributed equipment/apparel is returned.

KNOWLEDGE OF:
a. documentation methods
b. rules and regulations of applicable governing bodies
c. equipment/apparel replacement costs
d. marking and/or identification systems
e. necessary and/or mandatory documented information
f. accurate record-keeping
g. penalty system for non-returned items and items returned in poor condition

SKILL IN:
a. maintaining equipment database
b. legibly marking and identifying products
c. communicating retrieval knowledge with athletes and coaches

3. Establish a system of storage based on the characteristics and needs of the organization in order to ensure that stored equipment/apparel is properly secured, maintained, and available.

KNOWLEDGE OF:
a. storage systems to facilitate issue and inventory
b. storage systems to maximize available space
c. proper storage conditions (temperature, moisture, sun)
d. security systems to minimize theft
e. operational flow
f. penalty system for unreturned items
g. marking and/or identification systems

SKILL IN:
a. sorting equipment/apparel for proper storage
b. legibly marking and identifying products
c. communicating storage guidelines with athletes and coaches
d. complying with applicable rules and regulations governing safe and sanitary environments
e. complying with applicable rules and regulations when organizing equipment/apparel
f. utilizing security resources

4. Implement systems of distribution, retrieval, and storage based on the characteristics and needs of the organization in order to ensure that all equipment/apparel is accounted for at all times.

   KNOWLEDGE OF:
   a. accepted documentation methods
   b. accepted dissemination methods
   c. timelines
   d. rules and regulations of applicable governing bodies
   e. marking and/or identification systems
   f. necessary and/or mandatory documented information
   g. accurate record-keeping
   h. computers
   i. manufacturing specifications of each product
   j. fitting specifications of each manufacturer
   k. security systems to minimize theft

   SKILL IN:
   a. basic math
   b. maintaining equipment/apparel database
   c. legibly marking and identifying products
   d. communicating importance of equipment/apparel distribution
   e. communicating distribution knowledge with athletes and coaches
   f. utilizing security resources

Management

1. Maintain accurate documentation in accordance with established organizational policies and procedures in order to substantiate accountability.

   KNOWLEDGE OF:
   a. inventory systems and procedures
   b. methods used to evaluate inventory status
   c. product identification
   d. product characteristics
   e. accepted documentation methods
   f. budgetary restrictions and limitations (contracts, early-order incentive programs)
   g. timelines
   h. organizational policies
   i. applicable ethical standards

   SKILL IN:
   a. basic math
   b. maintaining equipment/apparel database
   c. accurately recording data and maintaining records
   d. writing specifications
   e. filing documents

2. Uphold the ethical standards of the AEMA and other relevant organizations by complying with appropriate practices and procedures in order to ensure professional standards.

   KNOWLEDGE OF:
   a. AEMA Code of Ethics
   b. Employer's Code of Ethics
   c. purchasing policies and ethics
   d. rules and regulations of applicable governing bodies
   e. organizational policies

   SKILL IN:
   a. upholding established Codes of Ethics
   b. adhering to accepted ethical standards
   c. recognizing ethical violations

3. Maintain budgetary guidelines through the effective use of available resources in order to perform all necessary tasks.

   KNOWLEDGE OF:
   a. budgetary restrictions and limitations (contracts, early-order incentive programs)
   b. organizational policies

   SKILL IN:
   a. basic math
   b. implementing budgets
   c. assessing budgets and contracts
   d. accurately recording data and maintaining records

4. Adhere to established human resources policies and procedures through knowledge of the organization's guidelines in order to properly hire, evaluate, discipline, reward, and educate all relevant personnel.

   KNOWLEDGE OF:
   a. employee performance standards
   b. crisis management techniques
   c. motivational techniques
   d. organizational policies
   e. personnel management techniques
   f. time management techniques
   g. organizational goals
   h. organizational structure

SKILL IN:

a. complying with applicable rules and regulations governing safe and efficient work environments
b. communicating motivational techniques to employees
c. supervising the completion of goals and objectives

5. Maintain the responsibility to continually educate one's self as well as other members of the athletic community by utilizing all available resources in order to further advance the profession of athletic equipment management.

KNOWLEDGE OF:

a. continuing education resources
b. rules and regulations of applicable governing bodies
c. organizational policies
d. organizational goals
e. organizational structure

SKILL IN:

a. accessing relevant resources
b. utilizing computer resources
c. maintaining knowledge of recent technological developments

Purchasing

1. Evaluate present inventory by counting and visually inspecting all items in order to determine available and/or usable equipment/apparel.

KNOWLEDGE OF:

a. inventory systems and procedures
b. methods used to evaluate inventory status
c. product identification
d. product characteristics

SKILL IN:

a. basic math
b. accurately recording data and maintaining records
c. selecting appropriate inventory techniques
d. differentiation of colors and sizes

2. Determine projected needs based on current inventory and the demands of the sport, function, and/or activity in order to maintain a sufficient inventory.

KNOWLEDGE OF:

a. past usage of equipment/apparel
b. approved contractual obligations/licensing agreements
c. specific needs of end-users (size, position, sport, performance)
d. specialized equipment/apparel needs of individual sports
e. new products/technology

SKILL IN:

a. determining cost/value correlation in formulating purchasing decisions
b. recognizing legitimate purchasing needs
c. forecasting equipment/apparel needs

3. Evaluate options by comparing inventory with projected needs in order to fulfill purchasing demands within budgetary constraints.

KNOWLEDGE OF:

a. budgetary restrictions and limitations (contracts, early-order incentive programs)
b. rules and regulations of applicable governing bodies
c. organizational policies
d. manufacturer or vendor selection
e. estimated cost and availability
f. product history and quality based on brand
g. purchasing policies and ethics
h. timetables
i. specific needs of end-users (size, position, sport, performance)

SKILL IN:

a. assessing budgets and contracts
b. interpreting rules regarding protective equipment (color, logo, size, number)
c. evaluating reputable vendors and manufacturers
d. communicating expectations to vendors
e. adhering to proper bidding procedures
f. attending trade shows
g. communicating product knowledge with vendors and manufacturers
h. reading catalogues
i. searching the Internet

4. Make purchasing decisions and/or recommendations based on budgetary restrictions, product knowledge, and/or pertinent information in order to purchase identified equipment/apparel.

   KNOWLEDGE OF:
   a. purchasing policies and ethics
   b. sports seasons and schedules
   c. vendors who can meet service demands
   d. computers
   e. budgetary restrictions and limitations (contract, early-order incentive programs)
   f. approved contractual obligation/licensing agreements
   g. products
   h. specific needs/preferences of personnel (size, position, sport, performance)
   i. sport-specific rules and regulations for equipment/apparel

   SKILL IN:
   a. communicating exact bid specifications
   b. interpreting contract language
   c. writing specifications
   d. communication of timetable
   e. communication of product knowledge with vendors and manufacturers
   f. computing and typing
   g. evaluating the input if others on purchasing decisions
   h. communication of purchasing decisions
   i. implementing budgets

5. Authorize payment by complying with appropriate organizational policies in order to complete the purchasing process.

   KNOWLEDGE OF:
   a. product identification
   b. product characteristics
   c. product ordering
   d. order restrictions and limitations (FOB, discounts, early-order incentive programs)

   SKILL IN:
   a. basic math
   b. accurately accessing data
   c. documenting payment authorization
   d. differentiating acceptable and unacceptable product substitutions
   e. interpreting vendors' and manufacturers' documents
   f. verifying prices

Fitting

1. Obtain pertinent information about the athlete through communication, measurement, and documentation in order to ensure the proper selection and fit of all equipment/apparel.

   KNOWLEDGE OF:
   a. basic muscular and skeletal anatomy
   b. medical terms
   c. specialized protective equipment
   d. injuries or medical conditions that require specialized fitting consideration
   e. sport-specific information

   SKILL IN:
   a. observing and identifying physical abnormalities requiring special fitting and/or medical equipment
   b. communicating to determine medical needs for specialized protective equipment
   c. making or developing specific adjustments to protective equipment

2. Select the appropriate equipment/apparel in accordance with the determined needs of the athlete in order to commence the fitting process.

   KNOWLEDGE OF:
   a. product availability
   b. specific measurements of athletes
   c. specific needs/preferences of various sport positions
   d. specific medical histories of athletes
   e. specific abilities and skills of athletes
   f. past experiences (injuries, sizes)

   SKILL IN:
   a. communicating product knowledge with vendors and manufacturers
   b. obtaining product updates
   c. obtaining products that meet specific needs/preferences
   d. measuring athletes
   e. recognizing specific needs/preferences of various sport positions
   f. recognizing specific needs/preferences of athletes
   g. documenting injuries
   h. maintaining athlete database

3. Fit the selected equipment/apparel by following established guidelines in order to ensure optimal fit.

   KNOWLEDGE OF:
   a. fitting specifications of each manufacturer
   b. basic muscular and skeletal anatomy
   c. specific measuring and fitting techniques

   SKILL IN:
   a. recognizing proper fit
   b. educating athletes on proper fit
   c. measuring athletes
   d. using various measurement tools properly
   e. making or developing specific adjustments to protective equipment

4. Educate the athlete through communication concerning the inherent risks involved with the misuse of the equipment/apparel in order to reduce the risk of injury.

   KNOWLEDGE OF:
   a. specialized protective equipment
   b. basic muscular and skeletal anatomy
   c. proper use of specialized protective equipment
   d. conditions and events that affect changes in fit
   e. fitting specifications of each manufacturer
   f. product liability
   g. product misuse
   h. product risks

   SKILL IN:
   a. communicating product availability with vendors and manufacturers
   b. communicating importance of protective equipment
   c. communicating importance of proper use
   d. observing and identifying physical abnormalities requiring special fitting and/or medical equipment
   e. educating athletes on performing daily visual checks of equipment
   f. educating athletes on warning labels
   g. educating athletes on proper fit

5. Perform continuous evaluations of the fit of equipment/apparel through routine checks in order to maintain proper fit.

   KNOWLEDGE OF:
   a. proper fitting protocol
   b. previous fitting history
   c. reconditioning history of product
   d. recent changes in medical history of athletes
   e. basic muscular and skeletal anatomy
   f. accurate record-keeping
   g. conditions and events that affect fit
   h. rules and regulations of applicable governing bodies

   SKILL IN:
   a. observing and identifying physical abnormalities requiring special fitting and/or medical equipment
   b. making or developing specific adjustments to protective equipment
   c. measuring athletes
   d. using various measurement tools properly
   e. performing daily visual checks of equipment
   f. recognizing fitting and equipment rule violations
   g. recognizing proper fit
   h. educating athletes on proper fit
   i. adapting equipment for atypical measurements

Maintenance and Repair

1. Inspect equipment/apparel through visual observation in order to identify needed repair.

   KNOWLEDGE OF:
   a. fitting specifications of each manufacturer
   b. rules and regulations of applicable governing bodies
   c. warranties and practices of each manufacturer
   d. manufacturing specifications of each product

   SKILL IN:
   a. inspecting equipment/apparel to ascertain necessary repairs

2. Repair equipment/apparel deemed necessary through observation and routine inspection in order to maintain functionality and safety standards.

   KNOWLEDGE OF:
   a. repair tools and supplies
   b. repair techniques
   c. outside repair vendors
   d. manufacturing specifications of each product
   e. fitting specifications of each manufacturer
   f. rules and regulations of applicable governing bodies
   g. sport-specific information

SKILL IN:

a. using various repair tools properly
b. differentiating between in-house repairs and outsourced repairs
c. prioritizing repairs
d. documenting repairs performed
e. complying with applicable rules and regulations when making repairs

3. Maintain equipment/apparel through established guidelines in order to prolong product usability.

KNOWLEDGE OF:

a. manufacturing maintenance guidelines for each product
b. specialized protective equipment
c. repair tools and supplies
d. repair techniques
e. outside repair vendors
f. maintenance documentation

SKILL IN:

a. maintaining equipment database
b. inspecting equipment/apparel to ascertain necessary repairs
c. repairing equipment
d. using various repair tools properly
e. differentiating between in-house repairs and outsourced repairs

4. Launder equipment/apparel using accepted methods in order to ensure proper cleaning and sanitizing of equipment/apparel

KNOWLEDGE OF:

a. manufacturing specifications of each product
b. fabric characteristics
c. laundry products
d. laundry facilities and machinery
e. manufacturing maintenance guidelines for laundry facilities and machinery
f. emergency first aid procedures
g. universal precautions

SKILL IN:

a. sorting equipment/apparel for proper cleaning
b. using proper laundry cycles and chemicals
c. maintaining laundry machinery
d. complying with applicable rules and regulations governing safe and sanitary environments
e. maintaining laundry machinery maintenance logs

AEMA CERTIFICATION MANUAL

CHAPTER 1

Accountability

By Mary O'Leary

ACCOUNTABILITY

"Accountable – answerable; responsible."
—*The American Heritage Dictionary*

The most important aspect of the athletic equipment manager's position is taking responsibility. Columbia Assessment Services (CAS) performed the "Job Analysis Report—Certified Equipment Manager" in 1989. This role delineation study surveyed 500 equipment managers throughout our membership to determine what portion of our jobs is spent on specific tasks. The study determined that accountability is one of five domains for our profession, comprising 17.6% of our time. (The study was reviewed and upgraded in 2002; please refer to "What is an Equipment Manager and What Does an Equipment Manager Do" on page viii.)

Athletic equipment managers are responsible to more than just the coaches and teams they serve. The job is varied and requires multi-tasking throughout the day to meet the demands of all the teams with whom we work, as well as various other groups of people. Below are a few aspects of the job that highlight how we are accountable to various groups we work with:

1. Inventory control of all the athletic clothing and equipment issued and purchased for our teams.
2. Record-keeping for equipment room personnel time sheets, budget reports, purchasing documentation, and documentation of safety checks on protective equipment.
3. The type of storage we utilize to protect and store the equipment and clothing.
4. The type of security system that is incorporated in the equipment room to discourage theft.
5. How each individual item is marked for identification and tracking purposes.
6. Knowledge of manufacturers' and industry safety specifications.
7. Knowledge of NCAA, state high school athletic association, or other rules pertaining to your venue governing equipment.

These few examples help to demonstrate the equipment manager's accountability for the equipment we issue and purchase for the athletic department. It may appear that a significant amount of time is devoted to accountability, but actually, rather than being a separate task, it should be a part of the daily routine.

Programs lacking accountability can face a multitude of issues that could damage their integrity. Not having the records to justify where thousands of dollars worth of equipment and clothing have gone could have you facing serious charges from your institution and your professional association. The AEMA has an Ethics Committee, which, if called upon, will look at charges brought against one of its members. The AEMA Ethics Committee takes accountability and the professionalism of its members very seriously. If a member is found to be in violation of the AEMA Code of Ethics, he or she can have his or her certification and membership revoked. There are also instances where a lack of accountability leads to criminal prosecution (see Chapter 2, "Management").

Having a conscientious work ethic makes the job easier, because having a defined and orderly routine in place will provide the steps necessary to perform tasks effortlessly, skillfully, and efficiently. Documentation is a vital and key part of this. Some good reasons to document your procedure protocol include the following:

1. When the written procedure is readily available to equipment room personnel, it can help to train workers even when the athletic equipment manager is not able to be with them.
2. A set routine establishes the protocol needed to complete the task to avoid mistakes and also to aid in problem solving when mistakes do occur.

3. In equipment room settings where several people may help to complete the same task, a set guideline makes it easier for a person to pick up where another has left off.

This chapter covers some of the main areas that athletic equipment managers are accountable for.

INVENTORY CONTROL

The Database

Maintaining records of all the clothing and equipment that comes through your area can be a tremendous undertaking. Getting the baseline established is one of the first orders of business that should be assumed when starting a new position. As ordering begins, records are updated with new items and items lost or removed from circulation are deleted. Records should reflect the cost of each item and from whom it was purchased, both for billing purposes, when athletes are billed for unreturned items, and to order replacements.

You should maintain a **master inventory** showing what items athletes received at the beginning of the season as well as their sizes. Changes to the inventory may be made as necessary but this document will determine what items athletes didn't return at the end of their season (see Table One, below). If the master inventory includes sizes and numbers for each jersey, it will save time when purchasing for the following year, because the records will provide a good predictor of sizes for the returning athletes.

The equipment should be recorded by the manufacturer's model number and serial number, if it has them, and the institution's inventory control number. Some institutions develop their own code for an inventory number. For example, it may include the date it was entered into inventory, how many are available, and the team that purchased the equipment. Example: a baseball pitching machine purchased May 15, 2002, that is one of three such machines purchased may have an inventory number of BB51502-1. Even though this machine has a manufacturer's model number and serial number, it's a good idea to have a separate control number to have a backup in case one of the numbers is damaged and you cannot distinguish which machine you are looking for. The equipment inventory should show the model number, serial number, and the control number assigned to each specific item.

Labeling uniforms/practice clothing involves a different type of marking system. Many institutions use one number inside an article of clothing with a permanent marker. Usually, this number is the athlete's game number, which is entered in an area that is easy to locate. For example, if an athlete competes as #12, then all the items assigned to that athlete will be marked with #12. Another method is to number each piece of clothing consecutively when it is first purchased. If 18 volleyball shorts are purchased they will be numbered 1-18. This system works, but if there is an athlete with all different numbers for individual clothing items, it is difficult to identify which piece goes to which athlete without having to look in the master inventory control records. One number per athlete simplifies the work and allows ready identification of who is missing an item or where a stray piece of clothing needs to go.

Daily inventories should also be taken. Not only are they very helpful in alerting your staff to missing items, but they may also alert you to uniforms and equipment that has been damaged or that have problems that need attention. When spotted early, routine damage to articles is much easier to repair. These daily inventories are also helpful when athletes are sure they returned an item but it isn't recorded on your inventory. This documentation gives you the credibility to notify the athlete and coach that an item has been lost or misplaced.

Another advantage of the daily inventory is that it shows exactly when an item is missing, thereby making it easier to track. If a team is on the road and an athlete leaves an article behind, then there is an advantage to

TABLE ONE

MASTER INVENTORY

SPORT ____________________ COACH ____________________

YEAR ____________________

PRACTICE GEAR												GAME GEAR									
# and Name	Rd. T	Wh. T	Gr. T	B.short	G.short	R.short	sock	loop	towel	sw.top	sw.bot	Miz.Jrz	Ad.Jrz	Nik.Jrz	short	short	short	WU T	WU B	T. Bag	Shoes
1. JANE D.	LG	LG	LG	LG	LG	LG	3 PR	3	3	LG	XLG	LG	LG	MD	MD	MD	MD	LG	LG	#1	10
2. MARY E.	LG	LG	LG	LG	LG	LG	3 PR	3	3	LG	XLG	MD	MD	LG	MD	MD	MD	LG	LG	#2	8.5
3. SALLY F.	XLG	XLG	XLG	XLG	XLG	XLG	3 PR	3	3	XLG	XLG	XLG	LG	XLG	LG	LG	LG	XLG	XLG	#3	9
ETC.																					

quickly contacting the site and possibly being able to have officials at that site find it and return it before the next competition. The more time that is allowed to pass between when the item is lost and when you first noticed it missing reduces the chances of finding it.

Storage

How uniforms and practice clothes are stored is an individual institution's choice. Most institutions allow their athletes to store two or more sets of practice gear in their lockers to simplify the individual workouts and multiple practice routines. If there are additional multiple sets that need to be stored in the equipment room, you may keep them separate from the game uniforms in a practice area for that specific sport.

Game uniforms should remain stored in the equipment room until they are required. Most institutions or teams cannot afford to buy multiple sets in the same numbers in case of loss or theft. Many equipment rooms store the uniforms by individual player during the season so a team can be packed quickly. Some institutions prefer to store the uniforms in number order by the style of each item. For example, the same style jerseys are in consecutive number order in storage ready to be handed out. This obviously is the method of choice for larger teams like football if you don't have adequate room to store the uniforms by individual athletes.

Storing items by each individual athlete does require more storage area, but it is much more efficient to issue when working with multiple teams. It also allows you to better utilize your staff because it can be set up ahead of time so that all that needs to be done is to pull the section off the pile you have preset. One trick is to put a separator (e.g., a towel or different piece of clothing) in the piles to separate what is needed on top from the items below, which are to remain in the cabinet. Out-of-season storage is generally done in number order so missing items are readily identified and earmarked for re-order.

All items should be cleaned and stored neatly to assure they are in good condition for the following season. Several factors affect clothing longevity. Laundering with the improper chemicals may cause unnecessary fabric breakdown. Drying at high temperatures may cause fabrics to deteriorate. Storing in a temperature-controlled setting with minimal UV rays will save your uniforms. Many schools drip-dry their game uniforms to keep the fabric and the lettering looking like new.

Equipment Distribution

When the time arrives to distribute the items to each athlete, it is important to record what each athlete receives. It is recommended that the athlete sign the property card or contract acknowledging receipt of said equipment and uniforms (see Table Two on page 5). A contract should include a statement explaining the athlete is responsible for the return of all items received, and that he or she will be billed for unreturned items through the athletic department.

Game-day issue should be laid out in plenty of time to allow athletes to check what has been packed and to add any personal items to their travel bags without being rushed. Distribution of travel gear before the final practice before departure allows athletes to check their gear with plenty of time to make corrections. This seems to work best, especially if you have a team that continually practices late and is then rushed to get on the bus. Sometimes the game or meet gear may need to be issued the day before departure if the athletes are coming straight from class to the bus. By issuing the day before, athletes can pack in advance and not be hurried when coming directly from their classes. Another helpful task to make sure athletes don't forget anything is to leave a note somewhere in their locker room detailing all the items they will need for the trip.

Equipment Retrieval and Processing

Daily practice gear should be laundered, inventoried, and returned to the athlete's locker in a timely manner. When items appear to be missing, the athlete should be informed and allowed the opportunity to recover what is missing. Sometimes, the items may not have been used or may be in the wrong locker. Equipment managers should check their own areas before billing the athlete to make sure the mistakes weren't caused by an oversight of the equipment room staff. This applies in particular to any items that are turned into the equipment room for laundering and points out the importance of the daily inventory of which items were laundered.

Protective equipment will need routine inspections by the equipment personnel. Protective gear is usually associated with teams that carry a high risk of injury, therefore increasing the risk of liability. The equipment manager should perform routine safety checks on helmets and shoulder pads and maintain a record of repairs and the reconditioning schedule for each piece of equipment.

Routinely, the equipment manager will be called upon to make adjustments in protective equipment for fitting purposes. It is extremely important that before adjustments are made there is an understanding of what the manufacturing specifications allow. A manufacturer is held responsible by law to provide safe equipment that meets the needs of the sport it was designed to protect, unless the equipment has been tampered with. If an unacceptable repair or adjustment is made to equipment

TABLE TWO

STUDENT-ATHLETE'S INVENTORY

SPORT: ____________________

NAME ____________________ LOCKER & COMBINATION ____________________

HOME ADDRESS ____________________ CAMPUS ADDRESS ____________________

____________________ ____________________

HOME PHONE ____________________ CAMPUS PHONE ____________________

ID# OR BANNER# ____________________

EQUIPMENT ISSUED:

	PRACTICE		***GAME***
T-SHIRT	______	TRAVEL BAG	______
SHORTS	______	GAME JERSEY	______
SWEAT TOP	______	GAME SHORTS	______
SWEAT BOTTOM	______	WARMUP TOP	______
SHOES	______	WARMUP BOTTOM	______
	______	SHOES	______
	______		______
	______		______
	______		______

I, THE UNDERSIGNED, agree to be personally responsible for the care and keeping of the above-named articles that I have received. I will be held responsible for their return at the conclusion of the season. Any items not returned will be billed to my account.

Awards may be withheld until all equipment is returned.

SIGNED ____________________ DATE ____________________

outside the manufacturer's specifications, the manufacturer's liability could be forfeited, in which case you and the institution could be held liable if a catastrophic injury occurs. (See Chapter 2, "Management," and Chapter 4, "Fitting Equipment and Clothing," for more on this.)

Paperwork must be processed for replacements of lost or damaged items. Many institutions require the athlete be billed for lost or unreturned items. This is usually a process worked out with the bursar's office so students can be billed through the institution.

At NCAA colleges and universities, Association rules do not allow athletes to retain their gear at the end of the season unless they have completed their eligibility.[1] Other NCAA rules also apply,[2] and your institution may have additional strict policies and procedures for when items are lost, non-returned, or returned in non-usable condition.

At the end of the season, all returned items should be checked against the master inventory. An inventory control form should be completed to record all items on hand and to show what re-orders need to be done for the next season (see Table Three on page 6). Action should be taken for any items not returned at the conclusion of the season, such as billing athletes, withholding awards, or any other policy approved by the athletic department.

A system utilizing checks and balances should be used when doing the final inventory and storage. One

---

1 A student-athlete may retain athletics apparel items (not equipment) at the end of the individual's collegiate participation. Used equipment may be purchased by the student-athlete on the same cost basis as by any other individual interested in purchasing such equipment. (Rule 16.12.1.6)
2003-04 NCAA Division I Manual, July 2003, Indianapolis, Indiana, pg. 230.

2 a) A student-athlete may retain and use institutional athletics equipment (per the institution's normal equipment policy) during a summer vacation period. (Rule 16.12.1.7)
2003-04 NCAA Division I Manual, July 2003, Indianapolis, Indiana, pg. 230.
b) A student-athlete may not accept athletics equipment, supplies, or clothing (e.g., tennis racquets, golf clubs, hockey sticks, balls, shirts) from a manufacturer or commercial enterprise. (Rule 16.12.2.5)
2003-04 NCAA Division I Manual, July 2003, Indianapolis, Indiana, pg. 231.

TABLE THREE

INVENTORY CONTROL

SPORT ______________________ DATE ______________________

ITEM & STYLE #	TOTAL #	PREV. # ON HAND	#PUR LAST YEAR	USABLE TODAY		REPAIR NEEDED	LOST	EST. NEED FOR NEXT YR.		
				NEW	USED			QUANTITY	$$$$	TOT. $$$

method would be to inventory all the items for the individual athlete by size and what numbers, if any, are on the uniform for every item issued to that athlete. Once the entire team has been inventoried, you then may pull all the "like" items and put them in number order to see if any are missing. This should match the inventory taken previously for each individual athlete. If it doesn't match, go back and find where the mistake occurred. For example: after completing an inventory for a team of 18 athletes, a complete list by size and number of what each athlete returned would be shown. Then, pull all the matching style jerseys and put them in number order. If you find #5 is missing a jersey, then the final inventory by individual athlete should also show that jersey missing.

Reconditioning Equipment

A check of the condition of all returned items needs to be performed regularly. This allows plenty of time for repairs and reconditioning. Maintaining a record of the items sent to a reconditioner will allow for a thorough check of the returns. It is very important you not only provide a list of what is to be repaired, but also where each item needs to be repaired. Sometimes it is very helpful to pin or mark the items in some way so the reconditioner knows exactly what area you were expecting to be repaired.

Helmet manufacturer's all have specifications their equipment should meet. Using a reputable reconditioner and knowing the manufacturer's specifications is your responsibility for the sports that use that equipment. Talk to your manufacturer's representative and your reconditioner to make sure these requirements are being met.

NOCSAE (National Operating Committee on Standards for Athletic Equipment) sets the level of acceptable performance for newly manufactured products used in football, baseball, softball, and lacrosse. NOCSAE has not yet established standards for equipment in other sports such as ice hockey and field hockey (goalies). It is, however, the various sports federations that adopt the NOCSAE standards for equipment like sports helmets and require those standards be enforced (look for the NOCSAE emblem on helmets). NOCSAE also sets standards for reconditioning football and lacrosse helmets. At this time, baseball and softball helmets may not be re-certified by a reconditioner.

Security

The security of the equipment room is one of the primary concerns of an equipment manager. Many equipment rooms are the storage areas for a number of teams and you have a responsibility to all of them to keep their equipment secure.

The locking system to the equipment room should be on a very secure key or coded system that only a few people have access to. If everyone is able to access the equipment room, you really have no control over what leaves the area. Some different kinds of security include locks, push-button controls, and computerized locks with an electronically coded plastic key, like many hotels use. The advantage of the push-button or computerized lock is that the code can be changed quickly and easily if there were an unwanted intrusion. When using keyed locks you may want to make sure the equipment room is on a master key blank different from the rest of the building. This will prevent someone with a master key in your facility from entering the equipment room.

Keeping uniforms and small equipment locked away in separate storage areas also is important for the security of your area. Storing equipment and clothing by sport also allows for quick and easy access to all the items you need for a specific team. If more than one storage area is needed, you may want to separate the equipment by functionality. For example, all the team's practice gear in one area and their game gear in another. This allows for ease of accessibility and prevents distributing the wrong items.

Each individual storage cabinet should have its own lock different from the other cabinets in the area. If someone were to intrude, they would have to know the following to successfully get into the items they wanted:

1. where keys are stored for each individual cabinet or storage area;

2. how to identify which key opens one of a multitude of cabinets; and
3. which cabinet in the area holds the items they are looking for.

The main objective to designing a secure area is to make it difficult for intruders to get what they want.

Some larger institutions use cameras in their facilities to discourage theft. This obviously is a monetary issue but one that probably pays for itself over time. Not all thefts involve persons outside our equipment area. There are many equipment managers who have been very disappointed to find that their own staff or student assistants have been helping themselves to the "goods." There is no place in the equipment room for naivete.

WORKING WITH YOUR ATHLETES AND COACHES

Communicating with your athletes and coaches helps build a working relationship, which, in turn, develops trust. Occasionally taking the time to visit with your coaches in their office may jar their memory of a matter they wanted to bring to your attention. Often, if this visit had not been made, the "matter" would have been forgotten until it became an "emergency." As equipment managers, it is much easier to do the job correctly when you have the time. Hurrying to get a job done is usually a recipe for doing the job wrong. For your part, thinking ahead of the potential problems your teams may encounter will make your job easier and help establish a positive working relationship with the coaches.

Take the time to talk to the teams about your responsibilities, the individual athlete's responsibilities, and how both can work together to make the intricacies of the job run smoother. This will help demonstrate your dedication and the concern you have for the athletes you serve.

The equipment manager cannot be expected to know the correct sizes for all the incoming athletes. Football teams usually provide a time during their first day on campus to fit their new student-athletes. Many of the other teams do not afford us that luxury, and we must make an effort to reach out to those athletes. Being available during the times they are in the locker room and letting them know you are there to assist them with changes is only one way to reach them. Many first-year athletes are shy and won't come and ask for changes right away. You may want to appear before or after a practice to check with the athletes and coaches to see if anyone is having problems. Sometimes, just going to a practice allows you to visually see who is in need of your services. When size changes are not possible because of budget and supply problems, then a reminder for the next year's budget should be noted to assure that the problem will be addressed the following year. (See Chapter 2, "Management," for more on communicating with athletes and coaches.)

LAUNDRY

For a comprehensive discussion of laundry practices, see Chapter 6, Laundry. Below is a brief discussion of some laundry issues as they pertain to accountability.

Laundry should be done as soon as possible following a practice or game situation to prevent bacterial growth on the clothes and to reduce fabric breakdown from the body chemicals present in perspiration. Body perspiration has natural oils and salt in its composition and allowing these to remain on the fabric causes the fibers to deteriorate.

Good laundry procedures and not over-drying garments allow them to wear better. If your laundry room allows the space for drip drying articles, this will really keep them looking like new for several seasons. Hanging laundry also allows gravity to position the article straight, thus removing any or all wrinkles from the washing machine. With time and attention to the folding, there is no need for an iron.

Once the laundry is completed, an inventory should be done as a follow-up to make sure each athlete turned in what he or she received. It is easier to address any problems immediately, especially if you need to contact the school where you last competed for return of the lost articles. Prompt attention can mean getting the articles returned in time. If you wait until the next game day and find out articles are missing, you won't be able to do much about it except hope you have an understanding coach. Even though there are days you don't think you have the time, remember, it is easier to do a job right the first time than it is to have to do the job twice.

The washing instruction labels should be on all the uniforms you purchase. If they aren't, you should contact your vendor or manufacturer for their recommendations. Many manufacturers pack detailed washing instructions in the shipping carton and most manufacturers will guarantee their product for a season; however, the condition of this guarantee is that you follow their washing instructions.

Sometimes, an athlete may have a skin reaction to the detergents or chemicals you are using in your laundry system. Working with your athletic trainer will help you determine if this is just a skin reaction or possibly a contagious skin disease such as ringworm. If it is an allergic response, you may need to wash the athlete's clothes separately in a very mild detergent such as Woolite. If a team has incidences of ringworm or other contagious skin diseases, it is imperative the contaminated items be washed separately from those of the rest of the team. Developing a good relationship with your athletic trainer will help you determine how these types of problems need to be handled. Including them in the process lends their expertise to determining the cause of the allergic reaction. Many times, I've had athletes complain about having skin reactions that they thought were caused by our laundry only to find out later they had changed their personal soap or shampoo, and that was actually the cause.

The equipment room is often faced with uniforms and training room towels infected with blood. The Occupational Safety and Health Administration (OSHA), a division of the U.S. Department of Labor, has established guidelines for the correct way to handle biohazardous waste. It is important that infected items be handled correctly not only for your personal safety but also for the safety of your coworkers and your athletes. Articles contaminated with blood need to be handled separately and treated with a special detergent that is a tuberculocidal cleaner (one that kills the bacteria that causes tuberculosis).

One separation method would be to have the athlete obtain the biohazardous plastic bags from the athletic training room to store his or her contaminated laundry and keep it from contacting the rest of the team's laundry. The threat of transmitting HIV and hepatitis-B through blood is a very real one when dealing with contaminated athletic laundry. It is the job of the equipment manager to take the necessary safeguards to protect anyone who could come in contact with such items.

GOVERNING BODIES AFFECTING ATHLETIC EQUIPMENT MANAGEMENT

There are several organizations that have rules affecting many aspects of our job. The most important of these include the NCAA, NOCSAE, and your athletic conference office or state high school athletic association. In addition to these governing bodies there are the individual sports rules committees. Each sport has a rules committee that reviews rules and initiates changes regularly. The coaches of the teams you are working with should have copies of these rules and should be able to make interpretations for you, if needed. The equipment manager should have access to any manuals and rulebooks so he or she can research any questions that may arise during the year.

NCAA Rules

The NCAA is a national association that looks out for the welfare of student-athletes at member colleges and universities. It is the main governing body for many of our collegiate athletic programs. It addresses rules, practice scheduling, academic eligibility, and benefits, which is where some of the equipment issues appear.

Rule interpretation and enforcement can be important in the equipment room. For example, many individual sports and conferences have specific rules about the lettering of game apparel. It is important for you to understand where and if placing memorial patches or U.S. flags are allowed on your team's uniforms. Your conference may have a patch it wants displayed in a specific location. These rules may vary from sport to sport; it is your responsibility to know each sport's requirements. Numbering the jerseys also may require knowledge of the rules. For example, many sports have a minimum and maximum numeral size regulation. It's important that you know and properly implement these rules. It could mean the difference between respect for your position or a negative relationship with the teams you represent should you or they run afoul of the NCAA or your conference.

Title IX

One of the more recent concerns gaining a lot of attention at all levels, from elementary schools to the federal government, is gender equity. For any school receiving federal funding, the passing of Title IX of the Educational Amendments of 1972 to the 1964 Civil Rights Act standardized the way women's athletic programs are run in relation to their male counterparts.

The following quote gives a quick idea of what Title IX set out to achieve:

> "No person in the United States shall, on the basis of sex, be excluded from participation in, be denied the benefits of, or be subject to discrimination under any educational program or activity receiving Federal financial assistance."
> —*Section 901(a) of Title IX of the Education Amendments of 1972 to the 1964 Civil Rights Act*

Subsequent to enacting the legislation, the Department of Education's Office for Civil Rights clarified their criteria for considering whether athletic benefits and opportunities were being fairly delivered:

> "In determining whether equal opportunities in athletics are available, the Title IX regulation specifies the following factors which must be considered:

- accommodation of athletic interests and abilities;
- equipment and supplies;
- scheduling of games and practice time;
- travel and per diem allowances;
- opportunity for coaching and academic tutoring;
- assignment and compensation of coaches and tutors;
- locker rooms and other facilities;
- medical and training services;
- housing and dining services; and
- publicity."

This law is not foolproof and, as is the case with many laws, has loopholes. However, it did set up a standard that gave women the opportunity to compete fairly. Title IX does not dictate that women receive equal money, but it does provide support, provisions, and expenditures for members of both sexes.

The equipment manager can play a very important role in assuring the equity of the overall athletic program at his or her institution. As noted in the quote above, equipment and supplies and locker rooms and other facilities are expressly mentioned as items that should be looked at when making sure the men's and women's programs at your institution are delivering services equitably. The bottom line as far as the athletic program is concerned is that male and female athletes need to receive equal opportunities for participation in athletics and support from all areas of the athletic department, including the services of the equipment manager.

Discrimination against women's athletics was a historical reality prior to 1972. Title IX merely forced the self-examination and re-evaluation necessary to untangle the years of discrimination. As an equipment manager, you need to make sure you are treating men's and women's programs equally in terms of both the material resources and the support and time you provide them.

In 1991, an NCAA task force published the results of a study that individually looked at several variables concerning gender equity at all the NCAA-member institutions. The Equity in Athletics Disclosure Act Gender-Equity Report has been carried out four times since then, most recently with the 1999-00 report. It can be found on-line through the NCAA's Web site, at www1.ncaa.org/membership/ed_outreach/gender_equity/index.html. The following quote, taken from this Web site, summarizes a quick and easy rule to follow when judging whether or not your services are equitable.

"An athletics program can be considered gender equitable when the participants in both the men's and women's sports programs would accept as fair and equitable the overall program of the other gender."
—*NCAA Gender-Equity Task Force*

COMPUTERS IN THE EQUIPMENT ROOM

Computers can play an important role in the equipment room. For most equipment managers the Internet and e-mail have become invaluable resources. The AEMA has a Web site (http://www.aema1.com) and discussion group for its members (mailto: aema-disc@aema1.com). The discussion group has become an invaluable tool for members to help each other solve problems. The Internet and a huge array of Web sites allow the equipment manager to research information quickly.

A computer database can be used to neatly input your inventories and make revisions or updates easily. Spreadsheets, such as Excel, allow the equipment manager to input purchasing orders and perform the necessary math to help reduce human error. Some schools allow the equipment manager to generate purchase orders online, which really adds to the processing speed. Many equipment departments can access the accounts payable department or purchasing department to see if purchase orders were paid or if they are still outstanding and need attention before the end of the fiscal year. Having quick access to this and a host of other purchasing information helps to make our jobs easier.

There are several companies who sell specific programs for use in the athletic equipment room. These programs are set up for the equipment manager to record the necessary information for their teams. They are designed to relieve the burden of inventories. Of course, these programs are only as good as the equipment manager. The equipment data doesn't enter itself, so the equipment manager must make a commitment to keep the files updated. One company uses bar codes on all equipment and clothing, which makes the job even simpler. Once the equipment information has been entered, you only need to scan each item with a portable scanner. The computer will complete the inventory for you once all the items have been scanned.

STUDENT AND FULL-TIME EMPLOYMENT

Since many equipment rooms hire students or full-time employment, it is important the equipment manager learn the rules about interviewing and hiring potential employees. If your school or personnel office offers informative sessions on employment law, you would be wise to take the time to educate yourself on these issues.

Federal and state laws protect potential employees from being discriminated against on the basis of sex, age, disability, national origin, race, and religion. Your role as a supervisor is to make sure the laws are followed in your area. The key to being prepared in employment issues is documentation. It is very important when discussing matters about employment with your employees that you document those conversations in case there is ever a dispute. In some cases, you may want the employee to sign off on a document verifying what was discussed or have a witness verify what was said in case a serious disciplinary session is necessary. There can never be too much documentation.

Many schools will require you to maintain records on your employees. Job evaluations should be conducted regularly and performed consistently and fairly. Allowing the employee to comment on the evaluation form is very important. Evaluations should be used as a means of communication between employer and employee. They can open the doors for good dialogue and help resolve problems before they get out of hand. (See Chapter 2, "Management," for more on this.)

There are also state and federal laws that pertain to the handling of public records and records of enrolled students in your educational setting. These laws are very specific about the definition of a public record. In some states, these are referred to as The Public Records Act or Sunshine Laws. Your institution should have guidelines on the proper procedure for handling such records and what information may be released.

The Family Educational Rights and Privacy Act, commonly called FERPA or the Buckley Amendment, was passed by Congress out of public awareness of government record-keeping and the dissemination of information commonly considered private in nature. This law allows for the right of inspections and prohibits unauthorized disclosure of educational records. This law pertains to any student in attendance at your institution.

CONCLUSION

Professionalism and integrity are the images you want to portray when working with your teams. You and you alone possess the ability to make that positive image by having an efficient equipment room and working hard to understand and meet the needs of all your teams. Pride in their appearance and support of your school sends an important message to the athletes and coaches you serve. Knowledge of the rules that apply to these teams demonstrates that you care about them. Taking good care of their uniforms allows them to look their best. Demonstrating to the teams you work with that you will work hard to help them also sends a strong message about your dedication. All these qualities define your desire to be accountable to the institution and the teams you work with.

One of the primary roles of an equipment manager is being accountable to his or her school, athletes, and coaches. Being a role model for your profession is a lifelong commitment. Demonstrating sound ethics and pride in your job help build respect and understanding for the work you perform for your teams. Everything we do for our athletes and coaches sends a message to those around us. An equipment manager is depended upon to do a multitude of tasks, many that our coaches and teams don't even realize are done for their team. Administrators also need to be educated about the importance of our work and how our jobs help the athletic department. A lazy or unethical equipment manager will never be forgotten and taking that path will only make your job even more difficult.

AEMA CERTIFICATION MANUAL

CHAPTER 2

ATHLETIC EQUIPMENT MANAGERS ASSOCIATION

Management

By Alan Ansell

MANAGEMENT

The athletic equipment manager is required to perform his or her duties in a wide range of venues from the most modest educational institution to the most complex professional organization. While the size and scope of the facilities in each equipment manager's charge can vary widely, along with the amount of support he or she receives, all equipment managers are confronted with the same basic management issues: communications, staffing, record-keeping, storage and security, and being aware of legal issues pertaining to equipment management. These are very broad topics that refer to a number of responsibilities. This chapter provides an overview of these functions that will serve to guide the entry-level equipment manager in his or her profession, while serving as a refresher and reference manual for seasoned professionals.

COMMUNICATIONS

The ability to communicate effectively with others is key to developing the necessary relationships required to provide for a healthy and productive work environment. This includes both verbal and written skills and involves knowing when and how to ask and when and how to tell.

Avoiding Misunderstandings

Communications theory provides a simple, but powerful framework for understanding how to communicate effectively with others. It postulates four elements of any communication: a sender, a receiver, a message, and noise. The role of the sender, receiver, and message are self-explanatory. Noise is anything that tends to alter the message as it travels from the sender to the receiver.

Noise can be physical noise, such as in a crowded locker room where the equipment manager's instructions are difficult to hear. But in a broader sense, it can be anything that alters a message—using words the receiver does not understand is noise, sending out memos whose meanings are unclear or with misleading typos is noise, and trying repeatedly to telephone someone and getting nothing but an answering machine is noise.

The most common type of noise, and the most difficult to detect, occurs between the sender's mouth and receiver's ears. The common term for this type of noise is misunderstanding—the sender believes that he or she is sending a message that means one thing to the receiver, and the receiver believes that he or she has received and understood the message. But, in fact, the receiver does not understand the message in the same way that the sender understands it.

The potential for misunderstanding any kind of communication is huge, no matter how simple that communication may be. For equipment managers, effective communication is largely a matter of avoiding misunderstandings.

The potential for misunderstanding is the reason that it is so important for equipment managers to take the time to make sure that their staff members understand the rules and procedures they are taught. In the case of physical procedures, such as sorting the laundry or fitting a shoulder pad, it is relatively easy to make sure that the message is understood. The equipment manager has only to ask the staff member to perform the procedure and watch him or her closely. Any misunderstanding will be reflected in the staff member's actions.

Misunderstandings about less concrete messages, such as equipment room policies, are more difficult to detect. It is not in the equipment manager's interests to wait until a staff member makes a mistake regarding equipment room policy to find out whether he or she understands it. It is far better to detect such misunderstandings ahead of time.

One of the simplest and best methods of ensuring that messages are understood is to ask the staff member to repeat the message, or to act out the tasks implied by the message. For example, the equipment manager might pretend to be a student who wants to borrow a piece of equipment without turning in a student ID as security. The staff member's job would be to handle the request consistent with equipment room policy.

Such "play acting" might seem silly or pointless to staff members, but it provides the equipment manager with a clear indication of a staff member's understanding, and it provides the staff member with clear guidelines for how to handle such situations.

It is also very important to listen to communications from staff members. Complaints that pop up regularly in staff meetings, for example, might point to an area in which equipment room procedures or policies should be improved or changed. Advice from staff members should be listened to carefully. Whether it is followed or not, it is better for staff members to feel that their advice is being heard than for them to feel that it is being ignored.

One of the most common communication problems is the tendency for individuals to judge the usefulness of information according to its source, rather than its own merits. Although it is true that new equipment room staff members may not have the accumulated experience and know-how of long-time staff members, they can still provide valuable insights.

Lines of Communication

It is important to learn how to properly communicate within your organization's framework. This starts with understanding the lines of communication, that is, to whom you report and who reports to you, and the social norms that govern your institution. For example, it is generally not acceptable to go "over the head" of your immediate supervisor or, in other words, outside the lines of communication.

Often, the most difficult aspect of this is determining the lines of authority. The athletic organization model usually has the equipment manager reporting, or subordinate, to a number of people. This can create problems due to the fact that the primary functions of an equipment manager are safety-related. This makes directives that compromise safety impossible to follow, no matter who they're coming from. It is therefore critical that equipment managers be able to express themselves clearly and professionally to people in authority, since they may be called on to defy them.

In addition to the equipment manager-coach/administrator communication line, other important pertinent communication lines are between the equipment manager and the rest of the equipment room staff and between the equipment manager and the athletes. There must always be a free flow of information along these communication lines. The need to make policies clear to employees and athletes alike is imperative to facilitate equipment room and sideline functions.

The final type of communication line is external: dealing with individuals outside your team or institution, such as vendors and other institutions. In such instances, you represent your organization. In doing so, one must be sure not to compromise the reputation of one's institution.

Coaches and Athletic Directors

It is just as important, if not more so, to communicate effectively with coaches and athletic directors as it is to communicate effectively with fellow equipment room staff. Most often, the equipment manager's responsibility in such communications is to make sure that the messages sent by coaches and athletic directors are being received and understood.

The key to avoiding misunderstanding messages from coaches and athletic directors is to be aware of the possibility of misinterpretations. If the phrasing of a memo or verbal request seems ambiguous or unclear, it is in the equipment manager's interest to immediately ask questions and to keep asking questions until understanding has been reached.

It is also important that the equipment manager not allow coaches and athletic directors to discount advice from the equipment manager because it originates from someone they may think of as a subordinate. Generally, an equipment manager knows his or her job better than anyone else on campus. This means that the advice of the equipment manager on matters relating to the equipment room is more informed than that of anyone else and should be considered carefully. Sometimes, this means that the equipment manager needs to educate new coaches and athletic directors about equipment management.

Although it may take time and effort for an equipment manager to educate others about the way an equipment room works, the payoff will always be worthwhile. Coaches and athletic directors who do not understand how the equipment room functions are more apt to have unreasonable expectations about the equipment room's abilities, and therefore, are more likely to make unreasonable requests.

Thus, it is an excellent idea to take new coaches and athletic directors on a tour of the equipment room and its facilities. If at all possible, show the laundry room in action. Describe the capacity of each washer and dryer and how long it takes to do a load of laundry. Explain how long it takes to prepare a team's laundry for an away game. List all teams that the equipment room serves. Explain how bags are packed, how inventory is controlled, and how equipment is maintained. This information will help the coach or athletic director when they are planning their team's activities.

Students and Student-Athletes

If the athletic director, or in some cases, team coaches, can be regarded as the equipment managers' bosses, the students and athletes that the equipment room serves can be regarded as its customers. They are the ones who actually need and use the services that the equipment room provides. Therefore, it is not surprising that many equipment managers report that establishing the right relationship with the athletes is as important as establishing the right relationship with coaches and athletic department management.

Athletes often perceive the equipment room as a less threatening part of the athletic department's structure than coaches or athletic trainers. Equipment managers, after all, do not pass judgment on athletes' abilities or their fitness to play.

Thus, athletes may come to equipment managers with problems that they might not bring to coaches or trainers. What begins as a complaint about badly fitting helmets, pads, or shoes may in fact be a disguised complaint about a mild injury that the athlete is not willing to tell an athletic trainer about. By being open and accessible to such complaints, and alert to the possibility that they might have their origins in mild injuries, the equipment manager can serve the athlete and the athletic department by recognizing the injury and seeing that the athlete is treated.

The key to good relations with athletes is accessibility and openness among the equipment room staff. Staff members who spend all their time working with the equipment, or who make checking out or distributing equipment a strictly mechanical procedure, are not as likely to hear from the athletes about problems with their equipment.

As one equipment manager put it, "When athletes aren't on good terms with the equipment room staff, they're more likely to just make do when they have problems with the equipment. We want to hear from the athletes when they have problems, so we can correct them."

Athletes who view the equipment staff as people they can talk to are also likely to take better care of their equipment. It is easy to abuse a piece of equipment when the equipment room is just an anonymous place. It is much more difficult to abuse it when you know the people who are in charge of maintaining it.

This analogy between athletes and students and business customers only goes so far, however. Its major flaw is that in the equipment room, the customer is not always right. There are times when the equipment room staff can and should say no to the students and athletes they serve. For example, when it comes to fitting safety equipment, such as football helmets or shoulder pads, the equipment manager's expertise is, or should be, much greater than the athlete's. While the equipment manager should be alert to complaints of discomfort or a bad fit, the equipment manager must make sure that the athlete wears the equipment properly while on the field, not only for the sake of the athlete, but also to avoid liability to the school.

Also, equipment room staff are charged with enforcing equipment room rules regarding things such as access to the equipment room and the hours during which athletic equipment may be checked out. This will periodically require telling an athlete no.

The key to doing so effectively and arousing as little anger as possible lies in making it clear to the athlete that the staff member is not denying the request for personal reasons. In the case of a recreational or physical education equipment room, it can be very handy to have a list of equipment room rules and hours posted at the point where equipment is distributed. This gives the staff member a simple means of demonstrating that he or she is only enforcing equipment room rules.

With athletes, education can be a powerful tool for making it easier for equipment room staff members to perform their functions. The equipment manager should take the time to explain the rules of the equipment room to all athletes at the beginning of each year, and to new student-athletes as they arrive on campus.

Coaches and athletic directors can help the equipment manager by making it clear to their athletes that they fully approve of the equipment manager's rules and will require the athletes to obey those rules. Equipment room staff members should make exceptions to the rules only when absolutely necessary. Occasions do arise when it might be necessary or advisable to allow student-athletes into the equipment room or to lend out equipment without going through the usual procedures. But when other students and athletes learn that some students or athletes are allowed to break the rules, they are more likely to take it as a personal affront when they are required to abide by the same rules others can apparently break. Evenhanded enforcement of equipment room rules ultimately makes the staff's job easier.

STAFFING

The term "staffing" is quite broad in scope. It includes the complete function of providing all necessary services to a particular group or organization. It includes, but is not limited to, understanding and, if necessary, creating personnel policy; figuring out your staffing needs; hiring the appropriate staff; training them; conducting evaluations; and determining and dispensing fair compensation.

It is essential that established organization policy is adhered to when dealing with staffing issues; if none exists, it must be created. When it is necessary to create policy, transparency will go a long way to eliminating confusion and misunderstandings. You should also be aware of local and federal laws that govern hiring and staffing practices. (See Chapter 1, "Accountability," for a brief discussion of this.)

Personnel Policy

The equipment room, like any other part of an educational or professional organization, is subject to strict formal guidelines in the form of personnel policies. These policies govern the employment of full-time and part-time staff, work-study students, and volunteers. They cover such matters as pay scales, the number of hours that can be worked over a given period of time, the amount of overtime that can be requested of an individual, how such overtime is compensated, and the personal conduct of both employees and managers. Uncompensated student volunteers generally are not subject to the same formal rules, but they are often asked to adhere to those that are not related to compensation and hours worked. These formal rules generally exist alongside the informal rules of conduct that govern each equipment room.

Equipment room managers should have formal, written equipment room policies and procedures. These are typically in the form of a chapter in the athletic department's handbook. As a general rule, written rules concerning the conduct of equipment rooms are regarded as immutable policy, and equipment room staff are expected to follow them or have a very good reason for not doing so. Typically, written rules describe equipment room policies in areas such as procedures for lending equipment to an athlete or student, circumstances under which a staff member might be excused from working, and procedures for securing the equipment room area when staff are away.

By contrast, many of the day-to-day functions of the equipment room are communicated through informal, verbal communications between equipment room managers and staff. These might include procedures for storing helmets and shoulder pads, for handling the laundry efficiently, and for preparing athletes' bags for away games. If, however, the staff is large or there is frequent staff turnover, it may be best to put all of this in writing.

Equipment room policy shouldn't simply be written in a binder somewhere and stuck on a shelf. It should be regularly reviewed and copies should be made available to all staff. Good communication skills are essential when dealing with equipment room policy. It is not enough to simply hand out a memo when there's been a change to existing policy—it is important to give staff members opportunities to ask questions and to make comments.

Proper implementation of equipment room procedures also requires that equipment room managers ensure that their staff understands the relationship between the equipment room and the other elements of the athletic department and the school or institution they're a part of. Equipment room staff should know such things as who has the keys to locked equipment lockers; under what circumstances coaches, student-athletes, and students should be issued what kinds of equipment; and who is permitted to enter secured areas of the equipment rooms.

Staff members should be informed not only about what equipment room policies are, but also about what their responsibilities are in enforcing those policies. In this respect, a written notice detailing equipment room policies can be very helpful to staff members, since it provides a backup for their decisions. For example, if the equipment room staff member acts according to policy and denies a student-athlete access to equipment after a set time, he or she will have the knowledge that he or she is backed by written policy. A student may be angry at not being able to obtain a basketball after 10 p.m., but if there is a clearly visible, posted notice to that effect, the student is less likely to be angry at the staff member who can point out that he or she is just enforcing the rules.

Staff members should be made to understand that although they are responsible for seeing that equipment room policies are followed, they are not expected or required to cope with physically or verbally abusive individuals. Physically abusive people should be referred to the campus police or similar authority, and those who are verbally abusive should be referred to their coach or instructor. Staff members should also be instructed to report incidences of abusive behavior to the equipment manager. Of course, policy and procedures should clearly state that equipment room staff members will be subject to penalties if they behave abusively toward a student, athlete, or other staff member.

Need

The level of need is a function of the task at hand—providing service to a single team will differ from providing for a complete organization. (Need should not be confused with financial limitations, which are always a factor in the decision-making process.) Whether the goal is to provide a full-service equipment room or "on-field" service, one must always determine the tasks to be completed and the level of personal contact required.

Taking the staffing of an equipment window as an example, the first step is determining the number of hours the window will be accessible to the athletes in any given day and the number of days per week, both in-season and out. It should be understood that a certified equipment manager is not always required to provide this type of service (although one should oversee all operations). This determination must be made in conjunction with the entire athletic department staff.

For example, say it is determined that the equipment window should be open 60 hours a week from August 15 to June 1. This could require as many as 10 students working four-hour shifts or as few as two employees each working 30 hours a week. Having 10 different people isn't necessarily better than having two, but keep in mind that the greater the number of employees, the greater the likelihood of inconsistency or error.

Providing athletes with items that have been predetermined for their use, as in the case of the equipment window, is far different from outfitting protective gear. Only qualified staff under the supervision of a certified athletic equipment manager should perform this task. Therefore, need is a factor of qualifications, time, and volume. There is no precise means of calculating this equation.

There will always be a need for certified athletic equipment managers in athletics, although the level of recognition of this need by teams and institutions varies greatly. It is therefore incumbent upon the certified athletic equipment manager to demonstrate the need for the role that he or she—and the rest of the equipment room staff—plays as part of the athletic family, from both a safety and administrative standpoint.

Selection

The process of hiring new staff for the equipment room will vary depending on the institution; however, several factors are usually present. Generally, a job description should be written up for any positions prior to hiring so that the eligibility of all applicants can be clearly established. Then, note all state or federal mandates, as well as institutional or departmental rules, regarding hiring. There may be rules in effect to encourage the hiring of students, minorities, or other special interest groups.

The use of a hiring committee is always recommended for positions that require any documented skills and, by extension, an interview process. Always verify the content of applicants' resumes prior to creating a shortlist for interview.

The interviews themselves should be consistent for all applicants. Have each athlete fill out an employment form (see Table One, on page 17). If several people will be interviewing the candidates, decide beforehand who will ask each question.

A response evaluation grid will greatly aid in ranking the candidates. This simply consists of a form with a list of criteria and corresponding questions, along with space for remarks on each candidate's responses. Decide the overall importance of each question, and accord each a percentage out of a total of 100. For example, one of the criteria may be "Management of staff," with questions such as "Describe situations where you've had to manage others. What were some of the major challenges you faced? What did you learn about managing others? Describe a time when you had to make difficult decisions regarding staff. How did you make your decisions and what did you learn?" Depending on how many criteria categories you have, this category may be accorded an importance of 20 percent. Someone should take notes on the candidates' responses to the questions during or shortly after the interview while it is fresh in their minds.

The evaluation grid allows someone else who was not at the interview to quickly see how each candidate responded to the important questions, and the interviewer's comments. Following the interview process, one should always take the time to formally notify all shortlisted candidates of the decisions of the hiring committee.

It is important to remain transparent throughout the process. Often, you will be presented with candidates for positions who have been recommended by someone in the organization or, even worse, a new staff member will come pre-selected for you. This latter case is practically impossible to overcome where protocols do not exist, and can be very difficult even when they do.

The process that one uses for unskilled student employment may differ greatly from the one used in the hiring of skilled employees; however, all prospective employees need to feel that they have been given every advantage the system allows. Take the time to indicate or post your policies regarding all of the different types of employment and the hiring process. It is also important to maintain a "bank" or list of people whom you may call on, and their availability, in the event of an emergency or short-term need.

Student Volunteers

Student volunteers can greatly enhance any equipment room. The availability of student volunteers depends to a certain extent on factors that the equipment staff cannot control, such as the popularity of and interest in the athletics program. But equipment managers can make a concerted effort to encourage and support student volunteers, and put the word out about the equipment program as much as possible, to increase the available pool of student volunteers.

It is possible to advertise for student volunteers in athletic department publications, game programs, and the student newspaper. Sports-related organizations, such as athletic booster clubs, can also be a source of volunteers.

Student volunteers should be shown that the staff and the members of the athletic department appreciate their efforts, but they should also understand that if they make a commitment to perform a task voluntarily, they will be expected to follow through on it. Thus, if they promise to help with the laundry or to be on the field to pack up equipment on a given day, they should be expected to fulfill that promise, just as a paid staff member would.

At the same time, student volunteers should not be expected to allow coursework to suffer because of what is, after all, a volunteer activity. Student volunteers should be used sparingly, if at all, during exam time. Good communication skills are extremely important in dealing with student volunteers. They should know that they are expected to tell the equipment manager as soon as possible of any conflict between their volunteer activities and their academic activities, as well as any other activities or problems that might prevent them from handling their assigned tasks.

The fundamental reward that motivates students to volunteer in the equipment room is feeling that they helped out when their team takes the field on game day. But equipment room managers can reward their volunteers in other ways. Trips to accompany the team on away games, warmup jackets, and other forms of recognition can be powerful motivators for student volunteers (as well as for paid staff). Certificates or letters of apprecia-

TABLE ONE

EMPLOYMENT FORM

NAME ______________________________ ID# OR DR. LIC.# ______________

LOCAL ADDRESS ______________________________

PHONE ______________________________ E-MAIL ______________

HAVE YOU WORKED ELSEWHERE ON THIS CAMPUS BEFORE? ❑ YES ❑ NO

IF YES, WHERE AND WHAT DID YOU DO? ______________________________

ARE YOU PRESENTLY WORKING IN ANOTHER DEPARTMENT ON CAMPUS? ❑ YES ❑ NO

ARE YOU A FULL-TIME STUDENT? ❑ YES ❑ NO NUMBER OF CREDIT HOURS ______________

BIRTH DATE ______________ TODAY'S DATE ______________

IN CASE OF EMERGENCY, CONTACT ______________________________ PHONE ______________

YEAR IN SCHOOL: ______________ WORK STUDY? ❑ YES ❑ NO

NUMBER OF HOURS WANTED WEEKLY: ______________ WORK WEEKENDS? ❑ YES ❑ NO

HOURS WANTED: ______________________________

DARKEN AREA WHERE YOU HAVE CLASSES OR OTHER COMMITMENTS

DAY	8:00	9:00	10:00	11:00	12:00	1:00	2:00	3:00	4:00	5:00	EVG
MON.											
TUES.											
WED.											
THURS.											
FRI.											
SAT.											
SUN.											

OFFICE USE ONLY:

Hired ______________ **Date** ______________ **Job Title** ______________ **Supervisor's Initials** ______________

tion—any kind of formal recognition from the athletic department—can also be useful in rewarding student volunteers for a job well done.

Recruiting Student Employees

Sometimes, students are not willing or able to volunteer their time. There will also be times that you will prefer to have the dependability—and accountability—of paid employees, even if they are students.

It is often possible to recruit student employees simply by posting a notice near the area where equipment is distributed announcing the position(s) available. Another productive technique is to place an ad in the student newspaper.

It is helpful to recruit student employees when they are just entering college. This decreases the amount of turnover in the equipment room staff, which, in turn, decreases the amount of time necessary for training.

Athletes who have been injured are another good source of equipment room employees. They are often interested in working in a sports-related field, and they already know at least some of the equipment well. Finally, asking coaches, staff members, alumni, and student-athletes about individuals who may be interested in working in the equipment room can be productive.

Student workers are a special case, because in addition to their equipment room workload, they have a classroom workload to handle. It is advisable to start them off with a relatively light schedule, somewhere between 8 and 15 hours a week. More hours can be added when and if they and the manager are comfortable with an increase.

Some schools may have rules concerning the number of hours that university departments may request student employees to work. It is important to find out about such rules before setting up schedules for student workers. If students are hired as part of a school-sponsored work-study program, make sure the equipment room's practices agree with the rules of the work-study program.

As student workers stay on and become more experienced in equipment room procedures, they can become extremely valuable members of the staff. They can be entrusted to handle the laundry by themselves, prepare bags for away games, and do some maintenance on athletic equipment. Such skills can come in very handy during an equipment room's peak periods.

Recruiting Full-Time Staff

The first and most natural place to look for full-time staff members is the equipment room itself. Part-time staff members and volunteers are a natural pool for full-time staff members. The key to finding good prospects for promotion in the equipment room is to keep an eye out for promotable people and to nurture them (there is more about this in the section on "Evaluating Staff").

It is not always possible, however, to fill full-time staff positions from in-house. Many part-time staff members are students who cannot interrupt their studies for a full-time job. Often, part-time employees work part-time not because full-time work is not available, but because limited working hours fit their needs.

Another potential source of full-time staff members is graduating seniors, particularly athletes. Graduating athletes may find that work in the equipment room is a way of continuing their interest in sports. It is also possible to recruit full-time staff members from other campuses, often from other equipment rooms, since the number of full-time positions in an equipment room tends to be low compared to the number of part-time positions.

Training

Once you've hired the right people for the job, their ability to complete all of their assigned tasks comes down to how well you train them. Almost certainly, anyone you hire, including volunteers, will bring with them some knowledge of athletic equipment and how it is used. Regardless of how much knowledge they come in with, however, it is imperative that each and every employee or volunteer be introduced to equipment room practices and procedures, how they fit into the big picture, and be given the necessary information and tools to complete all of the tasks at hand. Obviously, you cannot teach someone everything they will possibly need to know about the job in a couple of training sessions. Those training sessions are, however, crucial to allowing employees to make informed decisions and/or know where to find the answers, be it through other staff or manuals such as this one.

The equipment manager or a knowledgeable staff member should go over the following areas with new employees before putting them to work:

Equipment room procedures. Examples include how equipment is checked in and out, how equipment is stored, how laundry is handled, how equipment is inventoried, who is allowed to enter the equipment room, the equipment room hours, and how to fill out any forms that may be used in the equipment room.

Familiarity with equipment. The equipment manager should show the new employee each piece of equipment carried, and how it is used, fitted, and stored.

Equipment maintenance. This should include what, if any, maintenance procedures are used on each piece of equipment before storing it, what kinds of storage conditions are optimal for different kinds of equipment, and what situations can cause equipment to deteriorate.

Rules of behavior. The new employee should learn how equipment room staff are expected to work with and treat other equipment room staff, students, student-athletes, coaches, and others they will be dealing with. This includes such things as how to say no to a student or student-athlete.

Safety practices in the equipment room. All equipment room staff should be trained in basic first aid and safety procedures pertinent to the facility, such as handling potentially toxic chemicals used for laundry (see Chapter 6, "Laundry," for more on safety and first aid). Some equipment managers also train their staff members in fundamental lifesaving techniques, such as cardiopulmonary resuscitation (CPR). It is often possible to get skilled help from the athletic department's athletic trainers in these areas.

A popular way of handling the initial staff training is to give new employees an orientation on their first day in the equipment room. This should cover all the above topics briefly and the particular duties that the new employee will start out doing in greater detail. Any new staff member, no matter his or her level of previous experience, can quickly begin working in areas that involve straightforward, repetitive procedures, such as distributing equipment or preparing towels, following a few minutes of instruction from the equipment manager or an experienced staff member. Then, as the employee becomes more familiar with equipment room practices, and as time permits, the employee can be trained in new areas. Conducting such training in slack periods in the equipment room is advisable, since it makes the employee more useful during peak periods, when there is little time available for training.

A few points to keep in mind about training your employees: it is important to establish goals and objectives for your training program, monitor the progress of the participants, and provide an open forum for your staff to be able to discuss any problems that arise. It is also strongly recommended that the initial employee training be limited to as few individuals as possible. And remember, training is an ongoing process.

Evaluating Staff

Simply teaching equipment room staff how to perform their jobs is not enough. It is also important that the equipment manager or other staff members let new employees know what is expected of them. For example, all staff need to know what the equipment manager expects of them in terms of the speed and quality of their work. If staff members know that they are expected to fold and store a load of laundry in less than an hour, they are likely to work at a pace that will get the job done in time. If they do not know what is expected of them, they will have to guess at what is required—and they can't be expected to be right.

Try to find out as soon as possible how quickly and skillfully staff members can perform various tasks. Problems with speed and quality are most apt to show up during peak periods of equipment room activity, when they will cause the greatest disturbance and you won't have the time to address them. It is better to test the abilities of staff members during slack periods, when there is time for extra help and instruction if needed. Then, throughout the year, the equipment manager should evaluate how his or her staff is doing.

There are two kinds of evaluations that equipment managers make of their staff:

- formal—the sort that is conducted annually or semi-annually and filed with the employee's records; and
- informal—the ongoing assessment of an employee's personality, motivations, and interests that determine how the equipment manager will use the staff member within the equipment room.

Formal Evaluations

Equipment room managers may or may not be required to conduct formal evaluations. Some athletic departments or schools require such evaluations of all paid employees; others do not.

If formal evaluations are required, the equipment manager should conduct such evaluations very carefully, with an eye toward protecting the best interests of the athletic department and the employee. A formal, written evaluation that goes into an employee's file constitutes a permanent record that may affect his or her employment prospects long after he or she leaves the equipment room. Great care should be taken to avoid any comments that could be misconstrued by anyone who might read the record later. At the same time, failure to note major problems with an employee's performance that the equipment manager is in a position to know about could pose some liability for the athletic department.

The equipment manager's safest course in preparing a written evaluation of an employee is to get clear guidelines from the athletic department's business office concerning what areas should and should not be covered in the evaluation, and to adhere strictly to those guidelines.

Formal employee evaluations should be conducted at the same time every year. This lets everyone know where they stand, and also ensures consistency and helps lessen the fears naturally associated with an evaluation process. The evaluation process should afford both the supervisor and the employee the opportunity to engage in what may be termed a "quality conversation." This is not the time to identify work problems; rather, it is an opportunity to discuss an individual's response to job, policy, or other changes in the workplace. The centerpiece of annual or seasonal evaluations will be "how have we improved our ability to deal with pre-identified problem areas or new or changing techniques." It is, ideally, a positive activity.

The supervisor should not use this meeting as an annual dressing down of an employee nor should it be the place to bring new deficiencies to light. For example, when confronted with an employee who is habitually late for work, one needs to have a conversation with him or her as soon as the tardiness has been identified as problematic, preferably in private. Don't wait until evaluation time. If the situation improves, he or she should be commended; if it does not improve, another discussion needs to take place, followed, possibly, with disciplinary action. The formal evaluation meeting can then be used as a forum for both parties to discuss the improvement, or lack thereof, in the situation.

The formal evaluation meeting will also allow for goals, both personal and departmental, to be identified, discussed, and evaluated. It should also provide the employee with an insight as to where the organization is going and how his or her role may or may not change.

Informal Evaluations

An equipment manager should study the personalities and interests of staff members and consider these when scheduling staff activities and planning for the future. Informal evaluations of employees are necessary and useful in answering such questions as the following:

- Which employees should I consider for promotion?
- What tasks should be regularly assigned to which employees?
- Which employees should be assigned to work together?
- How many employees will be required to handle the workload for a given task?

Some equipment room staff members may be extremely outgoing and talkative, while others may be quiet, introverted, and show less interest in talking with others. The outgoing individual may consider staffing the equipment checkout window a pleasant, interesting task; the introverted person may consider staffing the window as boring and unpleasant. By the same token, the extrovert might consider working alone in the laundry room a great chore, while the introvert might find the same task relaxing and enjoyable.

This is not meant to imply that introverted people are necessarily better suited than extroverts to work in laundry rooms. It is also possible that an introvert might find the repetitive physical labor involved in loading, folding, and storing laundry more disagreeable than a particular extrovert would. The point is that everybody has his or her strengths and weaknesses, as well as preferences based on their personality. It's important for the equipment manager to work these factors into his or her staffing considerations.

Generally, the more carefully an equipment manager matches staff members to their work, the more productive and happy the staff will be. Unfortunately, the nature of equipment room work is such that some tasks are going to be much more pleasant and interesting than others. For example, it is a safe bet that during a football scrimmage, most equipment room staff members would rather be on duty on the sidelines than take inventory. Given this fact of life in the equipment room, the equipment manager should try to be evenhanded in dispensing the "pleasant" and the "unpleasant" tasks.

Compensation

Even if you are the head of your department, there will be limits to your ability to determine compensation for your staff—there will be established protocols for salaries and benefits for both regular and student staff. Be aware, however, that whatever salary scale exists should be reviewed, and may need to be updated, periodically. It is the supervisor's role to ensure that job descriptions are current and accurate and he or she should be prepared to put forward recommendations for change in classification when the opportunity arises. You may have to go to bat for your staff to get them better compensation. And be aware of ways to augment their pay—for example, fixed pay scales, especially for student help, could be augmented by including them in a department or team's athletic awards program.

The staffing process can be one of the most rewarding aspects of management when dealt with properly. To create a strong foundation for success one needs only to think of how one would like to be treated. The ability to positively interact with coworkers, subordinates, supervisors, and athletes alike will endear the equipment manager to respect and success.

RECORD-KEEPING

Keeping accurate records is an integral part of athletic equipment management. It allows the equipment manager to know what he or she has, who is using it, and what condition it is in. It goes beyond the obvious of simply what is on hand to include forecasting needs in order to avoid the embarrassment of shortages.

Equipment managers are required to record a wide assortment of information in the most practical format for their situation. This can range from the crudest of handwritten forms to elaborate computer software packages; the important thing is the information itself and how easily it can be accessed and revised. Records that all equipment managers should keep include inventory, allocation, and maintenance files. More information on keeping various kinds of records is available in Chapter 1, "Accountability"; specific information regarding purchasing records can be found in Chapter 3, "Purchasing."

Inventory Records

The inventory is the sum of all goods belonging to your team or institution for which you are responsible. In most cases, it is divided into capital and non-capital items. The former are usually large-ticket items that can be depreciated for insurance and/or tax purposes, such as video equipment. The item may cost $20,000, but the full amount is budgeted over time, such as over five years. In this case, each year, the budget would only show an expenditure of $4,000. During those five years the video equipment also depreciates in value, which needs to be taken into account if the item needs to be replaced after two or three years.

This also often creates a situation where items exist in the inventory that have zero book value. For example, if you bought video equipment and valued it over five years, and after that time it still works, it essentially has no value and can be replaced. But until is is replaced, it still needs to be included in the inventory.

Non-capital items are taken up by the general operating budget and comprise everything else, such as uniforms, most athletic equipment, etc.

The first step in preparing an inventory is to list every possible type of item you have and then determine the number of distinguishing features for each item listed, such as color, size, right or left, manufacturer, and/or style. There are a number of software packages that will expedite this process; however, it is recommended to start the old fashioned way by handling all of your items and physically seeing and noting the differences. This will allow for an inventory that meets your needs and capabilities. Table Two, above right, shows a sample inventory for shoulder pads.

TABLE TWO

SAMPLE SHOULDER PAD INVENTORY

Shoulder Pads (Total: 100pr)

	Manufacturer	*Size*	*Quantity*	*Style*
32pr	Wilson	Small	2	SB-10
			2	SQB-10
			2	SLB-10
		Medium	1	MB-16
			3	MQB-16
			3	MOLB-16
			1	MLB-16
		Large	1	LQB-20
			2	LOLB-20
		X-Large	4	XLRB-20
			2	XLWRB-20
		XX-Large	4	XXLLB-22
			2	XXOLB-22
		XXX-Large	3	XXXOLB-24
Etc.				

The sample shoulder pad inventory tells us how many pairs of pads and the number of each type we have. It does not, however, tell us whether or not they have been issued to someone and, if so, what their specific identification number is, or anything else about them. That information would be found in the maintenance and allocation files, which are discussed later in this chapter.

In addition to the information in our sample shoulder pad inventory shown in Table Two, it's important to further differentiate between items—not just that you have three XXX-Large shoulder pads. Traditionally, this identification has been tied to the year of purchase, the quantity on hand, and their sizes, and takes the form of a number marked on each piece of equipment. For example, the annotation 03-12-L could be used, where 03 is the year of purchase, 12 indicates the particular item number, and L represents its size (in this case, large). It should be noted that while size may very well be important, it is not always necessary to represent it in the ID number. Also, there are occasions where other identifiers are needed to differentiate between the "owners" of particular items. An example of this would be between the men's and women's teams or between different departments in an educational setting. Using the previous example, the ID number for an item belonging to the Physical Education Department could be written PE03-12-L. The goal in all cases is to be as specific as possible to enable the most accurate record-keeping.

It is important to utilize a marking system that will endure the day-to-day use of the equipment and its maintenance. In most cases, the use of indelible ink markers will suffice; however, permanent tags in cloth items and/or bar codes make for a neater presentation, although they take more work on your part. Whichever you use, the main thing is that it lasts and is easy to read.

When thinking about how to label items, it is also important to figure out the best place to put the label or mark and to always mark all items of a particular kind in the same place. For example, you may choose to put a helmet's ID number on the interior of the left ear flap. This will enable you and your staff to quickly identify the piece of equipment in question. When items are marked inconsistently, it makes it harder to locate the label and, often, items end up with multiple labels (when someone doesn't find the number in the first place they look, they assume the item hasn't yet been numbered and give it another number).

In any inventory, there are items that do not receive ID numbers, because they are handled on an in-and-out basis and are not to be returned or they are a consumed item. These may vary from one organization to another, but in general, items such as hockey sticks, baseball bats, and mouth guards would not receive an inventory number but would be identified after their issue simply for player identification. These items would be listed in the inventory simply by model, type, and/or manufacturer.

Table Three, below, gives an example of a few items that might be included in a general inventory. This general inventory does not differentiate between types in a category; however, one should have a subfile indicating all of the different subtypes of equipment (e.g., models, sizes, or styles of thigh pads) and their condition, if important. This example has a "WO/Purchased" category (written off/purchased) for items that are discarded or acquired during the year. While you may or may not keep them on hand after they have been written off, it is important to indicate that they have been written off so that the totals balance, much the same as you would indicate the acquisition of any new item.

This form also indicates the period for which it is valid, namely, September 2002 through December 2002. Inventory information should be updated at season's end to give an accurate statement of what is available, while enabling the equipment manager to forecast what he or she will have to purchase to ensure there's enough of a given product for the following season.

The third type of inventory file or report is item-specific and includes all pertinent information pertaining to that item, including the ID number. This type of form could be very similar to the Shoulder Pad Inventory shown in Table Two, if done manually (see Table Four, right). When using a software package, it would simply be a query for the established database. (For example, if one wants to know how many left-handed gloves he or she has in the inventory, he or she would simply query for the topic "left-handed baseball gloves" and the program would give the answer.)

TABLE THREE

SAMPLE GENERAL INVENTORY

September 2002–December 2002

Item	*No.*	*On Hand*	*Issued*	*WO/ Purchased**	*Grand Total*
Thigh pads	200pr	82pr	118pr	+10pr	210pr
Knee pads	150pr	75pr	75pr	-5pr	145pr
Shoulder pads	150pr	40pr	110pr	0pr	150pr

**WO = items that are written off (they have become lost or destroyed); Purchased = items that have been added to the inventory.*

Keep in mind that the inventory process is more than simply counting what you have and knowing where it is or to whom it has been assigned. The records you keep should also include notes about equipment activity, such as repairs and reconditioning, which will enable you to identify usage patterns and lifespan. While there is no sure-fire equation for ordering replacements, the data that is collected will go a long way to providing you with a good idea of annual needs. Obviously, interaction with the end-users, other equipment managers, and the vendors or suppliers is essential in allowing for a greater degree of accuracy.

Inventories also provide a means for keeping technical information on all equipment, including supplier information. It is also helpful to maintain current files on suppliers of similar or alternative equipment for future needs or comparison.

The annual or semi-annual inventory process is very time consuming, which makes some people question its importance. But it is invaluable in providing the equipment manager with the necessary information to make informed decisions with respect to purchases and

TABLE FOUR

SAMPLE RIDDELL HELMET INVENTORY

Size	*Model*	*ID #*	*Issued To*
Medium	VSR-4	99-01	
		99-02	
		00-01	
		01-01	
		02-01	
Large	VSR-4	99-03	
		99-04	
		99-05	
		00-02	
		00-03	
		00-04	
		00-05	
		01-03	
		01-04	
		01-05	
		01-06	
		01-07	
		02-02	
		02-03	
		02-04	
		02-05	
		02-06	
X-Large	VSR-4	99-06	
		99-07	
		99-08	
		00-06	
		00-07	
		01-08	
		01-09	
		01-10	
		02-07	
		02-08	

acquisitions. The inventory data also enables you to maximize your budget while minimizing the number of purchase errors.

Allocation Records

The records associated with the allocation of equipment are quite similar in form to inventory files. Their main difference is in their purpose—allocation files show to whom articles have been issued or allocated and by who. For example, if an equipment staffer wants to know where all the soccer practice shorts went, he or she would look in the allocation files and be able to see that 100 pairs went to the soccer team (given to coach so-and-so on such-and-such a date) and 20 pairs were put in storage. Allocation files are particularly useful when dealing with non-equipment items, such as towels. These items are not billed to any particular team, but it is important to track their whereabouts and know when they are expected to be returned. While in several instances the issuing individual's name will appear solely as a matter of record, when it comes to protective equipment, the issuer's name will infer that this individual has fitted the equipment in question.

The big picture of the total athletic department or team organization is very dependent on allocation files in that they indicate where in the scheme of things different items have been assigned and for how long. Being able to note the period for which the items have been assigned is incorporated into most databases or software packages; however, for those individuals preparing forms manually, it requires either a new listing annually or multiple entries per item. In most cases, these files are cross-referenced by records for each athlete or team with the individual item files as referred to in the previous section on Inventory Files.

Another important function of allocation files is being able to show when an item is lent from one group to another. This is very helpful when one encounters an unforeseen shortage in an item that is in surplus in another team's inventory, such as tube socks. While at larger institutions this type of sharing may not occur very often, it is a staple of smaller operations. In this case, the loan of the socks from one team to the other would be recorded in the allocation files to balance inventory until restitution is made, whether it be financial or simple replacement. The use of general allocation files is more prevalent in multi-sport equipment rooms where the same people handle items for a number of teams.

Maintenance Records

The need to keep accurate maintenance records is twofold: these records detail all maintenance activity of the items in your general inventory, and they also indicate the location of items that are out for repair or not available for issue because they are in need of repairs. The use of the information in these records will allow for informed decisions with respect to replacement of items and/or questions of durability.

These records often take the form of a journal (see Table Five, below). This format allows for the inclusion of a Maintenance Policy, which would state the general principles of your maintenance plan. In the case of protective equipment, this statement could simply be: "It is the goal of the equipment staff to physically check all protective gear on a weekly basis and to ensure that all items are properly prepared for use."

TABLE FIVE

SAMPLE MAINTENANCE RECORD

Date	*Item*	*Action*	*Location Return*
Feb. 12/03	80 Football Helmets See attachment for ID numbers	Sent for Reconditioning	Riddell
March 1/03	60prs Hockey Socks White game socks	Sent to seamstress	in-house

Personnel Records

In addition to recording and tracking all equipment, equipment managers are expected to keep records on their staff. These include information on hours worked, wages paid, work schedules, employee performance evaluations, travel records for equipment room staff who travel with teams, and any written descriptions of the requirements of each position in the equipment room.

In addition, it's a good idea to keep resumes received from people who have applied for work in the equipment room but who were not hired, along with any notes made if they were interviewed—sometimes, staff need to be hired quickly to replace a staff member who unexpectedly quits.

STORAGE AND SECURITY

The equipment manager's need to adequately store equipment and other items of the trade in a secure environment creates a never-ending challenge. The variety of institutions and professional organizations present numerous situations and solutions, and no two are alike. There are, however, some basic common issues and solutions.

Types of Equipment Facilities

The list of facility types is extensive; for the purpose of this manual, we will deal with Multi-Sport, Single-Team, and General Usage facilities. In doing so, we will define the identifying characteristics of each of these facilities, including specific needs and some storage and security solutions.

Multi-Sport

A multi-sport equipment room would be one that is the issue and storage area for more than one sport. It goes without saying that the level of service and equipment will vary by institution, but there are a few things they have in common. They are usually comprised of multiple storage areas, each designated for a particular team or activity, housed within a secure area. They often include a laundry facility in or adjacent to the equipment area. And they are usually manned by a large number of individuals under the direction of a variety of people who may or may not report to a single authority.

This type of equipment room is almost always used only by intercollegiate team members and is not accessible to the general public or regular student body. Its main function would be to ensure that all athletes and staff have access to the necessary equipment and services required in the performance of their sport.

Access to each team's storage area is restricted to the personnel associated with that team or sport by means of a key issue system. The key system can be either a series of independent locks or a fully integrated series, which would allow the head equipment manager to access all areas with a single key.

These areas would usually contain fixed or rolling racks on which uniforms can be hung and compartments in which items can be placed for storage. In some cases, these would also be lockable. The actual layout of these cupboards and the specific type of racks used would depend on each individual sport's needs.

Ideally, a multi-sport equipment room is centrally located in a larger facility, providing easy access to all while not being directly linked to a specific team room or series of rooms. Usually, they have poor or non-existent exterior access. The multi-sport equipment room can also be a satellite facility having no shipping or receiving functions, and, in some cases, they are not even equipped for laundry.

Single-Team

The single-team equipment room is probably the most common type in use today, and there's a huge variety within this type. The level of participation or funding usually dictates at which end of the extremes one's facility falls. The basic components of the single-team equipment room are the actual storage area, an issue "window" (this can take the form of an actual counter or Dutch door), and a laundry facility. The single-team area is usually self-contained and situated in or adjacent to a team's locker room. The storage and hanging racks are sport-specific and, depending on the actual size of the facility, may or may not be portable.

As the name indicates, this type of facility is for the exclusive use of one team, with access and service limited to team members. This allows for a more open approach to storage than the multi-sport equipment room.

General Usage

A general usage equipment room is one that caters to all of an institution's teams, clubs, and departments. It is most commonly found at smaller institutions, health clubs, or municipal recreation centers. This type of facility would be accessible to all and often doubles as the "check-in" area for a series of venues.

The general usage room would be comprised of specific storage areas for each sector that it serves while also providing service to a general population or membership. Typically, equipment is checked out by users who leave some sort of i.d. at the desk. This type of equipment room may or may not contain a laundry facility or a work area. It may be subdivided into areas for in-season and out-of-season supplies and equipment.

This type of facility would have the greatest number of authorized users and, therefore, presents the most control-based problems. Security in this type of room varies greatly, but often, items not in use are moved to a "dead" storage area, which would be secure and not easily accessible.

Layout

The physical layout of an equipment room can make or break its efficiency, regardless of the particular type of room in question. It's important to give some thought as to how the various elements fit and work together. The major elements of the equipment room usually include the following:

- a secured area where equipment is stored
- a locker room area where equipment is distributed to athletes
- a window where equipment is distributed to students
- a laundry room
- an office area where equipment room records are kept
- a "shipping and receiving" area where new equipment is received and equipment for away games is packed on trucks

The layout of a given equipment room depends on the nature of the services provided. It is common to have several different equipment rooms on a single campus providing various kinds of services. Furthermore, an equipment room should be closely linked with the laundry facilities that serve it and the locker rooms it serves. If at all possible, the equipment room, laundry rooms, and locker rooms should all be designed as a single functioning unit, with plenty of thought given to the way in which each room will interact with the others.

Physical education and recreation equipment rooms, for example, generally provide towels, basketballs, volleyballs, and other team sports equipment to students. Such rooms often have a secured area where the towels and equipment are stored, a bin or laundry cart for receiving used towels, and a window for distributing towels and equipment. Locker rooms for physical education and recreation facilities tend to feature many individual lockers for the temporary storage of students' clothing while they are in class or at play.

Equipment room staff do not have to stock lockers in these areas—all they have to do is supply towels and equipment as needed for each class. Therefore, the major consideration for such facilities concerns access to and from the area where towels are distributed and returned, and access to the laundry room.

The layout of equipment rooms for major sports teams is more varied and more complex, since it must provide a wider range of services. Equipping a major sports team can involve providing laundry and towel services to athletes during practices and home games, stocking athletes' equipment lockers, providing packed equipment bags for athletes during away games, loading trucks for away games, and storing bulky equipment between practices and games.

A competitive sports team's locker room can contain full-size, 72-inch lockers, half-size, 36-inch lockers, or basket-size lockers. The layout of a sports team locker room generally calls for an open area for team meetings. Some locker rooms are designed for men only and some for women only, and some of the newer ones are designed to be easily converted for use by either gender.

Since it is an excellent idea to locate the laundry room near the equipment room, the special needs of a laundry room should be considered. For example, laundry rooms can require special plumbing and electrical fixtures. In addition, it is useful to have surfaces for folding towels and clothing, and bins for storing these items, in the laundry room.

If you're in the enviable position of designing a new equipment room, it is imperative not to relinquish responsibility for the layout of the new facility to an architect or any other well-meaning individual. Most people will only have one opportunity in their careers to build a new facility. Therefore, plan carefully and study other facilities to help avoid the pitfalls of your peers.

There are a number of components that one should strive for in any design, the most important being the location. The equipment room needs to be adjacent to the team and laundry rooms and near the playing venue, and it should have exterior access and double doors. It is also important to ensure there is sufficient space for an office, storage, and a workshop area, in addition to a folding area in the laundry room. When a lack of space makes all of these areas impossible, one should be prepared to double-up or make due with less, depending on one's own priorities. How the equipment area coordinates with other athletic areas such as the locker rooms and medical facility should also be taken into account.

Finally, it's important to consider the human aspects of running an equipment room. Consider the example of rear-loading lockers. There is much disagreement about whether rear-loading lockers are a good idea. These facilities operate like post office boxes in a mail room—the equipment room staff has access to the rear of the lockers from the equipment room, while the athletes can access the lockers from the locker room. This arrangement is highly efficient for loading lockers, but some equipment managers dislike it because it minimizes personal contact between the equipment room staff and the athletes. They feel that personal contact helps keep the staff aware of the athletes' needs and makes the athletes more apt to care for their equipment and report problems when they occur. Whether or not something like rear-loading lockers will work best for a particular situation has to be decided on a case-by-case basis.

Security

One area where you can't afford to cut back is when dealing with security. The need for a secure equipment room is a major concern for all levels of play or work. It is not enough to ensure that all areas can be locked and that everyone makes sure to keep them locked. It is also important to control access; hence, we must address not only the locks but who has the keys.

The goal is twofold: keep the equipment in and unauthorized persons, including the players and coaches, out. One should always use a sign-out system for keys. They should be given out only to authorized personnel and they should be collected at an appropriate time, such as at season's end or upon termination.

Whenever possible, all storage areas, lockers, and cupboards should be locked with padlocks or deadbolt locks keyed to the locker room series. It is always a good idea to keep the number of keys issued, regardless of their level of access, to a minimum and to use independent deadbolts on keypad doors when out of season. The security controls in place to prevent the loss of equipment and supplies also helps keep all other items from being tampered with. The limited access and the presence of an inventory/issue system will ensure that everything is where it should be and in the expected condition.

Venues

In today's athletic society, we find "home" games being held further away than some road contests and the ever-increasing use of multiple practice venues. For example, many small colleges' sports teams practice at nearby facilities that are rented out—if the school doesn't have a hockey facility, the hockey team may practice and play at the local public rink or at a nearby school. On the other end of the spectrum, colleges, particularly large schools, are increasingly playing in their local professional sports facilities. So, even when you're the home team, increasingly, it's much like being on the road.

In all such cases, it is imperative to communicate with the host agency to ascertain what is available for your use and when it can be made available. This could entail numerous communications with the stadium or arena authority where you will be practicing or playing. Likewise, as a host, you should prepare documentation for your opponents listing all of the amenities you will provide and the procedure for obtaining these items. Campus or facility maps are also important items to provide for your visitors. If possible, this information should be placed on your athletic department Web site.

Regardless of where a game or practice is taking place, it is imperative to ensure that you have everything you need at easy access and that all of your team's equipment is secure, along with all of the players' and coaches' belongings. Every effort must be made to eliminate the opportunity for theft without hindering the free flow of your team's operation. This requires that you be prepared to lock doors and trunks and/or restrict access to team facilities and ensure that access policies are well communicated to all concerned.

LEGAL LIABILITY

You may do everything in your power to ensure the safety of your athletes—regularly inspecting and upgrading equipment and facilities, training your staff to perform at the highest levels, etc.—but they will still get injured. And, sometimes, their injury can be perceived to have resulted from something the equipment room staff did or didn't do. It's never been more important than in today's litigious society to be aware of the legal issues surrounding one's work.

Basis for Legal Liability

The majority of legal liability cases in sports are torts, or lawsuits. Tort cases seek to achieve socially acceptable results by resolving the conflicting interests of two parties. In these cases, an injured party must have a reason to take action against another party in an effort to recover damages for the injury.

As this pertains to equipment managers, an athlete may sustain an injury and take action against several parties, the equipment manager among them. For example, a football player is seriously injured when his helmet comes off during a play. He or his family files a lawsuit that may include as defendants the helmet manufacturer, the coaching staff, the athletic department, even the school he plays for, as well as the equipment manager. This is based on the injured party's belief that each of these people or groups of people is in some way responsible for his injury. The legal criteria for finding someone responsible fall under the following seven categories:

1. intentional harm to the person
2. intentional harm to tangible property
3. negligence
4. strict liability
5. nuisance
6. harm to tangible personal interests
7. harm to tangible property interests

Most sports law cases are the result of negligence. In determining whether someone acted negligently, his or her actions are compared to those expected of an ordinary, reasonably prudent person under a certain set of circumstances. If the person in question did not take those types of actions under the same or similar circumstances, he or she may be found negligent and be held liable for that conduct. There are five factors that further help determine whether someone can be found liable for their actions (or lack thereof):

1. ignorance of the law
2. ignoring the law
3. failure to act
4. failure to warn
5. expense

It should be noted that there are no concrete criteria for determining negligence, because each case stands on its own set of circumstances. But the above factors are all considered when attempting a tort liability case with a charge of negligence.

Ignorance of the Law

The old saying that "ignorance of the law is no excuse" was never more true than it is in cases of sports liability. It is our job as equipment managers and facility supervisors to know the regulations and laws that pertain to our areas of responsibility. If you are uncertain about these rules, make sure you contact lawyers, manufacturers, and other equipment people—or anyone who can increase your awareness in the field—to find out the correct procedures and guidelines.

Ignoring the Law

Once you familiarize yourself with the laws, you must take care not to ignore them. Some people involved in athletics choose to ignore rules, regulations, and laws until they are forced to comply by court order or are threatened with a lawsuit.

One of the most common examples of this problem is guardrails for bleachers in most sports facilities. Many states have safety codes requiring these rails in sports facilities. Also, many countries have a national code designed to protect spectators who use these bleachers. Studies have found, however, that many facilities have no guardrails, or the ones they have are substandard. This pattern of ignoring a law may not only put people at risk physically, but, concurrently, it leaves the door open for lawsuits.

Failure to Act

When we become aware of the law and stop ignoring it, the next step is to take action on what we know. Failure to act is the leading cause of liability for a sports manager. Some facility/equipment supervisors have good intentions, but they lack the drive or ability to act until a serious injury or accident occurs. Two examples drive this point home.

A high school athletic director in Kansas attended an in-service workshop on sports programs liability. He came back from this session with the good intention of inspecting his facilities. According to his report, he became busy and failed to carry out this inspection. Soon after, a spectator at a track meet was hit in the head by a discus thrown into the stands. A Kansas court awarded the spectator $100,000 in damages because the location of the discus throw was too close to spectators in nearby bleachers. It ruled that the athletic director and school were guilty of negligence.

In a case at the college level, an athletic director requested that an indoor swimming pool be painted a lighter color so supervisory personnel could observe swimmers in the pool more clearly. The athletic director volunteered to paint the bottom of the pool himself if the paint was supplied, but the request was denied because of lack of funds. The day following his paint request/denial, a student was found at the bottom of a neighboring college's pool by swimmers in an afternoon class. The student had drowned during a morning class, but because of the dark color at the bottom of the pool, the student had gone undetected until that afternoon. Needless to say, the athletic director's paint request was immediately approved in spite of the alleged lack of funds.

This level of care extends to the equipment room and equipment staff, as well. Equipment managers must ensure that the equipment area is as safe a working environment as possible.

Failure to Warn

A safety-conscious sports manager never hesitates to act when he or she sees potential danger. But some dangers cannot be eliminated from sports no matter how safety conscious everyone involved is. When dangers cannot be eliminated, participants must be warned of the risks involved. Failure to warn is one of the key factors in sports litigation today.

Football helmets have been closely scrutinized in failure-to-warn cases. Several landmark cases occurred in the early 1980s. In 1981, a Texas court awarded Mark Daniels, a high school football player, $1.5 million for a crippling injury he received when the top of his helmet caved in while he was making a tackle. The court emphasized the importance and necessity of warning participants in sports activities of the dangers involved in the sport. It also declared that "the failure to warn was negligence" and added that "a product that does not include a warning is dangerously defective."

Courts didn't always feel that it was important to warn participants of the dangers of sport. For example, in the 1962 case of *Vendell v. School District #26C* (Oregon), a high school football player was rendered a paraplegic when he was struck on the head during play. The court in this case ruled:

> "Body contacts, bruises, and clashes are inherent in the game. There is no other way to play it. No prospective player need be told that participants in the game of football may sustain injury. That fact is self-evident."

The fact that athletes may be injured in any sport is no longer "self-evident." The courts have decided that sports are not inherently dangerous (with the exception of boxing); they only become dangerous in the way that they are conducted. No matter how obvious, it is important that all parties involved take the necessary precautions to ensure that participants are advised of the risks involved in their sport.

In this regard, equipment managers must, at the very least, make sure warning labels are properly affixed to all equipment requiring them, such as football helmets. This tenet also extends to the equipment room and equipment personnel. Equipment managers should ensure that all staff understand the risks associated with working in certain areas, such as with certain chemicals used in laundry.

Expense

Expense is of primary concern to sports administrators, but it also must concern equipment managers and facility supervisors. When there are budget cuts, or sports managers are unwilling to appropriate funds, maintenance of equipment and facilities will usually suffer. The following two cases illustrate how the lawsuits will invariably cost more than the extra dollars required for equipment and facilities.

In 1981, a New York jury awarded the wife of a deceased high school worker $1,400,000 after it found the school liable in his death. He fell to his death when the railing he grabbed trying to get onto a platform from a stepladder gave way. During the trial, it was found that a nut and bolt that should have secured the railing was not in place. The school was found liable because it failed to produce a program of preventive maintenance or inspection.

This case, and hundreds of others like it, makes it clear that facility safety improvements and routine maintenance inspections with follow-up repairs are a budget priority. So, the next time someone denies your request for funds and tells you to "let it slide this time," remind him or her of the potential for liability.

Parties Involved in Liability

When someone is injured, there is often a need to shift the responsibility—to find someone to blame. Rarely will there be an obvious guilty party—in athletics, fortunately, it isn't often that someone purposefully injures someone else. As described above, there will still be people who can be found to be in some way responsible for the injuries. When an athlete is injured, that list of people can include anyone and everyone who had any part in the athlete's participation, from the school/club, administrators, coaches, manufacturers, athletic trainers, and equipment managers.

Participant/Plaintiff Liability

First, it is necessary to look at the degree to which the injured party is responsible or liable for his or her own actions. When the plaintiff chose to play his or her sport, he or she should have been warned of the possibility of injury. This knowledge leads to an assumption of risk, because all persons take responsibility for their own safety. In situations in which the athlete has knowledge of the dangers of the sport (see Failure to Warn, above), he or she must assume the majority of the liability; however, if the athlete is not warned of the dangers, he or she assumes none of the risk. If the athlete has no knowledge of the dangers and makes no effort to determine the hazards, he or she may be considered to be contributing to the negligence. This situation is called contributory negligence.

Contributory negligence would prevent the injured party from recovering damages because that person was in some way, no matter how slight, responsible for causing his or her own injury. The court will decide this responsibility, and what action is appropriate, by considering factors such as the person's age, physical capabilities, and training before it decides fault.

Some states have also enacted the concept of comparative negligence, in which case the damages are prorated according to degree of negligence. In these states, contributory negligence is no longer a factor. For example, there was a case of a student at Occidental College in California who stepped on a loose basketball and ran into an unpadded gym wall during intramurals. The court found the college 75 percent at fault and the student 25 percent at fault under the comparative negligence concept. The student was seeking damages of $60,000, and therefore received $45,000 ($60,000 x 0.75); if he had lived in a contributory negligence state, he would have received nothing.

Staff and Supervisor Liability

Just as the participant is liable for his or her actions, we must consider our personal liability as equipment managers and coaches who issue equipment. Normally, equipment personnel are not the sole targets of a lawsuit, but can be named as co-defendants along with their employer. The reason for lack of financial responsibility is twofold—the "deep-pocket" concept as well as the doctrine of respondent superior.

The first is fairly self-explanatory: The plaintiff must recover a large dollar amount to cover the damages from a catastrophic injury; therefore, the plaintiff will name as a defendant the entity that can pay a large settlement. The wealthier the equipment supervisor is, the more vulnerable he or she is to liability suits.

We must remember that lawyers will be compensated with a percentage of the plaintiff's damages, so they have an interest in finding the deep pocket for their client as well as to recover their own fee. Because equipment supervisors are generally not as wealthy as their employers or an equipment manufacturer, they are not usually the sole targets for large lawsuits.

The second reason that the plaintiff will not choose equipment personnel as the sole defendant when seeking damages is the doctrine of respondent superior. This doctrine means that an employer can be held liable for an act committed by an employee if the act can be considered to be within the scope of his or her employment. The liability is transferred wholly to the employer, because he or she created the situation whereby the employee did what he or she did. This is true regardless of whether or not the employee is properly supervised by his or her employer or the employee is acting on the employer's orders. Respondent superior does not relieve the employee of direct liability; however, it does give the plaintiff a reason to aim at the deep-pocketed employer. It must also be pointed out that in a case in which respondent superior is used by the plaintiff, the employer is named as sole defendant with the employee's negligence as a basis, but the employee may be sued individually in a later case.

For the equipment manager, this lack of financial responsibility is a relief, but it should not give you a false sense of security. As the trends in litigation in recent years are to include everyone in lawsuits, the danger becomes more pronounced. Damages in personal lawsuits must be paid in full, and, in the absence of adequate insurance, they come out of your pocket (or your wages) and cannot be dispelled by declaring bankruptcy. Therefore, always take care to act as a reasonable, prudent professional and be aware of your own liability.

In addition to the financial dangers, being named as a co-defendant or as a basis for negligence in a respondent superior case can be professionally devastating to the equipment supervisor. This is more evident when you look at things from your employer's viewpoint. If you are considered negligent for your actions, the employer is not being responsible or prudent in continuing to employ you. Likewise, it would not be prudent for any other employer in the field of athletics to employ you for the same job function in which you were negligent.

This vicarious liability (employer assumes employee liability) makes supervision and hiring of competent employees a crucial issue for administrators, including equipment managers. Managers can be held responsible when the standard reasonable care requirement is not met by anyone for whom they are vicariously liable. There was a case of a student being awarded more than $1 million following a gymnastics injury. It was found that the instructor was guilty of negligence, but the administrator was also included in the suit for failing to supervise the instructor.

Administrators will further expose themselves to liability if they do not hire competent personnel. This goes for volunteers, too. Any volunteers under the equipment manager's guidance need to be fully able to perform whatever functions he or she assigns to them. The administrator must exercise reasonable care to check volunteers' qualifications, just as if they were salaried employees.

Manufacturer/Product Liability

Equipment and facilities liability begins with the manufacturer's product. A product is considered any consumer good and the container in which it is sold. A vacant lot that is changed by an earth mover into a baseball diamond becomes a "product" and the earth moving company can be held liable for bumps and holes in the field that cause injury.

Product manufacturers can only be held liable in cases where the product is being used for the purpose intended by the seller, and the consumer must prove there was a defect when the product left the control of the manufacturer or seller or that the product was inherently dangerous. A case involving a product that is deemed defective can create numerous defendants—anyone involved in the chain of construction and distribution.

To see how product liability relates to the equipment manager, let's take a look at which defendants are affected and how they are affected. In a $2.5 million liability suit, *Halbrook v. Oregon State University,* the defendants (accused of causing a baseball player's death due to faulty artificial turf) included the artificial turf manufacturer, the artificial turf installer, the asphalt subsurface manufacturer, the asphalt installer, and the university that was responsible for the selection, maintenance, and repair of the field. The manufacturer is responsible for reasonable care in both the manufacture and design of their wares to ensure consumer safety when these products are used in the manner for which they were intended. In addition, if a product could be dangerous even if used properly, it is the duty of the manufacturer to warn the consumer. However, it is not the responsibility of the manufacturer to produce the safest or best designed product—only to meet legal standards involved in the manufacturing process and to be considered "reasonably" safe when compared with similar products.

The responsibility for comparing various manufacturers' products falls on the seller, whether it be the retailer or wholesaler. The seller has the duty to inspect all products that he or she sells, particularly those he or she knows or has reason to suspect are dangerous. An interesting twist to this occurs in the laws of several states where if a new, improved product is introduced, the older, less advanced product is considered instantly obsolete and unsafe. Thus, a seller and manufacturer can be held liable for any injuries resulting from using the "old" product. In this situation, as in any other when a seller may be aware of product danger, the seller must warn the purchaser of this hazard to avoid liability.

CONCLUSION

As this chapter points out, when there is a liability suit, everyone involved in the athletic world surrounding the plaintiff and defendant is affected. All the parties involved must work together to ensure that reasonable care is taken so that a participant is as safe as possible. The scariest part of all is that as an equipment manager, you can do all the things you think are reasonable and prudent and still find yourself involved in liability cases.

Should we just give up and hope we are lucky enough not to be involved with a catastrophic injury case? No, as equipment managers, we must care for the athletes' equipment and facilities as if they were to be used by our loved ones. We must always strive to be informed of the latest developments in our field. And we must train our staffs and supervise them so that they can perform their duties to the best of their abilities.

The position of athletic equipment manager today requires those who aspire to occupy it be capable managers of more than just equipment. They must possess good communication skills while understanding their role within their organization; they need to be record-keepers who are computer literate; and they must be innovative when it comes to storage and police-like in terms of security. They will also need to be well-versed in human resources and pertinent government and institutional policy to ensure day-in and day-out compliance. And they need to understand and help minimize the risks associated with participating in sports.

AEMA
CERTIFICATION
MANUAL

CHAPTER 3

ATHLETIC EQUIPMENT MANAGERS ASSOCIATION

Purchasing

By Dale Strauf

PURCHASING

The need to establish sound purchasing plans for athletics, physical education, intramural, and recreation has never been greater. Regardless of the economy, available funds for the areas equipment managers are responsible for always seem to be tight. Budget increases rarely coincide with increases in the cost of equipment.

To successfully manage equipment with the budgets provided, it is important to make wise purchasing decisions. This section of the manual offers some suggestions that will help establish an efficient purchasing system for your organization.

PURCHASING EQUIPMENT

Purchasing athletic, physical education, intramural, and recreation equipment and supplies is an ongoing process. At any point in the year, equipment personnel are reviewing inventories, gathering product information, compiling requests for new equipment and submitting them, gathering bids from suppliers, tracking orders, and restocking shelves. When one team is in one place in the process, another is somewhere else. Which is why it's so important to be organized and to keep the purchasing process moving as efficiently as possible. Here's an overview of that process:

1. *Initiation.* The available stock is inventoried, establishing a need for equipment. A request is then made for equipment to fulfill, augment, supplement, or improve the program's stocks. Individual requests are received from coaches as well as from physical education, recreation, and intramural directors. Each department is encouraged to request the items it feels are needed for its programs.
2. *Review of requests.* The proper administrative personnel will approve or reject requests after careful consideration of need has been established. The high school athletic director or college equipment manager will usually have this responsibility. Information pertaining to existing inventories, anticipated program size, and condition of equipment will establish a need to purchase.
3. *Review of budget allocations.* A budget code number is assigned after availability of funds in that category has been determined. The business manager sets the budget. In athletics, money budgeted for equipment will be divided among individual teams. The size of the squad and the nature of the sport will determine the funds needed to equip the sport. For example, it takes a great deal more money to equip a football team than it does to equip a basketball team. There are more players on a football team, and they need protective equipment because of the contact involved. Basketball is not a contact sport; therefore, it requires little or no protective equipment.
4. *Preparation of specifications.* Specifications that give exact requirements are prepared in detail and made available to prospective contractors or vendors. The following are examples of specifications:
   a. Wilson football (Cornell imprint) GST 1003 NCAA; 100 each; no substitutes.
   b. Baseball-type coach caps; Big Play; 36 each large to x-large size range; red cap with white block "C" feathered in black 2"; 18 mesh back, 18 solid back; no substitutes.
5. *Receipt of bids.* The contractors and vendors must submit their bids on or before the stated deadline. After the bids are received, they are compared and awarded to the lowest responsible bidder. When reviewing the bids, care must be taken to make certain that prices given are for the items on the bid sheet, not substitutes. If you are concerned about the reliability of a vendor, do not send that vendor a bid.
6. *Issue of purchase order to supplier.* After the bids have been evaluated and awarded, the business manager prepares specific recommendations for approval. After approval, a purchase order is issued that fulfills the requirements at the most competitive bid price.

   At Cornell University, we usually do not notify successful bidders—the award of a purchase order will indicate success in the bidding process. We do not notify vendors who are not successful in the bidding process. If they inquire, we share only the information that is permitted by our central purchasing department.

7. *Following up.* If any questions concerning goods purchased surface, contact the vendor by e-mail or telephone to satisfy the question. For example, each purchase order has a requested delivery date. If the items purchased have not arrived by the requested date, contact the vendor by e-mail or telephone to check on the status of the items in question. Continue to make this inquiry periodically until the items are received.
8. *Central receiving.* Central receiving is responsible for receiving incoming goods; signing and checking the carrier's delivery notice; identifying and recording incoming goods; reporting receipt to purchasing, inventory control, and quality control personnel; and making prompt disposition to the appropriate department.
9. *Tracking.* The entire purchasing process is recorded electronically, generating a computer record for each order that carries a unique number it can be tracked by. A hard copy is also printed out and placed in a file sorted numerically by sport. A notebook journal also records all purchase orders. Receipt of items is recorded on the hard copy in the individual file for each sport. The date the items are received is recorded on the copy next to the item. All shipping documents are also filed with the hard copy of the purchase order. When an invoice is received, an electronic record of the items as received is entered into the computer and the invoice is paid. If we have experienced any problems with delivery, billing, or the product, notes indicating the problem are placed in the individual file. Depending on the nature of these notes, future purchasing decisions could be affected negatively or positively.

INVENTORY

Before contemplating the purchase of any item, a need should be established and justified. This starts with a detailed inventory of what's in stock. The inventory should be itemized and it should include the quantity and quality of the equipment. Comparing the inventory to the needs of the members participating in each area of responsibility (e.g., each sport) should furnish an accurate need to purchase.

The inventory should be conducted at the conclusion of a sport season and just prior to ordering equipment for the following season. For example, if your football season ends in November and you order your equipment for the following year in March, your reconditioning and inventory should take place in December, January, and February.

The inventory should be conducted in a meticulous manner. Items should be counted and totals recorded in categories depicting the condition of the equipment. Suggested categories are new, good, and poor. This will help estimate the longevity of the item.

All records must be accurate and legible. Computerization is a great method of keeping records neat. Once the information has been keyed into the computer, it is easy to change and retrieve. There are several programs available for athletic type inventories. Many equipment managers build inventory systems to match their needs using a database.

Bar coding is a relatively new method of conducting inventories in the athletic equipment management profession. Each item is coded and a scanner is used to count and record inventories. This method of inventory is extremely accurate and saves a great deal of time, so it's not surprising that bar coding has experienced a great deal of success in athletic equipment management. With the added emphasis on accountability, the use of bar coding systems will continue to increase in our profession.

The following are some helpful hints to aid in your inventory process:

1. Hang all numbered items—jerseys, jackets, and warmups. This makes it easier to store these items. It also helps in counting, checking numbers, and making repair decisions. Hanging helps the equipment manager to easily locate and examine these items.
2. Group similar items together:
   - helmets—hang on a helmet tree or on wall hooks, according to style and size
   - shoulder pads—hang on a rack, according to sport, type, and size
   - accessory pads—pair and stack or bag sets of pads
   - cloth items that cannot be hung (shorts, tees, girdles, pants)—fold with the fold facing out and stack according to size and style
   - shoes—box new shoes and stack them according to size and style. Used shoes should be tied together and stacked according to size and style
3. Separate all equipment repair items—screws, hangers, buckles, laces, and straps.

REQUESTS

Requests usually originate with physical education teachers, coaches, or managers in charge of various instructional programs within the organization. Usually, requests are received by a central agency such as an equipment or business office. Decisions to grant or deny requests are based on inventories, priorities, and total budget allocations.

This procedure will encounter problems if the decision-making people are not sensitive to the equipment needs of all areas in the organization. In athletics, physical education, recreation, and intramural, funds are allocated to each section by the business manager and the athletic director. The most efficient purchasing method seems to use a designated person who is familiar with all aspects of equipment management (ideally, a certified member of the AEMA) to coordinate all purchases.

That central person will still need to work to a varying degree with others in the athletic department. For example, before any purchase order is processed, it needs to be approved by the designated level of administration. Depending on the institution, this could be one person or a group of administrators, such as the athletic director, an associate athletic director, the business manager, and/or the coach. Athletic directors typically address issues like style, color, and program priorities. Business managers address budgetary issues. Coaches and equipment managers address all equipment issues pertaining to the individual program. The extent to which the various administrators are involved can vary greatly depending on your institution.

Coaches can offer a great deal of information when selecting equipment. In addition to making decisions about their own programs, they should also be among the decision-making party when purchasing equipment that is uniform in nature, such as practice sweats that all teams will use. Coaches usually have their convention at the conclusion of their season, where they have an opportunity to see all the latest equipment for their individual sport.

Knowledge of equipment sources and product information is essential for any efficient purchasing system. While the person responsible for purchasing relies on information from individual coaches, managers, and physical education instructors, the following are some additional sources of product information:

- Web sites established by manufacturers and organizations contracted to furnish product information and sources
- catalogues furnished by suppliers
- trade journals containing articles on new products and substitutions, information on suppliers and personnel, and the advertisements in these journals
- industrial advertising material sent to organizations in the trade
- trade exhibits where suppliers exhibit and provide detailed data on their products (e.g., AEMA National Convention, Super Show)
- sales representatives who furnish valuable information and service on their products
- maintenance of a source databank that classifies and stores information on suppliers for reference and quick retrieval

With the increasing demand on manufacturers for equipment, it is important to adhere to a strict ordering schedule. If an institution waits too long to order its equipment, it jeopardizes timely delivery. It is important to receive early delivery on equipment so it can be added to the inventory, labeled, and made ready for issuing. The following is a recommended schedule for ordering athletic equipment. If these ordering schedules are used, there should be no problems with late equipment deliveries.

1. Fall sports (football, volleyball, soccer, field hockey, cross country)—March 1.
2. Winter sports (basketball, swimming, gymnastics, wrestling, ice hockey)—June 1.
3. Spring sports (baseball, softball, lacrosse, track, tennis)—October 1.

Pre-budget approval has been the main obstacle to early equipment ordering for many institutions. The fiscal year begins on July 1 for many schools and colleges. This necessitates making purchases after the fiscal year begins. Initiating purchases at such a late date jeopardizes delivery of equipment for fall sports. If fall sport teams were allowed to order equipment in March, and the equipment was not received until June, it would not be necessary to pay the invoices until after the budget year had started in July. The amount of money budgeted for fall sports would need to be estimated if this schedule is used.

PURCHASING POLICIES

Basically, nine purchasing policies should be considered before any purchasing of equipment is initiated:

1. *Standardization of equipment.* Standardization of equipment is a common expression used among people who handle or purchase athletic equipment. It means that a school adopts a certain color, type, and style of equipment that is maintained over a period of time. For example, athletic departments standardize equipment such as travel bags, game warmups, sideline jackets, practice underwear, and practice sweats. When these items are standardized, reordering is much easier and equipment control is much more efficient. It is also cost effective when many teams share a common item of equipment. When items are shared, the necessity to keep large inventories is reduced. In addition, when a certain type of ball is

standardized for athletics, physical education, recreation, and intramurals, it is possible to take advantage of quantity discounts when purchasing.

2. *Quality merchandise.* The best policy is to purchase the better quality or grades of equipment. The manufacturer who has been supplying quality equipment for a long period of time can usually be depended upon to continue doing so when purchasing considerations are made. If a new company is being considered, it is a good idea to ask for samples that can be field-tested before a determination to purchase is made. If the company has confidence in their product, they will usually allow field-testing. You can also determine quality by asking an institution that is already using the product. When in doubt, buy the better brand-name equipment. An established company will usually provide the best service on the equipment it sells.
3. *Purchasing from reputable businesses.* This is a corollary to purchasing quality merchandise. It is essential to deal with companies that have a proven reputation for sound business practices. Established companies offer a greater degree of service on the materials they supply. Smaller, less well-established companies should be investigated before a purchasing contract is finalized. They need to have the capacity to service what they sell.

   As mentioned above, when considering using a new vendor, ask for references. You'll want to know what other organizations have used this particular vendor. Contact the references to establish vendor efficiency and quality. We also ask manufacturer's representatives who call on us if the vendor can supply the types of items we purchase.
4. *Buying within the range of the ability to pay.* Spending more than you are budgeted can jeopardize employment and vendor relations. Although vendors are in business to make a profit, schools must adhere to an established budget. Bad relationships are created between the vendor and the school when payments are delayed because of a lack of funds.
5. *Ordering early.* When equipment is ordered early, the school enjoys early delivery, better equipment management (marking and storing), and better quality equipment. If equipment is ordered late, the manufacturer is pressured to produce the product in a short period of time. When a job is hurried, the quality of workmanship can be compromised, and the chances of having orders filled inaccurately increase. It is essential in athletics to have the equipment in-house and ready to issue before the season begins. There are also times when early order discounts are given when equipment is ordered before a certain date.
6. *Considering the best interest of the school.* Personal gain should not influence purchasing. If a vendor makes an offer of personal gain in exchange for purchasing considerations, that vendor should be avoided when future bids are distributed. Accepting a bribe jeopardizes an equipment manager's career.
7. *Establishing friendly relationships with vendors.* When dealing with suppliers, certain businesslike actions foster a good relationship. For example:
   - Avoid requesting bids or quotations unless you sincerely expect to consider the supplier.
   - Furnish fair and clear specifications to the greatest extent possible.
   - Conduct business in a fair, competitive atmosphere.
   - Respect the confidence of the pricing and other proprietary data furnished by a supplier as a basis for selection.
   - Do not take unfair advantage of suppliers' errors.
   - Avoid favoritism—do not give some suppliers another opportunity to amend bids or quotations and exclude other suppliers from doing the same.
   - Suppliers should make prompt and fair adjustments when there is a deficiency in performance, such as poor quality or less than timely delivery.
   - If they ask, courteously advise unsuccessful suppliers in the bid process of their rejection with an explanation that does not betray the successful supplier's confidence (we withhold the name of the successful bidder and/or the successful bid amount).
   - Respond promptly to correspondence or telephone communications.
   - Do not take samples unless you intend to examine or test them and furnish the supplier with a report of the results.
   - Avoid any obligation to a supplier outside strict business obligations.
   - Cooperate with a supplier in any area of the business transaction not described in this article.
8. *Take advantage of legitimate discounts.* The following are some legitimate discounts that are commonly offered:
   - quantity discounts (discounts are based on the size of an order)
   - discounts for early orders (discounts are based on when an order is placed)
   - close-outs (usually offered at the end of the year on items that didn't sell)
   - promotional discount (if a program wears a certain brand, free items are offered)
   - inventory reduction discounts (year-end sales on excess inventories)
   - discounts on blemished articles (discounts on slightly defective equipment)

- trade discounts (discounts that are offered by manufacturers of certain items)
- cash discounts (percentage discount is given if the bill is paid by a certain date)

9. *Bids and specifications.* At least three bids are usually required. Some states use a state contract system whereby vendors, including physical education suppliers, provide a standing bid on specified items for a period of time (six or 12 months).

   There are two common classifications of bids: formal and informal. Formal bids require public advertising and public opening, and are awarded to the lowest responsible bidder. Informal bids can be made by telephone quotation or written quotation; the latter is preferred. Informal bids are usually used if the dollar amount is small.

   In bidding, it is important to furnish fair and clear specifications giving all participants an opportunity to be successful. Small purchases ($200 to $500) can be made without bids. Usually, departments will issue select staff credit cards that are to be used to purchase specific items that cost less than $500.

   Your bids should be sent out as soon as a need for products can be established. Your need will depend to a large extent on your end-of-season inventory. If your soccer season ends in late November, your bid requests should be completed in mid-January. The central purchasing department documents and distributes the bids by early February. The due date for the bids to be returned by the participating vendors is three to four weeks after they have been distributed.

WRITTEN FORMS

There are many written forms that are exchanged during a purchasing transaction. The following paragraphs describe the most common of these forms:

1. *Requisition.* A requisition form is sent to the administrative department to request that certain articles of equipment be ordered. The brand name, style, and quantity of each piece of equipment should be clearly indicated on this form. If the specifications are complete, future misunderstandings can be avoided. Requisitions are often made informally, without necessarily submitting a form.
2. *Purchase order.* This is the instrument by which goods are purchased to fill a request. Often, it starts out as a bid sheet, or request for proposal, which is sent out to prospective bidders with an explanation of institution policy (see Appendix A on page 39). Every purchase order should include the following information: the name and address of your school, the name and address of the vendor, complete specifications on the equipment being ordered, the number of items being ordered, the unit prices, the total prices, the payment terms, the arrival date, FOB (Free on Board) information (which refers to the cost of shipping and which party—the buyer or the seller—pays for it), the date, the account code, the order number, the department of internal reference, the requisition number, and a signature. (See Appendix B on page 42.)

   The purchase order gives the physical education or athletic director, purchasing agent, and administrator a record of all purchases. Many institutions use an electronic purchasing system whereby purchase orders are entered through the computer. Compared to keeping handwritten notes, this system is faster, offers more efficient record-keeping capabilities, and facilitates receiving and accounting operations. The electronic system also gives the business manager better control over who is ordering what items. Only certain responsible staff members are given the proper clearance to process purchase orders.

   It is important to write complete specifications for the items being purchased or requested. There should be no doubt about what items are being purchased, or the requested quantities. There should be no opportunity for prospective bidders to substitute items. Sizes should be furnished, if applicable. Colors and lettering specifications should be complete, if applicable. If there is still an element of doubt concerning the product being requested, samples should be requested. Before bids or purchase orders are processed, all product information must be provided. This will eliminate the possibility of substitutions or receiving the wrong items.
3. *Voucher.* A voucher is an institution's own form on which it can be billed. The voucher, in duplicate, is sent to the vendor with the purchase order. When the order is received and the voucher is returned by the vendor and found to be in order, the bill is paid. Much of this procedure is often done electronically by fax. The voucher generates an electronic form that is sent to the person responsible for receiving. The items listed on the purchase order are received electronically, and the bill is paid. This expedites the entire purchasing process. Electronics have made the receiving and payment process prompt and accurate, with excellent record-keeping capabilities that facilitate accountability. A procedure that once required a week to finalize can now be completed in hours.

PERTINENT QUESTIONS

Regardless of the number of people involved in the selection process, the following 11 questions may serve as guides when considering the purchase of equipment for use in physical education, athletic, recreation, or intramural programs:

1. *Is it safe?* The National Operating Committee on Standards for Athletic Equipment (NOCSAE) has done a great deal to make athletic equipment safer. Since its inception in 1969, NOCSAE has been a leading force in the effort to improve athletic equipment and, as a result, reduce injuries. Some NOCSAE efforts include the development of standards for football, lacrosse, baseball, and softball helmets and facemasks. This research has led to a better understanding of the mechanism of head and neck injuries. NOCSAE is currently working on standards for hockey helmets that are near implementation. The uniqueness of the NOCSAE organization is that it is comprised of representatives from almost every group with an interest in athletic equipment—the manufacturer, re-conditioner, dealer, and consumer. These diverse interests have joined forces in an attempt to arrive at a common goal of improving athletic equipment. Wayne State University, long pre-eminent in research on head and neck injury and protection mechanics, directs the research for NOCSAE.
2. *How about the quality?* A company that has been supplying a good product for a long time can be considered an established company. When you buy from an established manufacturer, there is usually a high degree of quality in the product. An established company will also service the equipment it sells. When purchasing equipment from a new company, be sure that you are receiving the same quality that an established company offers. Requesting the opportunity to field-test equipment from a new company is a good practice.
3. *Has it been tested in use?* There are several methods of assuring that equipment has been field-tested. For example, check with other schools that have used the equipment in question, ask for samples and conduct your own field-test, and check for a seal that would indicate that the equipment has been tested by a certified testing agent, such as NOCSAE.
4. *Is it guaranteed?* This will usually be stated in the purchasing agreement. When purchasing a new product from a young company, it is a good idea to ask for a written guarantee. When purchasing from an established company, the company will stand behind the equipment it sells.
5. *Will replacements be available later?* This will not be a problem when stock items are being purchased. When custom uniforms are being purchased, however, it is a good policy to order extra uniforms in an assortment of different sizes. When purchasing numbered uniforms, order extra blanks and have them numbered as needed. When standardizing an equipment item, ask for a commitment from the company representatives that they plan to offer the item for a certain period of time. When purchasing items that will need to be replaced, it is a good policy to buy from an established manufacturer.
6. *Is it cut to fit properly?* When ordering custom uniforms, it is recommended that the vendor receiving the order size the uniforms. The vendor can come to the institution and measure the team members, or a list of measurements can be supplied by the institution. This will make the vendor responsible for sizing; if mistakes are made in the cut of the uniforms, the vendor will be accountable for making the proper adjustments. When ordering stock uniforms for athletes, be certain to ask for a cut to match the level of player with whom you are working (youth, high school student, college player, professional athlete). If, for example, a certain percentage of your athletes are tall, ask for extra length in that number of uniform pants being purchased. It is a good idea to keep a sizing card on all returning athletes. This will take the guesswork out of purchasing uniform items.
7. *Is it attractive?* Beauty is in the eye of the beholder. Each individual team must decide on the style of uniform it wants to purchase. The colors will usually be determined by department or school policy. A uniform should never be designed so that it will cause athletes to become self-conscious of what they are wearing. When purchasing uniforms and equipment, make sure the companies you are dealing with can manufacture them in the colors you require. If your school colors are black and a specific shade of green, for example, you want to make sure you can get the right shade of green, and that you can continue getting the same color year after year.
8. *If ordered, when will it be delivered and be available for use?* One area on the purchase order gives the date by which the equipment should be received. When the vendor accepts the purchase order, that company agrees to deliver the equipment on or before this date. The date entered in this column should be well in advance of the date by which the equipment is needed.
9. *Is it priced competitively?* This question will usually be answered if the bidding system is followed. The lowest responsible bidder should be awarded the

purchase order. When using telephone quotes, at least three vendors should be contacted.

10. *Is it easy to maintain?* Equipment that needs expensive maintenance will be a drain on the athletic reconditioning budget. Buttons and zippers should be avoided when selecting athletic uniforms. Uniform materials should be colorfast, wash and wear, and shrink-resistant.
11. *Is it a priority need, and are funds available to purchase it?* This question should be resolved when the requisition is reviewed. The inventory will indicate whether or not the equipment is needed. When the bids are received and the totals are compared to the budget, funds available will be indicated. Protective equipment should be given the highest priority when determining budgets.

SAMPLE SCENARIOS

Purchasing procedures and requirements vary from one institution to another. It is hard to develop a purchasing scenario that will mirror every program involved in athletic equipment management. Below are some specific purchasing situations and the steps to be taken when making purchases that vary in regards to the amount of money involved:

Large purchases (in excess of $5,000)

Cornell recently standardized a practice short that will be worn by all athletes. After polling representatives from all levels of involvement, we decided on the fabric and construction of our short. We contacted selected manufacturers of shorts and asked that a sample be constructed and sent to us for evaluation.

After the samples were evaluated by our program representatives (athletes, coaches, equipment staff), they were field-tested by our athletes. During our field-testing, the samples were subjected to in-house laundry procedures in an effort to evaluate wear and maintenance of the material. Based on the results, we made a decision on the manufacturer and developed specifications to be used in the bidding process.

We relied on the manufacturer to provide information that would create clear specifications that would be fair and equal to all vendors involved in bidding. After the bids were completed, they were sent to a central purchasing department for documentation. The purchasing department set a date at which the bid was offered along with an identification number for the bid. The formal bid also established a due date and explained all purchasing policies involved in the bidding procedure. The bids were sent to selected vendors who provide items that are specified on the bid. When the bids were returned to the central purchasing department, they were recorded and returned to the requesting program.

All things being equal, the program manager should select the vendor who has offered the product for a price that is in the best interest of the organization. When the purchase order is processed, the bid number is indicated. The purchase order will specify payment terms, shipping terms, account distribution, delivery dates, quantities, and individual and total prices. The same specifications used for bidding should be used for the purchase order.

Example: Don Alleson red mesh short w/drawstring #HD590P; 7" inseam; white 1.5" athletic block lettering on left thigh; sizes: 30 dz. medium, 80 dz. large, 50 dz. x-large, 20 dz. xx-large.

The shorts were ordered and tracked. They were received by the requested date, inspected, inventoried, and distributed, with some going to teams and some going into storage for distribution later in the year. Notes were kept on the entire process, along with copies of all the forms involved.

Small purchases (less than $500)

Many institutions furnish procurement cards to individuals who have purchasing privileges. After permission is given to purchase, the card serves as a credit card to complete the purchase. This procedure eliminates much of the paperwork involved in purchasing. This method of purchasing should be reserved for situations that occur at the last minute and cannot be predicted. It would be cost-effective to secure telephone price quotes from at least three vendors who supply the items being purchased. Planned purchases, regardless of their sizes, should always be subjected to the bid process, even if informally done over the phone.

Blanket purchase orders

It is hard to predict the quantities that need to be purchased with certain items. These items are subjected to the bidding process, but when the purchase order is initiated, the quantities may not be finalized. These situations are addressed with a Blanket Purchase Order with a certain dollar amount. For example, the need for hockey sticks is hard to predict, because an unknown number will invariably break during the session. Sticks are ordered as needed against the blanket order. If the total is reached, the order is closed or the dollar amount is increased. If there are remaining funds on the order, you pay for only the items ordered. This method of purchasing saves time and addresses the needs of the program when those needs are not clearly identified.

APPENDIX A

Sample Request For Proposal Form

REQUEST FOR PROPOSAL NO. 05001-008-03
CORNELL UNIVERSITY
ATHLETICS
ATHLETIC EQUIPMENT
April 2, 2003

GENERAL INFORMATION

Cornell University Department of ATHLETICS has a need to acquire ATHLETIC EQUIPMENT as per the requirements outlined within this RFP.

Answers to all questions on the following pages are required. Answers should be presented as follows:

1. Specific—For any questions requesting specific information, such as numbers, names, locations, etc., please answer directly or indicate a reason for not answering (e.g., "company policy prohibits release of this information"). Although optional materials are welcome, answers to direct questions should contain all specific information requested rather than making extensive cross-reference to supporting material.

2. General—For questions requesting more general information, answer directly to highlight important items or refer to supporting materials, as appropriate. If vendor complies completely with a question/statement as written, response should be "Comply."

3. Order and Numbering—Answer specific questions in the order of appearance in this RFP. Number each answer as the questions are numbered.

Questions not answered as specified above will be considered non-responsive.

Any optional materials which will be useful in our evaluation are welcome.

Any questions or clarifications of this RFP should be directed to the department for technical questions (DALE STRAUF, 607-255-4115) or to the Purchasing Agent. Cornell will not be responsible for comments or inquiries directed elsewhere, either written or oral. This RFP shall in no way be modified by anyone other than the responsible agent in conjunction with the requisitioning department.

EVALUATION CRITERIA

All proposals will be evaluated jointly by the Office for Purchasing Services and department staff. Evaluation and selection of vendors to provide products and services as defined in this RFP to Cornell will be based on price, warranty, vendor support and references, quality and technical evaluation information as provided by vendors or as available through other sources, completeness of information provided in response to this RFP and other various business issues as outlined herein.

It is Cornell's intention to source all products from one vendor, but reserves the right to award individually by item.

Sample Request For Proposal Form, continued

RFP 05001-**008-03** Page 2

DIRECT QUESTIONS

1. BUSINESS PROFILE

1.1 Purchase Order Terms and Conditions
Cornell's purchase order terms and conditions (revision dated December 8, 1992) as provided with this RFP along with the vendor final proposal response will be the controlling documents with regards to terms and conditions. Any exceptions to these Terms and Conditions must be submitted in writing. (If vendor requires completion of any additional agreements, software licenses or order forms, a complete copy of those must be provided with your response.)

1.2 Invoice Terms
Invoice terms will be Net 30 days upon receipt of equipment and receipt of vendor's invoice. If vendor offers discount terms for payment in less than 30 days, please advise those terms.

1.3 Business Profile—Other
Provide any other relevant information on the vendor's business or technical experience and capabilities.

2. PRODUCTS AND PRICING

2.1 Pricing
Quote FOB CORNELL UNIVERSITY (Ithaca, NY) to include all shipping and insurance charges, and provide itemized pricing to meet or exceed specifications as requested on the enclosed Attachment A.

Exceptions—Please answer directly to each of the items listed with either the statement "comply" or if exceeding specification, with item being quoted. No exceptions listed indicates vendor complies with specification as requested.

2.2 Products and Pricing—Other
Provide any other relevant information on vendor products and pricing.

APPENDIX A (CONTINUED)

Sample Request For Proposal Form, continued

RFP #05001-008-03 Attachment A
Purchasing Agent: Melinda Sweazey
Men's Lacrosse Equipment

If not meeting specs as shown, list exceptions Item	Description	Mfr. Name	Mfr./Model or Part No.	Vendor Catalog #	U/M	Qty.	Listed Unit Price	Net Unit Price	Net Ext. Price
1	Dual Digital Field Clock to record penalty time				ea	1			
2	Goals Nets Heavy Duty, White Treated	Bacharach	4 mm		pr	2			
3	Balls White (Blems, if possible)				dz	50			
4	Scorebooks	Bacharach	LSB		ea	1			
5	Sport Helmet Face Mask Black, C Pro 2 Style				ea	6			
6	Mask Helmet Hardware Sport Helmet, C Pro 2 Style				sets	50			
7	Mask Snap Attachments Sport Helmet				sets	50			
8	Sport Helmet White, Sizes: TBA, C Pro 2 Style				ea	15			
9	Sweat Suits Crew Top as per Lacrosse Specs Top lettered as per practice tees, bottom lettered as per game tees, Sizes: TBA	Reebok			sets	50			
10	50%/50% Tee Shirts, Size: XLarge	Reebok			ea	50			
11	Red/White Reversible Scrimmage, Size: XLarge As per lacrosse specifications Blank but quote numbered prices #9, 23, 30	Reebok			ea	12			
12	Collared Team Shirts for Travel Specifications & Sizes: TBA	Reebok			ea	50			
13	Spandex Shorts Under Armour 0026, Black				ea	12			
14	Tee-Shirt Body Armour, White, Size: XLarge				ea	12			
15	Away Game Shorts as per Lacrosse specifications, Sizes: TBA 6 white / 6 red	Reebok			ea	12			
16	Arm Pads, Slag	Brine			pr	6			
17	Shoulder Pads	Brine	SP9		ea	6			
18	Shoulder Pads	Brine	SP4		ea	6			
19	Arm Pads, Blue	Brine	LAP12A		pr	6			
20	Arm Pads, Blue	Brine	LAP9A		pr	6			
21	Arm Pads, Rag	Brine			pr	6			
22	Traditional Kits	Brine			ea	60			
23	Monster Mesh Kits	Brine			ea	18			
24	Dura Mesh Kit	Brine			ea	18			
25	Goalie Hard Mesh Kit	Brine			ea	8			
26	Goalie Soft Mesh Kit	Brine			ea	8			
27	Shooting String White (Spools)				ea	2			
28	Heads (White): Edge Cyber Edge Plus Warp	Brine Brine Brine Brine			ea ea ea ea	10 12 14 14			
29	Goalie Heads (White): SG Goalmaster	STX			ea	8			
30	Brine Shafts: F15 Attack Defense				ea ea	30 30			
31	Goalie Protector (The Eliminator)				ea	1			
32	Socks Twin City Heel and Toe, White		RQ010		dz	8			
33	Brine Shafts: F15 Power-Grip Attack Defense				ea ea	15 15			
34	Brine Shafts: F22 Attack Defense				ea ea	20 20			
35	Brine F15 Goalie Shafts				ea	12			
36	Grass Shoes current comparable model Sizes: TBA, 20-63332	Reebok			pr	50			
37	Turf Shoes current comparable model Sizes: TBA, RJ32	Reebok			pr	50			
38	Cross Trainers (Dry Turf) current comparable model, Sizes: TBA, Iversons	Reebok			pr	50			
GRAND TOTAL OF ALL ITEMS									

APPENDIX B

Sample Purchase Order Form

PO
NUMBER:
DATE:

CORNELL
UNIVERSITY

DEPARTMENT QUICK ORDER

State Contract:
Commodity Group:

Ordering Department: R03
ATHLETICS

REQ. No.: 03411
INTERNAL REF:

SEND INVOICES TO: (in duplicate)
CORNELL UNIVERSITY
Invoice Processing
PO Box 4040
Ithaca, NY 14852-4040

VENDOR NAME AND ADDRESS:
TO
ATTN: LEN PARROT
PARROT SPORTS
123 CRACKER BLVD.
TAMPA, FL 12345
1-800-555-1234

DESTINATION OF GOODS:
SHIP
ATTN: DALE STRAUF
CORNELL UNIVERSITY
ATHLETICS
XXX SCHOELLKOPF HALL
ITHACA, NY 14853
607-255-4115

PAY TERMS: NET 30 FOB: FOB DESTINATION, FREIGHT PREPAID AND ADDED
REQUESTED DELIVERY DATE: 02/12/04 CORNELL BID QUOTE REFERENCE:
QUOTED SHIPPING DATE: VENDOR QUOTE REFERENCE:

SEQ.	Cornell Item No. Item Description	Supplier	Cat. No.	Qty.	U/M U/M	Unit Desc.	Price ($)	Extended Price ($)
PAGE NO. 1								
001	HOCKEY THROAT PROTECTORS	VAUGHN	VPC7000	2	EA LARGE (EACH)		$XX.XX	$XX.XX

Dept. Contact: DALE LEROY STRAUF
Phone: 607-255-4115

TOTAL COST: $XX.XX

Cornell University terms and conditions of purchase (updated December 8, 1992) as previously supplied shall apply. A copy is available from Cornell University if desired. Phone: 607-255-3804.

PAGE NO. 1 END OF ORDER

DEPARTMENT QUICK ORDER PAGE NO. 1

APPROVED BY: George Marshall Date: 8/15/03

AEMA CERTIFICATION MANUAL

CHAPTER 4

Fitting Equipment & Clothing

By Don Barnes

FITTING EQUIPMENT AND CLOTHING

One of the primary roles of athletic equipment managers is to outfit athletes in equipment and clothing that is comfortable, durable, attractive, and, above all, protective. This chapter covers the primary areas equipment managers are involved in when it comes to fitting equipment and clothing: football helmets and pads, uniforms, and shoes. Equipment and clothing has greatly evolved and continues to evolve. This chapter provides an overview of the fitting process. Experts—equipment manufacturers, experienced equipment managers, etc.—should always be consulted when confronted with a new piece of equipment, particularly if it's one that, if not maintained or fitted correctly, could put athletes at risk.

FITTING FOOTBALL HELMETS

One of the predominant reasons for the emergence of professional equipment managers was the need for qualified athletic personnel to fit football helmets. It was not until the advent of the plastic shell helmet, which contributed to a more intense contact game, that the number of injuries in the sport greatly increased. This increased focus on the need for safety standards for manufacturing of the equipment and specially trained athletic personnel to assure that athletes are properly fitted.

The high incidence of football injuries and fatalities seen in the 1960s was attributed to 1) spearing, coupled with 2) improper fit. Further, a study of football injuries in California revealed that 95.3 percent of the injured athletes were wearing improperly fitted helmets. The occurrence of serious head and neck injuries has dropped dramatically as a result of rules banning spearing and an earnest attempt to better fit the football helmet.

A properly fitted football helmet is not only desirable for reducing injuries, but also helps to foster confidence when the athlete wears the helmet. This is achieved by maximizing the athlete's visibility, comfort, and hearing. Impairment in any of these areas disrupts a player's concentration, leading to poor judgment and making that player more prone to mistakes that can result in faulty performance and injury. Another serious consideration in obtaining and maintaining a properly fitting helmet is the possible liability involved. The more recent lawsuits against helmet manufacturers have concentrated on the "failure to warn" athletes and their families about the dangers of football and the limits of helmets to protect players in the game of football. Coaches also are not warned enough about the dangers of improper coaching techniques. However, failure to properly fit the helmet has been cited as a secondary claim in many of these cases. The equipment manager, the coach, and the dealer's and manufacturer's reps have all been named in the lawsuits if they had any hand in any facet of the fitting process, and one of these parties will always be involved in that process. (See Chapter 2, "Management," for more on legal liability.)

A properly fitted helmet is one that is custom fit to the individual player's head. Each and every athlete is going to have a different head size and shape and you can never just hand a player a helmet and expect it to fit. The head must first be measured and the proper size helmet must then be fitted for that specific head size and shape. A helmet needs to be fitted to a "firm but comfortable" level. The helmet must fit snug and not be able to move or rotate on the head, but also maintain a fit that will allow the athlete a certain level of comfort.

Following are some of the key points to consider when fitting football helmets. Much of the general discussion also applies to fitting other types of helmets. When in doubt about how to fit a certain type of helmet, always consult the manufacturer's guidelines.

Assume a Professional Attitude

Earning the player's respect and trust is imperative when fitting that player's helmet. This begins with the equipment manager's attitude.

The best method of achieving this success is not to present a casual attitude, but to treat the task with the respect it deserves, especially in the case of younger athletes. Get them off on the right foot in their attitude toward their equipment. Do not let the athletes control you when doing the fitting by telling you what they want. You tell them what is needed.

Assuming a professional attitude will help the athlete gain confidence in you and the equipment you fit.

Educate the Athlete

Use the fitting time to educate the athlete about the equipment. Athletes spend most of their time concerned about the X's and O's and their coach's approval. When fitting them for their helmet, you have a small segment of time with their full attention. Use it. Explain what you are doing and why, and keep it simple. Also explain the need for daily checks and how to make them (see Appendix A on page 61). Encourage the athletes to come to you with any equipment problems and to not try to solve them for themselves.

Keep It Simple—Follow Manufacturers' Guidelines

With the many rules, regulations, and warnings concerning helmets, coupled with a multitude of sizing parts, the fitting of the football helmet can become a maze filled with mystery and fear. Keep everything in perspective and remember that the ultimate goal is to end up with a helmet that is in firm but comfortable contact with the head. Everything else is secondary.

Every helmet manufacturer provides various fitting pamphlets with each helmet sold detailing how to fit the helmet. These instructions *must* be followed. Always keep current copies of the pamphlets on file. Because the pamphlets are updated frequently, be sure to read those provided with each new helmet shipment you receive and to replace any old versions.

Often, larger "poster" versions of the fitting pamphlets are also shipped with new helmets. These posters should be posted in the area(s) you commonly use to fit helmets. If these are not available, call the manufacturer or post the smaller pamphlets provided with the helmet.

NOTE—**Because the manufacturers' fitting guidelines are updated every few years and new helmets are periodically introduced or discontinued, a complete listing of the manufacturer's guidelines for each helmet will not be presented here. This allows this chapter to avoid becoming dated in a short period of time. It remains the equipment manager's responsibility to obtain and keep current fitting pamphlets on file.** ***The fitting guidelines that follow are only intended to summarize and supplement the guidelines provided by the manufacturers, not to replace them.***

Fitting Guidelines

STEP 1: Prepare Helmets

Before beginning any helmet fitting session, all the helmets should be properly prepared, as follows:

1. Clean and sanitize each helmet. If you need to fit a helmet that is not new or just returned from being reconditioned, sanitize the inside of the helmet with a germicide to clean it before passing it on to the next athlete. Sweat and oil might still be in it from the previous user. Make sure all of the visible dirt is cleaned off, and clean any areas that may come into contact with the head or skin or that may harbor bacteria. This is easily done by simply spraying the entire inside of the helmet with a germicide. Then, with a clean towel, scrub the inside of the helmet and wipe it dry. It is important to dry the helmet completely; failure to do so will promote rust.
2. Inspect each helmet, inside and out (see checklist, Appendix B, on page 62, and Chapter 5, "Maintenance and Repair," for more on this).
3. Be sure that all needed repair work has been completed.
4. Check each helmet to assure that it bears a *current* NOCSAE (National Operating Committee on Standards for Athletic Equipment) certification stamp (see manufacturer's recommendations for their definition of current).
5. Be certain that the helmet warning label is clearly legible on the outside of the helmet.
6. Be sure there is a full range of sizes ready to be issued (see Appendix C on page 63).

STEP 2: Organize Fitting Area

The next step is to organize your fitting area. Any helmets not ready to be issued should be removed from the fitting area and clearly marked so they are not used accidentally. After assuring that all helmets are ready to be issued, organize your area to ensure a smooth flow. Then, make certain all necessary paperwork is ready (see Appendices D and E on pages 64 and 66), that you have plenty of writing utensils on hand, and that your measuring tools are accessible. A clean, well-organized fitting area will make it easier for you to do your job and reinforce athletes' images of your professionalism.

STEP 3: Obtain Information From the Athlete

Athletes should be questioned informally at the beginning of the fitting process concerning the following:

POSITION

Determine what position they will be playing; this helps you decide later on the appropriate facemask and sometimes affects the style of helmet used.

MEDICAL HISTORY

Check for any prior medical problems. If athletes have a history of concussions, you will want to keep a close eye on them. If they have had allergic reactions to some of the helmet materials that come in contact with the skin, you may need to change to another helmet with a different type of liner material. If they have suffered a broken nose on more than an isolated occasion while out on the field, you will need to determine whether it was the result of a poor fit or whether the style of helmet they used just did not grip their particular head shape well enough. If there is a prior medical problem, make a permanent note. When necessary, consult your athletic trainer for advice.

PAST EXPERIENCES

Ask athletes what type or types of helmets they have used in the past. Get their opinions on how the helmet performed. If they have had problems, simple questions such as, "Did it move on your head?" "Was it comfortable?" "Did it have pressure points and, if so, where?" all provide little clues that can be added up to give you a good indication of their past experience with helmets. This information will be valuable in determining what type of helmet to select and allows athletes to provide input into the fitting process, helping them to be more comfortable with the fitting and giving them more confidence in the end result. Do not put a helmet on an athlete just because he wants to wear it, however; it has to fit well.

PHYSICAL CHARACTERISTICS

Visibly check the athlete's head for any unique physical characteristics. Use your hand to feel the areas of the head covered by hair. Examples of abnormalities might include a severely sloping forehead, lumps beneath the skin, an overly extended brow, an extra-large occipital bone, protruding moles or warts, scars, or any other unusual occurrences that may cause problems with the helmet's fit or comfort.

STEP 4: Obtain Measurements

CIRCUMFERENCE

There are two head measurements commonly used when fitting helmets. The first is the head circumference measurement taken with a tape measure. There are specially designed tapes for taking this measurement. They have a metal loop at one end and a full range of head sizes marked, so that the head can be measured by head size and not just in inches. However, a common cloth type will suffice. The measurement can be noted in either inches or by head size (see Table One, below, for converting between the two) and should be recorded on the athlete's records.

Begin by placing the tape around the athlete's head at the widest point (see Figure One on page 47). The tape should be one inch above the eyebrow in front and on the occipital lobe in the back. The tape should be over the hair, but check to make certain it is not over the ears. Pull the tape snug and take the measurement. To be certain of what snug is, first pull the tape tight then back off just a little without letting it become loose.

CALIPER

The second measurement is taken with a head caliper (see Figure Two on page 47). Begin by having the athlete sit in a chair so the caliper can be read more easily. Place the caliper one inch above the eyebrow in front and on the crest of the occipital lobe in back. Carefully read the measurement before removing the caliper from the athlete's head. As before, record the measurement on a permanent record for the athlete.

TABLE ONE

HEAD MEASUREMENT CONVERSION CHART

HEAD CIRCUMFERENCE IN INCHES	HEAD SIZE
20 1/8	6 3/8
20 1/2	6 1/2
20 7/8	6 5/8
20 1/4	6 3/4
21 5/8	6 7/8
22	7
22 3/8	7 1/8
22 3/4	7 1/4
23 1/8	7 3/8
23 1/2	7 1/2
23 7/8	7 5/8
24 1/4	7 3/4
24 5/8	7 7/8
25	8
25 3/8	8 1/8
25 3/4	8 1/4
26 1/8	8 3/8
26 1/2	8 1/2

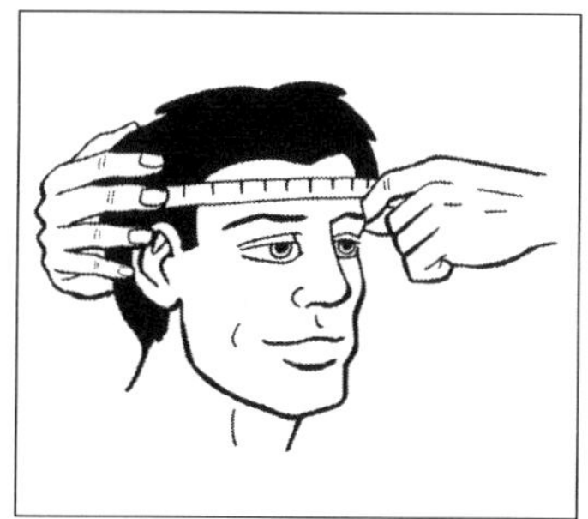

FIGURE ONE
Measuring head size with a tape measure.

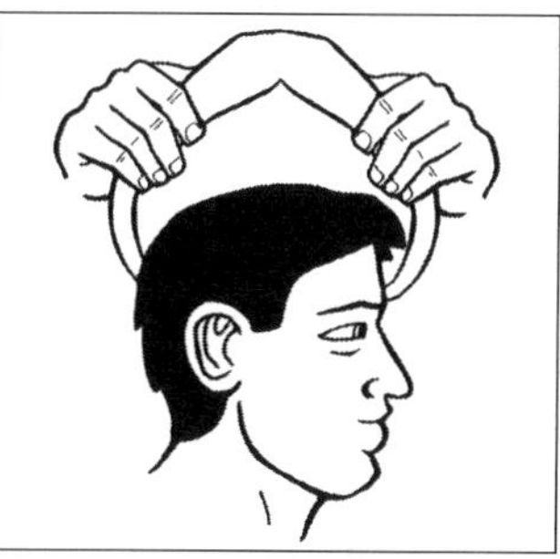

FIGURE TWO
Measuring head size with head calipers.

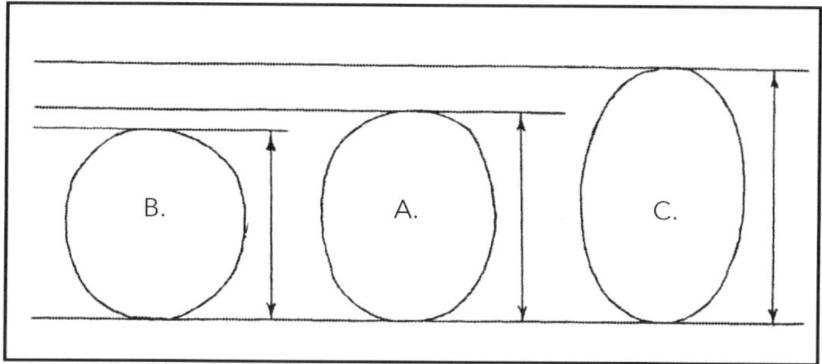

FIGURE THREE
Common head shapes.

It is highly recommended that both measurements be taken, because they can be compared, providing information about the overall head shape you are fitting. The "ideal" head shape should produce circumference and caliper measurements that are equal. This will not always be the case, however. Then, depending on the difference, you will have either a "short, squatty" head shape or a "long, oval" head shape (see Figure Three, above).

Assume that all three head shapes have an equal circumference. If you compress the normal head shape (A) into a more circular shape (B), the caliper measurement would be smaller. If you stretched head shape (A) into a "long oval" (C), the caliper measurement would be larger.

A variance of one to two head sizes is somewhat common; however, a variance of two to three head sizes or more usually means that you have an unusual-shaped head that will require special attention.

STEP 5: Select the Helmet

STYLE

The first decision in selecting an appropriate helmet for the athlete is the style to be used. It is recommended that you not limit yourself to only one style of helmet, as the various styles tend to fit different types of head shapes differently; some are better than others. Before choosing a style, consider the athlete's past experience, any abnormalities you have noted, and the level of play. At this point, you must combine your product knowledge of the various helmet styles, your experience in fitting, and all the information on the athlete to choose the best helmet for the situation. Seldom are there clear-cut answers. Product knowledge comes from reading available literature and attending workshops and equipment shows; experience comes from working with the athletes and other seasoned equipment managers.

SIZE

Once the style has been selected, choose the appropriate size. First, check the athlete's measurements; second, refer to the appropriate sizing chart for the helmet style selected. Each helmet manufacturer publishes a complete sizing chart for all their helmet styles. These charts should be readily available for quick reference. The helmet size you choose should be considered as only a starting point; you may need to size up or down after completing the next step.

STEP 6: Initial "Positioning and Sizing" Check

PREPARATION

Before the athlete tries the helmet on, it is recommended that you wet his hair down to approximate the sweaty conditions under which the helmet will be used. With younger players, a quick review of how to put the helmet on properly is very helpful. The use of a facemask during the initial check is discretionary, as manufacturers have shown proper fitting procedures both with and without a facemask on the helmet.

NOTE—The following procedures and the order in which they occur vary depending on the helmet brand and style you are fitting. You MUST follow the manufacturer's guidelines and use the following only as supplemental information.

PREPARE AIR-FILLED PADS

If the helmet you are fitting uses air-filled pads for fitting purposes, you will need to follow the manufacturer's recommended procedures for either inflating or deflating the pads before placing the helmet on the athlete's head for fitting.

HEIGHT

Ask the athlete to put the helmet on. The first check will be for the correct height. The frontal rim of the helmet should be one inch (or one finger width) above the eyebrow. If the height is incorrect, follow the recommended procedure for adjusting the height. The correct height must be established before continuing the fitting, because many of the remaining fitting checks will vary depending on the height (see Figure Four on page 48).

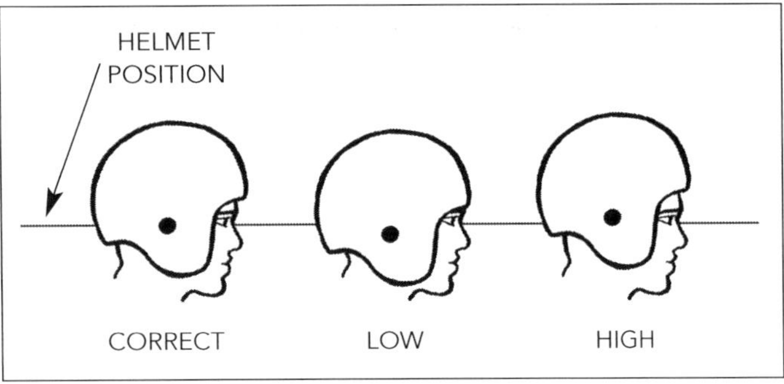

FIGURE FOUR
Correct helmet positioning.

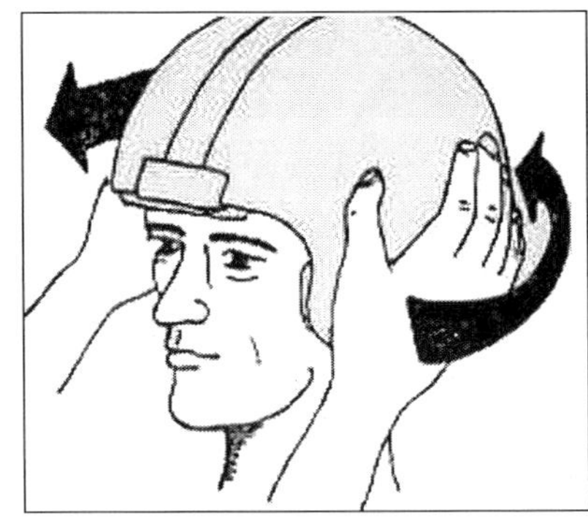

FIGURE FIVE
Checking for a good front-pad fit.

CHIN STRAP
Once the correct height has been established, the chin strap must be correctly fastened; this will keep the helmet in the proper position while you check and adjust the remaining pads in the helmet. Hold the chin cup squarely on the athlete's chin, and then adjust and fasten the front straps and then the back. Make certain that the tension is equal on all straps and that none is pulled out of alignment.

NECK
Use your fingers to feel just under the posterior rim of the helmet. The padding should be in firm but comfortable contact with the head. The neck padding is one of the major areas that grips the head to keep the helmet from sliding down onto the athlete's nose. If there are any gaps or if the helmet is too tight, follow the manufacturer's guidelines to make any necessary adjustments.

BACK AND FRONT
The fit of the front and the back pads should be checked at the same time, because they affect each other. The very center of the back pad cannot be reached, but the sides can be checked somewhat by placing a finger into the ear hole and feeling for firm contact with the head.

The front pad is visible, and several types of checks are recommended for this area. First, grip the helmet firmly on each side and rotate it gently from side to side, then up and down (see Figure Five, above right). The skin of the forehead should move with the helmet. If the helmet slips without moving the skin, adjustment needs to be made. Second, standing in front of the athlete, lock your fingers behind the athlete's head and pull firmly toward you. If a gap appears between the front liner and the forehead, adjustments will have to be made to increase the thickness of the front and back pads. Care should be taken in this procedure, as too much force can cause a gap even if there is a good fit.

The last check requires that the helmet be on the athlete for at least one minute. After that time, remove the helmet and immediately check the color of the athlete's forehead. There should be no hint of whiteness or pale discoloration of the skin, which indicates a loss of circulation (the helmet is too tight). A little redness, however, is acceptable.

SIDES
The sides can be partially seen from the front and can be felt by slipping a finger through the ear hole. Check for firm but comfortable contact with the skin. If the sides are too tight or loose, follow the manufacturer's recommendations and make the needed adjustments.

CHEEK PADS
The cheek pads can be clearly seen from the front. As much of their surface area as possible should be in firm but comfortable contact with the skin without squeezing the cheeks into a puckered position. The cheekpad has evolved with the helmet and today's cheekpads offer more protection than those of old. Some manufacturers have added an inflatable cheekpad to their lines and these are much like the inflatable bladders within the up crown and back of the helmet. Like the fitting of the helmet, the air management bladders in the cheekpads should be fit like the non-inflatable pieces. You want the cheekpad to be firm but in a comfortable position. Do not rely on the air for fitting; air should be used for comfort, not to fill space. The more direct padding in contact with the athlete, the more energy that is absorbed during a direct blow.

FACEMASK
Check your paperwork to determine the position the athlete plays (it should have been recorded earlier). Then, use the manufacturer's guidelines to select the proper style and size of mask based on the athlete's position and helmet size. Follow the manufacturer's instructions to attach the mask, then check the fit. The clearance between the end of the nose and the inside of the mask should be two to three finger widths. Also, ensure that the athlete's vision has not been impaired by the placement of the horizontal bars.

The facemask should be attached to the helmet using only the manufacturer's recommended parts, which must be in good working order. Do not use any pieces that are rusted, stripped, misshapen, or discolored. Always follow the manufacturer's guidelines for properly attaching the mask to the helmet.

ADJUSTMENTS
Air-filled pads are the easiest to adjust, simply by inflating or deflating the appropriate cells. Padded cells require a little more work. If any pad within the helmet does not fit properly, replace it with the appropriate-thickness pad. Each manufacturer supplies various thicknesses of pads that can be interchanged without voiding their warranty. This helps ensure the athlete gets a custom fit. If you are unsure of which pads to use, consult the helmet manufacturer, a reputable helmet dealer, a reconditioner, or a certified equipment manager with experience in this area.

STEP 7: The Final "Grip" Check

The ultimate goal in fitting a football helmet is to obtain a firm yet comfortable grip on the head. There are several quick methods to assure that this goal has been attained. With the helmet fully assembled, have the athlete put it on and affix the chin strap.

CROWN CHECK
Lock your fingers on the very top of the helmet and firmly pull straight down on the athlete's head. Ask the athlete where the pressure is felt. Be cautious not to "lead" the athlete into giving you an answer. If the pressure is felt evenly distributed all over, then you have a good fit on top. If the athlete says that pressure is felt on top, the answer is still acceptable. However, if the athlete feels pressure mainly in front and back, then the helmet is too tight from front to back and you will need to make more adjustments.

LATERAL MOVEMENT
Place your hands on each side of the helmet and ask the athlete to hold his head still. Gently force the helmet from side to side, watching the skin on the forehead. It should move with the helmet. There should be a firm resistance to the helmet. The cheek pad should bunch the cheeks, but not slide around toward the nose. If there is too much movement, check the cheek pads, side pads, and chin strap.

VERTICAL MOVEMENT
Again, place your hands on each side of the helmet and ask the athlete to hold his head still. Gently force the helmet up and down. The skin on the athlete's forehead should move with the helmet, and with enough force it will eventually slip a little, but it should catch on the eyebrows without coming down on the nose. If it does come down on the nose, check the neck pad first, as it is designed to grab the base of the occipital lobe to keep the helmet from sliding forward. Also check the chin strap and the front and back pads. Be cautioned, however, that with enough force, even a good-fitting helmet can be brought down onto the nose, especially if the force is exerted on the facemask and not the sides of the helmet.

FINAL CHECK
When you have completed the fitting, ask whether the athlete is comfortable with the helmet, and let him know that you are pleased with the fit. This will help build confidence in the equipment and the player's trust in you. You are like a salesperson making the final sale. Just be sure that you do have a good fit before you make that final sale.

COMFORT
Comfort is a relative term, at best. The phrase "firm but comfortable" has been used throughout the fitting process already described but I'd like to clarify what that means. The sensitivity of each individual will determine what is comfortable for that person. Some players, particularly those with little skin fat in the head area, will be more sensitive, and they will not feel comfortable unless the helmet fits loosely. In such cases, it is more important that a firm fit be maintained, sacrificing some of the athlete's comfort.

RECORDING
Make certain that all pertinent information on the athlete's helmet has been permanently recorded in a file that is easily accessible. This information will be needed during future maintenance, inspections, and inventories. More important, it provides solid documentation if it's ever needed in a court of law. Also, each helmet should be clearly marked with some type of serial number, so that both the equipment manager and the athlete can clearly distinguish them from each other.

Appendices D and E on pages 64 and 66 show examples of forms for recording necessary information for issuing and tracking football equipment. Each is two pages long. (When used at the University of Wisconsin-Madison, the sheets are copied back-to-back to keep all the information on one sheet of paper.) These forms are only samples to provide the reader with an idea of what could be used. As each institution's needs differ, the forms may need to be altered to accomodate individual needs.

Customized Padding

It is preferable to obtain a good fit without customizing the helmet. However, if customizing is needed, helmet manufacturers provide various pad thicknesses, allowing for considerable customization when fitting the athlete. It is imperative that you follow established guidelines when changing these pads. Following are some key points:

1. Never interchange pads between different brands of helmets.
2. Pads are often made to fit within a specified shell size, for example, M, L, or XL. Make certain that you are using the correct pad for the given shell size.
3. Never alter a pad by cutting it down in size.
4. If you must add padding and already have the thickest pad the manufacturer provides, be careful not to inhibit the function of the helmet as designed by the manufacturer.
5. In the rare circumstance that you cannot get a helmet to fit firmly but comfortably, and you are unsure how to customize the helmet, call the helmet manufacturer for advice. Never attempt to customize a helmet unless you know how to properly achieve your goal.

Customized pads or inserts to the helmets should be checked by the player on a daily basis and by the equipment manager on a weekly basis.

Many helmet manufacturers have specialized pads already designed for some of the more common problems. These pads include such items as the "Denver front" for severely sloping foreheads; side shims for the long, narrow head; and special crown pads to lift up low-riding helmets. If you do not have any of these items, contact your helmet dealer for further information.

Fitting—A Continuous Process

The fitting process has only begun. The fitting of the football helmet will last as long as the athlete is with your team. The athlete will need to make daily checks, and the equipment manager should make weekly spot checks (see Appendices A and B on pages 61 and 62). At the beginning of each season, each athlete's helmet should be thoroughly checked for proper fit, even if the athlete is wearing the same helmet from the previous season. The goal is not only to obtain, but also to *maintain a firm but comfortable fit.*

New Improvements

With the ever-changing technology in today's society, the safety and fit of the helmet is constantly evolving and getting better and better. Many manufacturers have responded to players' complaints about the weight, heat, comfort, and safety of the helmet. The responses have been well received by the consumer—today's helmets are lighter, safer, stronger, cooler (due to added air vents), and more comfortable (with the addition of things like inflatable cheek pads).

A recent study conducted by the independent consulting firm Biokinetics & Associates found that a new helmet testing procedure was needed to test the Head Impact Power (HIP) Index. It was determined that the strength of the old helmets lay in the frontal and rear sections, while the sides of the helmet did not test as well. The occurrence of side-impact concussions was not on the decline as much as a front and back concussion location has been on the decline. New helmets are now being developed and tested that address this.

FITTING SHOULDER PADS

Shoulder pads are designed to provide protection to the musculature and skeletal parts of the shoulder, back, and chest without restricting mobility. Some of the design features can help protect the athlete's shoulder area from bruises. The shoulder pad cannot prevent dislocations or separations, however, or bruises caused when certain body parts are stressed by blocking and tackling.

A shoulder pad must fit properly to provide the protection for which it was designed. An improperly fitted shoulder pad could result in serious injury to the athlete.

Before beginning the discussion about fitting shoulder pads, it is important to understand basic shoulder anatomy, common shoulder injuries, and the components that make up the shoulder pad.

Basic Shoulder Anatomy

The following lists the muscles and bones of the shoulder protected by the shoulder pad (see also Figure Six on page 51 and Figure Seven on page 52).

MUSCLES	BONES & JOINTS
Latissimus dorsi	Sternum
Rhomboids	Clavicle
Biceps	Scapula
Deltoids	Humerus
Trapezius	Glenohumeral joint
Triceps	Acromioclavicular joint
Pectoralis	

Common Shoulder Injuries

Acromioclavicular (AC) Joint Sprain

The AC joint is the point at which the clavicle and the acromion process of the scapula come together. It is tied together by ligaments. There is no or very little musculature present.

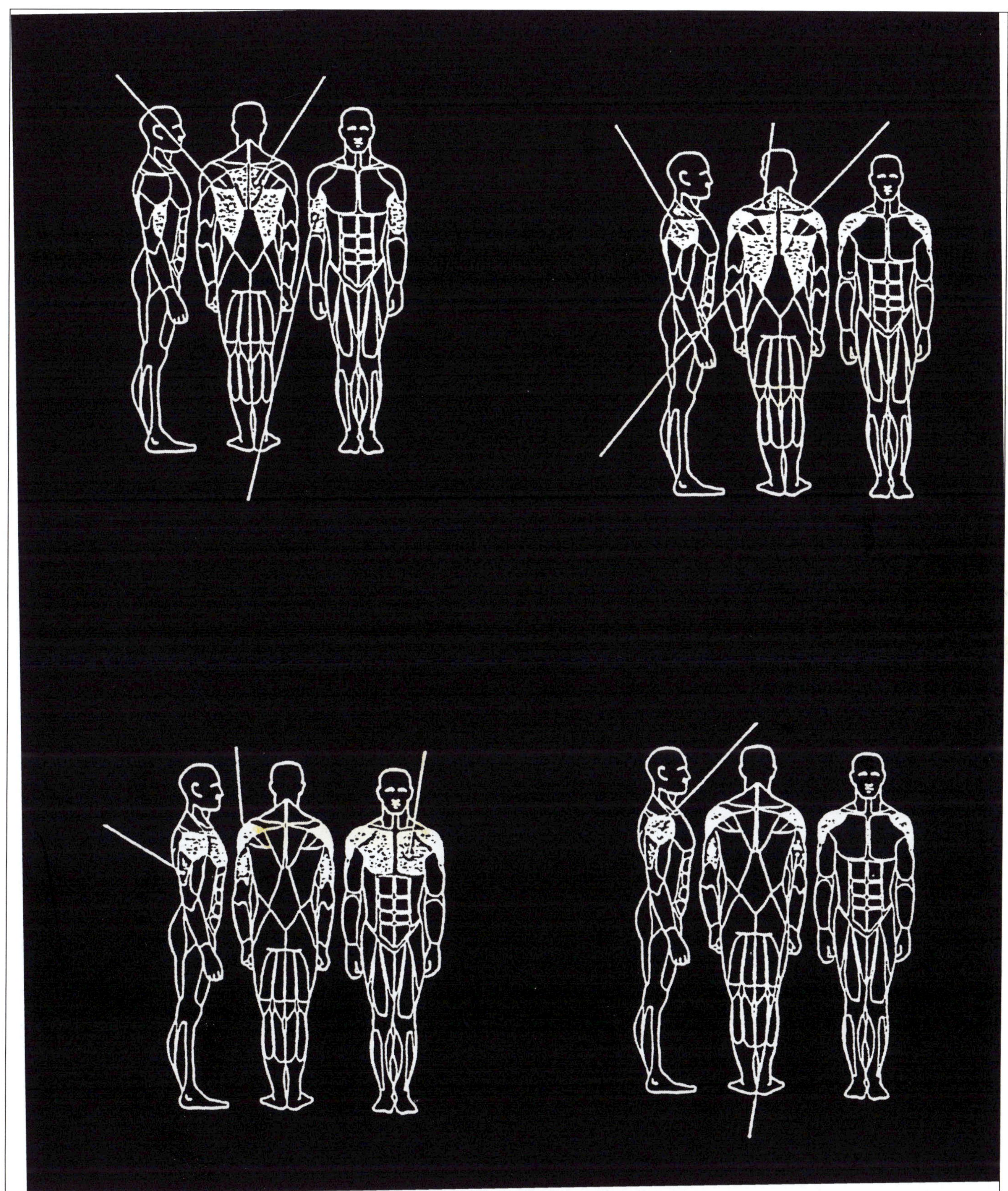

FIGURE SIX
Muscles of the shoulder, back, and chest.

The AC joint is the most commonly injured part of the shoulder. It is also the most difficult to keep free from injury because of the variety of ways that an injury can occur.

An AC sprain is an irritation of the joint, mainly caused by the stretching of ligaments. The clavicle will go upward with sprains or even fractures. AC sprains occur in various degrees, including a complete AC dislocation.

One way that this injury commonly occurs is as a result of an athlete landing on an outstretched arm. The force is transferred to the shoulder area, which causes an upward movement of the clavicle. Another common way of experiencing this injury is by receiving a direct blow to the AC joint.

The primary goal of a properly fitted shoulder pad is to protect the AC joint from a direct blow. The AC joint should fit within the "AC channel" of the shoulder pad and remain untouched. The shoulder pad cannot protect against injuries that occur when the athlete lands on an outstretched arm or elbow, causing subluxation.

Burner (Stinger)

The burner (or stinger) is the most common cervical injury. It is caused by the stretching of the brachial plexus, a network of nerves that run from the spine through the shoulder and into the arm (see Figure Eight, below right).

The burner occurs when the shoulder is driven down and the head is pushed laterally away from the force. The nerve becomes stretched; it then is unable to activate the muscles. The results are transient loss of strength and function of the arm. The athlete could experience numbness, burning, or a tingling sensation down the arm and possibly into the hand. There could also be weakness in the deltoid and bicep muscles.

This will usually last several minutes. If recurrence becomes a problem, however, or if the episode lasts longer than one hour, a physician should be contacted to conduct a neurological examination.

To help prevent burners, extreme cervical motion must be restricted. While first-time burners are not easily prevented, subsequent injuries are preventable with the proper use of a neck roll. Equipment managers should also make sure there isn't an excessive gap between the athlete's neck and the collar to the shoulder pad. During the off-season, athletes can strengthen the cervical musculature to help prevent recurrence of a burner. Coaches can also work with athletes who have suffered burners to improve blocking and tackling techniques.

Each athlete should be treated individually with this or any type of injury. Some athletes may have strong enough cervical muscles so that future burners are not likely, while others may be prone to this type of injury and require more neck support and padding.

Shoulder Pad Components

The components of the shoulder pad work together to spread the force of the blow over a large area. The components are as follows:

- clavicle (or AC) channel—padding should be structured so there is a gap between the pad and the AC joint
- arch—the plastic shell covering the sternum, pectoralis, rhomboids, and latissimus dorsi
- sub arch—structures beneath the arch to strengthen it and help it retain its shape
- epaulet—flap
- snubbers—help keep epaulet, cap, and arch secured
- cup cap—covers deltoid and humerus
- metal grommets—protect and strengthen the openings for eyelets, T-hook, and keyhole buckles

FIGURE SEVEN

Skeletal structures of the shoulder, back, and chest.

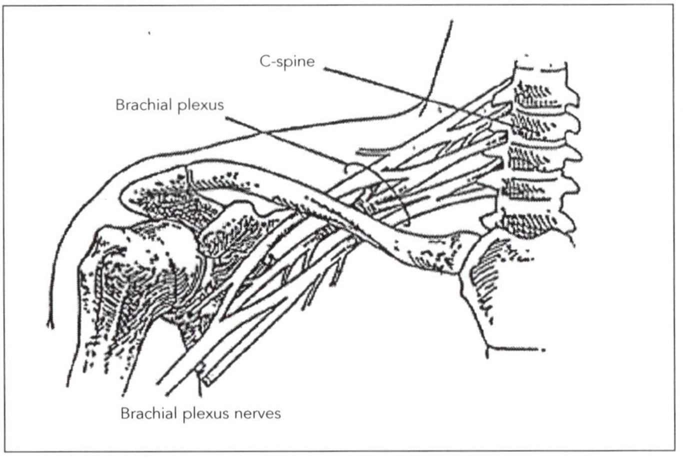

FIGURE EIGHT

The brachial plexus.

- cantilever—spreads force to front and rear of the arch. An inside cantilever gives shape and support to the arch. With flat shoulder pads, cantilever is formed by pulling the belts securely.
- padding system—body of the pad
- collar—protects neck area, trapezius
- deltoid pad—extends from body of pad

Making the Fit

To fit shoulder pads properly, keep these points in mind:

- athlete's personal history of injuries (contact athletic trainer or physician)
- birth defects
- fit without shirt or T-shirt only

Determine the athlete's shoulder width (use a tape measure to measure shoulder tip to shoulder tip) and/or chest size and, possibly, weight. Next, determine the playing position(s) of this athlete. Match the player's position and shoulder width with a corresponding shoulder pad.

Remember: This is just to get you started.

Try the pads on the athlete. Secure the straps and laces. Be sure the sternum and spine are covered.

Anterior View (Front)

1. Check for proper AC joint coverage. The pad should extend 1/2 inch over the deltoid.
2. Check for proper pectoralis muscle coverage.
3. The collar should provide comfortable range of motion to the neck (1/2 inch). Arms raised in an upward motion should not pinch the neck.
4. Check coverage of the deltoids (the cap should fit snugly).
5. Check trapezius coverage.
6. The arches should meet evenly, with no overlap.

Lateral View (Side)

1. Check for proper AC channel. Check to see whether it is off the AC joint.
2. Check for proper coverage of the caps over the deltoids.
3. Check the clavicle. The padding should be in contact with, and completely covering, the clavicle.

Posterior View (Back)

1. Check coverage of the rhomboids and the latissimus dorsi. The pad should fit neatly over this region, and the arches should not overlap.
2. Check the neck area again.
3. Check the straps.

Final Check

1. The shoulder pad should fit snugly over the entire shoulder region, yet still allow for range of motion.
2. Player should be able to raise his hands above his head.
3. Player must be able to make a football stance.
4. Straps should be snug.
5. Pads should not choke or pinch the athlete.
6. Make sure there is no restriction of movement of the extended arm.
7. Pads should rest back into place after movement.
8. Medial portion of the neck should be snug to the neck; movement should not scissor the neck.
9. Properly worn jerseys and sleeves help keep the pad in place.

Check Again

Fitting of shoulder pads isn't complete the first time they are fitted correctly. Consult with athletes during the season to make sure they are getting the protection they need and still have the range of motion and flexibility they desire. While checking with the athlete to determine his satisfaction with the shoulder pads, make a quick inspection to determine that all of the rivets are still in place, the epaulets are still connected, and the foam or air packs are all still attached and functioning.

Shoulder Pads—Troubleshooting

During equipment managers' day-to-day work schedules, they will be confronted with various things that go wrong with shoulder pads. The following troubleshooting guide should help equipment managers when these problems occur.

1. Bottoms Out

Possible causes:

- loose-fitting pad
- broken pad part
- bent plastic shell (arch)

Solutions:

- tighten strapping
- check shoulder supports (cantilevers)

Preventive measures:

- check strapping—keep tight
- check cantilever before issuing pads
- use webbed strapping instead of elastic (belts could also be worn). Replace old elastic straps with new ones.

2. **Loose Padding**

Possible causes:
- broken rivets/snubbers
- worn padding

Solutions:
- fix with T-nuts and washers
- cover T-nuts with moleskin

Preventive measures:
- maintenance (visual) checks for pad wear

3. **Odor**

Possible causes:
- sweat accumulation
- poor ventilation in locker room area

Solution:
- hand wash with mild soap

4. **Breaking Laces**

Possible causes:
- weak laces (cotton)
- singular lacing

Solution:
- replace laces

Preventive measures:
- use nylon laces
- use double laces

5. **Bouncing Pads**

Possible causes:
- incorrect fit
- cut or improperly fitted jersey

Preventive measures:
- fit for tight jersey
- do not cut jersey

6. **Cracking Neck Roll (Collar)**

Possible causes:
- dry or brittle neck roll (collar)
- improper storage
- dried-on sweat

Solution:
- cover with moleskin

Preventive measures:
- use leather conditioner to soften
- wash on a regular, routine, maintenance schedule
- recondition and store properly

FITTING UNIFORMS

Fitting uniforms is a topic that not all equipment managers need to deal with, but is helpful for all to know. Further, departmental constraints will govern what you can do as far as uniforms. For example, some budgets might be too small to allow you to do much with customizing uniforms, even insofar as fit is concerned. If you're in this position, not only will you be forced to use the same uniforms for several years, but you will need to keep the fit rather broad. With that in mind, the following is a general discussion of the major considerations of fitting uniforms.

The easiest and most efficient method of fitting a uniform is getting a sample size run from the vendor and trying it on each athlete. This allows you to order the exact size that each athlete needs/wants. You might not want to get too personal as far as the fit to each athlete if you need to use those jerseys for multiple years and/or for multiple athletes. If you don't have the budget to get a personal fit for each player, just do the best you can. For most sports, the best fit is the one that the athlete is the happiest with and that allows him or her to perform to his or her optimum potential.

Several new fabrics are available today that are lighter, thinner, more breathable, more comfortable, and have water wicking abilities. These are discussed in detail in Chaper 6, "Laundry."

Basic Uniform Types

The fitting of athletic uniforms varies significantly from sport to sport. Football is the one contact sport that the uniform has a major impact on the fit of the protective padding and how it stays in place. The tighter the fit of the jerseys, the tougher it is to grab, and the better the pads will stay in place on the shoulder and back.

Football uniforms are mostly composed of a dazzle cloth yoke with either a pro-bright, a dull, a tricot, a porthole, or a cordura type of fabric, with a Lycra/Spandex insert up the side of the jersey. The pant is almost always a dazzle/warp knit type of fabric.

A key to selecting these fabrics is to get a nylon fabric in the colors you will need, but in any white sections that are to be contained in the uniform, have them made with a polyester fabric. This will not only help the uniform as far as durability and repair, but polyester fabric does not accept loose dyes in the wash (nylon accepts residual dyes that typically are released when washed at high temperatures).

Hockey, although it is a contact sport, has not adopted the tight-fitting uniform. The protective padding found in hockey gear is smaller than football padding and has good adherence to the location it needs to be in. Range of motion and player comfort are key in this sport.

Wrestling, volleyball, track (especially sprint and relay events), and swimming are all sports that prefer a tighter fitting uniform but that do not have significant considerations as far as protective padding that has to be kept in place. Lycra and Spandex have been popular in the makeup of these uniforms. These fabrics provide a tight fit, yet they have the stretch and flexibility to allow comfort and the range of motion desired by athletes in these sports. Distance runners and field events athletes tend to wear the loose-fitting traditional nylon uniforms.

Basketball has seen a shift in the last 20 years from a short/tight uniform to a long/baggy uniform. The fabric has gone from wool to silk to polyester to dazzle. It is really a personal preference of the individual team you are working with.

Women's volleyball has seen a shift from long-sleeved jerseys with a short "bun-hugger" type bottom, to a short-sleeve, tight-fitting top made of a water-wicking fabric combined with a tight bicycle-style short with a 3" to 5" inseam. The cut of the mens' shorts hasn't changed significantly, but the fabric for both tops and bottoms has also shifted to a water-wicking fabric.

Gymnastics uses a skintight leotard for wind resistance and comfort, as well as for safety.

Baseball and softball have seen the shift go from wool to polyester to a new blend of poly/cotton fabric that brings the cotton on the inside of the uniform for comfort on the body and has the polyester on the outside for durability.

Lacrosse has many of the same characteristics of the football uniform, except that the lacrosse jersey is not as tight.

Fitting Women's Athletic Uniforms

Women's athletic uniforms used to be one of the worst fitting on the market. At best, they covered the athlete's body, but they failed to give the athlete the freedom and range of motion required by active sports. Many manufacturers actually cut their pattern from misses-style patterns.

Today's female athletes participate in extensive strength and conditioning programs, which result in thicker waistlines and more chest expansion because of the stronger back muscles. These dimensions directly affect the fit of women's uniforms. This should be kept in mind when you look at those uniforms on catalog models as opposed to athletes.

The best way to alleviate as many problems as possible is to ask for a sample uniform from which to size your athletes. Look for tight fits around the arm, neck, and leg openings. Simple 1/2-inch to two-inch adjustments may be needed in these areas. The rise—the distance from the waistband to the crotch—is an important measurement to ensure a comfortable fit. The inseam measurement is the length of the pants or shorts down the inside seam. Generally, the inseam on shorter athletes is fine, but taller athletes may need some added inches. (Table Two, below, lists new uniform sizes for men and women.)

Yes, these extra measurements mean extra dollars tacked onto the cost of the uniform. We have found, however, that the time saved in mending repairs and the lack of complaints from the athletes and coaches warrant this added expense.

TABLE TWO

NEW UNIFORM SIZES

(SGMA International☆ standard sizes)

MEN'S	XS	S	M	L	XL	XXL*	XXXL**
Shirt	36	38-40	42-44	46-48	50	52	
Pant	26	28-30	32-34	36-38	40-42	44	46

**10% extra, **20% extra*

WOMEN'S	XS	S	M	L	XL	XXL*
Shirt	28-30	30-32	34-36	38-40	42-44	46
Pant	21-22	24-26	26-28	30-32	34-36	38
Dress	4-6	8-10	12-14	16-18	20-22	24

**10% extra*

(☆ formerly Sporting Goods Manufacturers Association)

FITTING ATHLETIC SHOES

Shoes provide a stable base for the foot to use as it controls movement of the lower body. The purpose of this section is to improve the equipment manager's knowledge of athletic shoes. Improved knowledge can keep an athlete in shoes that accomplish all of the following:

- protect the foot
- assist natural movement
- improve performance
- fit properly
- are comfortable
- can overcome some physiological problems
- are designed for the sport or activity in which the athlete will be engaged

The Equipment Manager's Role

Athletic shoes are designed for specific types of individual athletic activities. For example, there are several different types of shoes for one position in a team sport, and the athletes' requirements can be broken down even further by playing surface, injury history, and weather conditions.

The fitting of athletic shoes is a very complex issue. The modern equipment manager must be the guide who wisely selects shoes that will allow athletes to perform to their potential; that is, ensures that the shoes are designed for the activity in which the athletes are participating, as well as for the playing surface and weather conditions. The shoes chosen must protect the foot, fit properly, and reduce the chance of injury.

Proper athletic shoe fitting requires an understanding of foot and lower-body anatomy and biomechanics, as well as how modern athletic shoes are constructed. These are discussed in Appendices H and J at the end of this chapter.

There are a ton of new shoe models that come out on almost a weekly basis. We have chosen to not go into depth on any one for the simple fact that this Manual would have old information by the time it was printed. Manufacturers are continually coming out with design "improvements," few of which stand the test of time. In general, new shoes are lighter, but sometimes manufacturers sacrifice traction and support for the sake of weight.

When selecting a shoe, the first concern should be picking a shoe to match the athlete's sport. Weight, support, strength, and traction are all points to be aware of when selecting the proper athletic shoe.

The Eight Steps in Fitting

The following eight-step process will help ensure that athletic shoes are functional and fit properly.

STEP 1: Measure the Feet

This step is similar to measuring an athlete's head to fit a helmet or the chest for shoulder pads. It does not determine the exact size of shoes an athlete will wear, but it will provide important information about the shape of the athlete's feet, prevents the equipment manager from putting the athlete in shoes that definitely will not fit because of the shoe's design (for example, measuring the width of an athlete's foot will eliminate styles of shoes that are too wide or too narrow), and provides a starting point from which to begin having the athlete try on shoes to see whether they fit.

The best way to assess an athlete's foot for fitting shoes is with a foot-measuring device. Refer to Appendix F on page 68 for instructions on how to use the Brannock Foot-Measuring Device.

Before using the device, several points should be understood that affect the accuracy of the information it can provide. First, try to measure and fit shoes as late in the day as possible—feet expand as much as one whole size during the day. In addition, always measure the foot when the athlete is wearing the maximum number of socks that will be used. If the athlete is required to have the ankles taped or wrapped, this can affect the fit. Have the athlete pull out on the ends of the socks to prevent them from curling in the toes and providing a "short" reading.

To ensure consistency when obtaining measurements, ask the athlete to stand and position your head so you are looking straight down. (NOTE—This position is recommended when measuring with the Brannock device. There are other foot-measuring devices; instructions for these devices may recommend a sitting position when measuring. Be sure to follow the instructions that pertain to your device.) Measure both feet. Sometimes there are large differences between a person's left and right foot, so much so that some people have to wear two different-size shoes to get a pair.

A foot-measuring device provides three measurements:

1. **Total Length.** Total foot length is measured from the heel to the end of the longest toe (see Figure Nine on page 57). This measurement gives an adjusted shoe size. Brannock estimates three quarters of an inch to allow for toe-box room.
2. **Arch Length.** The arch length is the distance from the heel to the ball joint (see Figure Nine on page 57). This tells you how far forward the widest part of the foot is (long or short toes). The widest part of the foot must be in the widest part of the shoes. If the

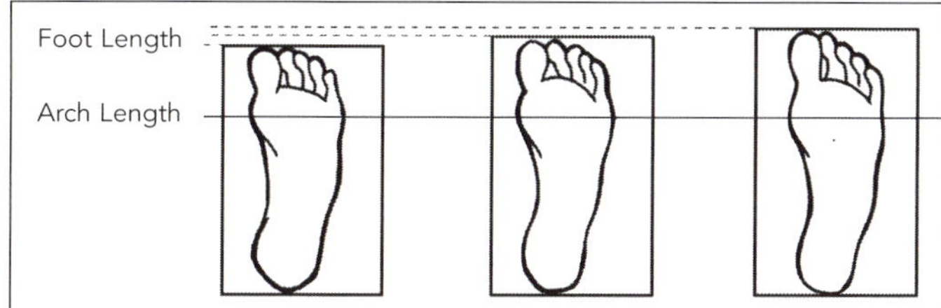

FIGURE NINE
Measuring total foot length and arch length.

arch length is longer than the total length, the athlete may have to wear a shoe size that is larger than the total length would indicate. With athletic shoes, the extra space at the end of the shoe can create problems. There will have to be give and take (and trial and error) to get the correct foot placement.

3. **Width (Girth Measurement).** There are 12 letter widths that tell how wide a person's foot is (AAAAA to EEEE: A widths are narrow; E's are wide; and B's, C's, and D's are in between). Knowing this measurement allows the equipment manager to put athletes in shoes of the proper width (when style comes in more than one width) or to steer them to different style shoes that are wider or narrower lasted when a style with variable widths is not available. Standard widths will vary from one manufacturer to another and even from one shoe type to another in the samc manufacturer's line.

STEP 2: Question the Athlete

The athlete is the person who will have to wear the shoe. An effective discussion with the athlete can pinpoint specific problems and/or successes the athlete has had with shoes, and any history of past injury. It will let the equipment manager know what the shoe will be used for and what type of shoe the athlete wants to wear.

Questions for a football player might include, "What position do you play?" "What type of shoe have you worn in the past?" "Did you have any problems with this shoe?" "Will this shoe be worn for practice or for games?" "Have you ever sprained your ankle or hurt your knee?" "Have you ever had other types of injuries to your feet?" "What type of shoe would you like to wear?"

Answers to these types of questions provide valuable information about an athlete. What have the athlete's past experiences been? If they were good, you may not want to change things, but if they were bad or painful, the pattern should not be continued.

Some types of football shoes are preferred for playing certain positions. You will often want to place an athlete in a more comfortable and protective shoe for practice and move the athlete to a lighter shoe that provides more traction for a game. If the player has a history of sprained ankles, you might want to use a high-top shoe or a shoe with a built-in ankle brace.

Rearfoot control is very important to people who have knee problems, because a shoe that allows overpronation causes excessive twisting at the knee. Athletes with knee injuries should stay away from shoes with excessive flare in the heels, whereas people with a history of ankle sprains need more flare at the heel, knee allowing. Shoes with midsoles and wedges help the Achilles tendon when it does not stretch enough, or you might have to cut off the top of the Achilles tendon protector if it is rubbing on the tendon and irritating it.

Many times, an athlete's mind will be made up about what is best. Asking about the athlete's desires and discussing them help both of you understand what is going on and what you are trying to achieve.

STEP 3: Examine the Old Shoes

When an athlete brings you a pair of shoes to be exchanged for a new pair, you are being handed very valuable information about the athlete that has tremendous value to you as the guide.

Stand the shoes on the edge of a flat surface and look at the heel counters. If they lean in, the athlete probably overpronates and the replacement shoes should have good rearfoot control. If they slant out, the athlete is susceptible to ankle sprains and should avoid shoes with a varus wedge, which makes the foot tilt out even more (see Figure Ten, right).

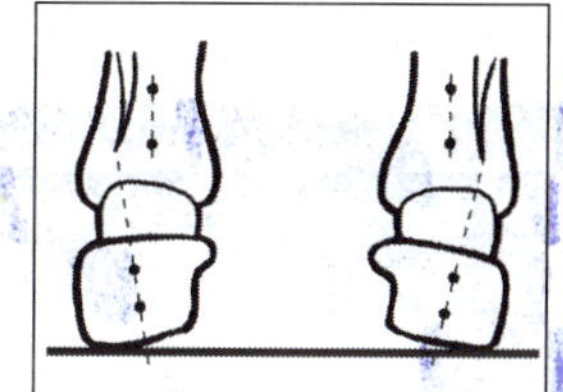

FIGURE TEN
Rearfoot varus.

With the shoes still on the flat surface, turn them around and look at the fronts. If both sides hang over the soles, the athlete needs a larger or wider shoe.

Next, check if either the inside or the outside of the shoe is deformed or especially worn out. Synthetic materials will usually be ripped, and it will tell you the direction of the foot force. For example, if the shoe is worn on top of the toes, more toe box room is needed.

Look at the eyestays. Parallel, U-shaped eyestays are normal. If they V out, the shoe may be too narrow; if they pull in, it may be too wide.

Look at the midsole and wedges. If the shoe has thinned considerably in one area, make sure to look for a shoe that is thicker in this area. Emphasize to the athlete the importance of a shoe creating a flat base and not continuing to use a shoe that has worn out.

Outsoles are a good indicator of foot problems. Rearfoot strikers will wear out the outside back edge of the outsole and will need a shoe with good rearfoot control. If the wear is mostly on the outside front, then the athlete is probably a midfoot or forefoot strider.

Asking the athlete a few questions about his or her present shoes will also help both of you to select the next pair. For example, you can ask the following: "Did you get any blisters?" "If so, where?" "Did your toes ever get numb?" "Did you get black toenails?" "Were you comfortable in the shoes?" "Did you like the shoes?" "Do you want the same type of shoes again?"

STEP 4: Examine the Feet and Legs

Have the athlete take the wet foot test to determine his or her arch type. This test is very simple. Have the athlete wet his or her feet, step on a smooth surface, and then step away. Compare the footprints to the diagram in Figure Eleven, below. You can also determine the arch type by observing the arch with the athlete standing (see Figure Twelve, below right). If the arch type is normal, the athlete will be able to wear a wide range of shoes.

High arches need special consideration. There are two types of high arches, rigid and flexible. Rigid arches have a limited range of motion in both flexion and extension, but especially in supination and pronation. The rigid-type arch cannot act as a shock absorber, as the normal foot can. This foot must have a shoe with good impact-absorption qualities. The rigid, high arch does not require a shoe with good rearfoot control, because this is already built into the foot. The flexible, high arch will need extra support, because it has large unsupported areas. Supports that mold to the feet may need to be added in shoes worn by people with flexible, high arches. With both types of high arches, shoes with good cushioning are needed.

Flat feet have given up the fight against pronatory forces and have taken a resting position in which the long, inside arch has fallen or disappeared, and the rearfoot is in a pronated position. Such a foot may or may not need help. Straight-lasted shoes tend to help people with flat feet. Shoes with strong arch bandages will also be beneficial. Rearfoot control is a priority for people with flat feet, because it will provide resistance against pronatory forces.

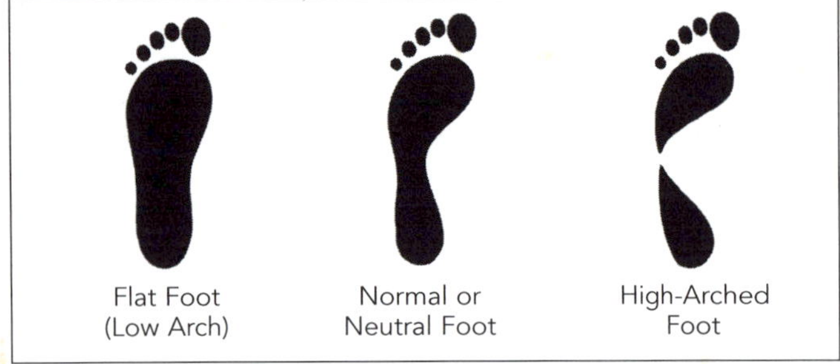

FIGURE ELEVEN
Determining arch type with the wet foot test.

Look at the rearfoot. Does it slant in? If so, a varus wedge might be used. If it slants out, the athlete must stay away from shoes with varus wedges because these will compound the problem.

Look at the tops of the athlete's feet. Are there any unusual bumps or projections? Check especially over the toes and joints. Nylon uppers will not break in as leather shoes will. If a nylon shoe is causing problems, it will continue to do so as long as the shoe is worn. For people with these types of bumps, leather is a better choice of material for the upper. Leather will mold to the feet, and shoe stretchers are available that can stretch the shoe in specific spots to help with problem areas.

Determine how closely the size of the athlete's two feet match. Fit the shoe to the wider, longer foot. Choose a shoe with variable-width lacing or use an alternate lacing method (refer to Appendix G on page 71) to close the upper on the smaller foot. Also consider padding, such as heel cups, to fill out extra space.

STEP 5: Match the Shoe to the Conditions

In this step, the information from the previous steps is combined, and decisions are made concerning the activity for which the shoe will be used, the playing surface, and the weather conditions.

For example, when fitting football shoes for an offensive lineman with wide feet, you might want to begin the fitting process with a high-top (more protective) EEE shoe (for wide foot) with a turf plate (spring-steel plate in the forefoot to prevent hyperextension of the great toe).

Next, it's important to consider the playing conditions. If playing on dry grass, a 7-stud or molded-bottom shoe would be best. If playing on wet grass, a 7-stud screw-in works best. We use a BBX or flat-bottom turf shoe for when athletes are playing on dry artificial turf. If playing on wet or frozen artificial turf, it's best to have the players try different shoes on to find the one they like best. Usually, a destroyer or Wet Rat is best for these conditions. Finally, if playing on a Field Turf field (wet or dry), we will also have athletes wear the destroyers.

This example shows that the equipment manager combines the players' physiological needs with the sports-specific demands and matches them through

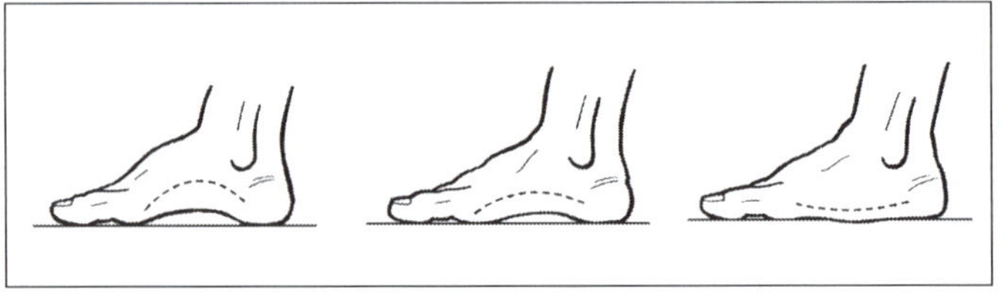

FIGURE TWELVE
Determining arch type by observing the athlete standing.

product knowledge of the shoe or shoes that will allow the athletes to perform so they can reach their potential as injury-free as possible.

STEP 6: Check the Fit

Lace both shoes properly and ask the athlete to try on both of them. (Refer to Appendix G on page 71 for alternate lacing methods that may help athletes with specific problems.) The following are several points that are repeated here to make it easier for you to keep them in mind as you have the athlete try on the shoe selected.

1. Try to fit shoes as late in the day as possible.
2. If possible, have the athlete taped, padded, and wearing the number of socks that will be used.
3. Shoes made using mostly modern, synthetic materials will not break in. The fit you get the first time is the fit you will have throughout the life of the shoe. Leather shoes will break in and mold to the shape of the foot.

When fitting the shoe, check the toe area, ball joint, eye stays, arch, flex point, and heel. Each of these is discussed below.

THE TOE AREA

This is the measurement from the heel to the end of the toe. There should be enough room so the toes are not bunched or cramped. In addition, there should be approximately one-half inch between the longest toe and the end of the shoe (press down on the end of the shoe). The toe box should be big enough so the upper does not touch the nails. (NOTE—A more pointed toe area may require a longer shoe to prevent the toes from being bruised.)

THE BALL JOINT AREA

This is the heel-to-ball measurement, and this area is the widest part of the foot. There should be enough room for the foot to flex and spread, but the foot should not drift or "slop around." The foot's girth should fit comfortably yet firmly. Check for bulges, pressure points, and excessive wrinkling. These are to be avoided. To check for slack material, use your thumb to press the upper down onto the lasting insole. All toes should be on the insole. Toes should not press the upper over the feather edge.

THE EYE STAYS

This is the same step used when checking an athlete's old shoes. This lets you know whether the shoe has to overadjust in this area. The eye stays should be parallel. If they V out, a wider shoe might be the answer; if they pull together, a narrower shoe might be better. (NOTE—Eye stays on hockey and figure skates are cut wider because the shoes must fit more snugly to give the support needed for these activities.)

THE ARCH AREA

Athletes with high insteps and arches are usually helped by more support in this area. People with pronated feet and low arches have trouble with arch supports. In most shoes, the arch support can be removed. It can be realigned in many shoes to put it where it will do the most good. Some arch supports are too soft to be beneficial. Knowing what type of foot an athlete has, and discussing how the shoe feels, will allow you to guide the athlete to a proper fit in the arch area.

THE FLEX-POINT AREA

The flex point is across the metatarsal joint, not in the middle of the shoe. Many cleated field shoes have flex paths. **It is critical that the flex path on the bottom of the shoe be centered on the flex path of the foot. The inflexible parts of the shoes must never be placed under the flex point of the foot.** Two ways to improve the flexibility of shoes are to press the toe up to the top line of the shoe and hold it there for a few minutes (which breaks down the adhesion of the sole and insole) and, in severe cases, to make a small cut across the sole along the flex path.

THE HEEL AREA

Are all seams smooth, not causing any irritation? Make sure the Achilles tendon protector is soft and flexible and not causing irritation. Also, make sure the heel counter is sturdy enough for the activity the athlete will perform. Is there enough heel room? If there is slippage in the heel and the fit is good everywhere else, you might try a different lacing system or go to a higher-cut shoe, or you might add a heel cup to take up the extra space.

STEP 7: Perform a Wear Test

Allow the athlete to get a feel for the shoes. Ask him or her to walk and run in the shoes and to try to perform as many activities that will actually be performed in the shoe as possible. Asking a few key questions will lead you to some important information. For example: "How do the shoes feel in the toe area?" "Do the shoes bunch or cramp your toes?" "How do the shoes feel over the ball of the foot?" "Is the shoe flexible enough in this area?" "How tight is the shoe across the widest part of your foot?" "Does your foot slip on the forefoot?" "How does the shoe feel in the arch area?" "Does the shoe slip on the heel?" "Is the heel area big enough?" "How do you like the shoes?"

STEP 8: Evaluate and Make Adjustments

Equipment managers have a real advantage over shoe stores. When shoe store clerks fit a person in a pair of athletic shoes, they most likely will not see the person again. Equipment managers, on the other hand, work with the athletes they fit every day. Watch your athletes at practice. Discuss what they like and dislike about the shoes they are wearing. Work to solve their problems, and build on successes. Both of you will learn, and performance can be improved and injuries reduced.

Women's Shoes

Everything discussed thus far about fitting shoes goes for both men and women. There are, however, a few additional considerations when fitting women's athletic shoes.

When possible, fit women with shoes that are available in women's sizes, if function and quality are not compromised. When this is not possible, remember that women's shoes are approximately 1-1/2 to 2 sizes smaller than men's sizes (for example, a woman's size 7 would be approximately a man's size 5). In addition, women's feet tend to be shorter and narrower than men's.

Although less of a concern these days, the change from high-fashion heels to low athletic shoes can cause Achilles tendon, ankle, calf, and knee problems for women (good heel lift and cushioning are very helpful). Finally, for women with children, the additional weight gained during pregnancy may flatten out the longitudinal arch and/or cause the forefoot to turn out.

Children's Shoes

The fit of children's athletic shoes is extremely important. Often, children's shoes are expected to last "one more season," which can have very harmful effects on the wearer. Children should be given new shoes to accommodate their growth; shoes should not be expected to wear out before they are replaced. **Never pass down shoes from one child to another; this passes on foot problems in the formative years.** The following chart shows how often a child's shoe size should be checked with a measuring device.

CHILD'S AGE	MEASURE THIS OFTEN
2 to 6	Every one to two months
6 to 10	Every two to three months
10 to 12	Every three to four months
12 to 15	Every five to six month
15 to 20	Every six months
20 and older	Every time shoes are purchased

Children's shoes should fit snugly in the heel, and the ball of the foot should be comfortably centered in the widest part of the shoe. From birth until a person is about 18 years old, the bones of the foot are changing from cartilage to bones. Pressure from improperly fitting shoes and socks can cause bones to align improperly at the joints, especially under the heavy stresses of athletics.

APPENDIX A

PLAYER'S SUGGESTED DAILY HELMET INSPECTION CHECKLIST

by the
National Operating Committee on Standards for Athletic Equipment (NOCSAE)

Each player should inspect his helmet before each usage, as follows:

1. Check foam padding for proper placement and any deterioration.

2. Check for cracks in vinyl / rubber covering of air-, foam-, and liquid-padded helmets.

3. Check that protective system or foam padding has not been altered or removed.

4. Check for proper amount of inflation in air-padded helmets. Follow manufacturer's recommended practice for adjusting air pressure at the valves.

5. Check all rivets, screws, Velcro, and snaps to assure they are properly fastened and holding protective parts.

IF ANY OF THE ABOVE INSPECTIONS INDICATE A NEED FOR REPAIR AND/OR REPLACEMENT, NOTIFY YOUR EQUIPMENT MANAGER.

THIS IS YOUR RESPONSIBILITY!

NEVER WEAR A DAMAGED HELMET

APPENDIX B

SUGGESTED WEEKLY HELMET INSPECTION CHECKLIST

by the
National Operating Committee on Standards for Athletic Equipment (NOCSAE)

NOTE—These should be completed by qualified personnel.

1. Check helmet fit for agreement with manufacturer's instructions.

2. Examine shell for cracks particularly noting any cracks around holes (where most cracks start) and replace any that have cracked.

DO NOT USE A HELMET WITH A CRACKED SHELL

3. Examine all mounting rivets, screws, Velcro, and snaps for breakage, distortion, and/or looseness.

REPAIR AS NECESSARY

4. Replace face guards if bare metal is showing, there is a broken weld, or if guard is grossly misshapen.

5. Examine for helmet completeness, and replace any parts that have become damaged, such as sweatbands, nose snubbers, and chin straps.

6. Replace jaw pads when damaged. Check for proper installation and fit.

7. Examine chin strap for proper adjustment, and inspect to see if it is broken or stretched out of shape; also inspect the hardware to see if it needs replacement.

8. Read instructions provided by manufacturer regarding care and maintenance procedures. Always follow these instructions.

CAUTION: Only paints, waxes, decals, or cleaning agents approved by the manufacturer are to be used on any helmet. It is possible to get a severe or delayed reaction by using unauthorized materials, which could permanently damage the helmet shell and affect its safety performance.

FOOTBALL HELMET SIZE RANGES FOR DIFFERENT LEVELS OF PLAY

HELMET SIZE RANGE FOR HIGH SCHOOLS

HELMET SIZE	% OF USE	SQUAD SIZE 30	35	40	45	50	55	60	65	70	75	80	85	90	95	100	105	110	115	120	125	130	135	140	145	150
6 5/8	1%	0	0	0	0	1	1	1	1	1	1	1	1	1	1	1	1	1	1	1	1	1	1	1	1	2
6 3/4	2%	1	1	1	1	1	1	1	1	1	2	2	2	2	2	2	2	2	2	2	3	3	3	3	3	3
6 7/8	3%	2	2	2	2	3	3	3	3	4	4	4	4	5	5	6	5	6	6	6	6	7	7	7	7	8
7	9%	3	3	4	4	5	5	5	6	6	7	7	8	8	9	9	9	10	10	11	11	12	12	13	13	14
7 1/8	13%	4	5	5	6	7	7	8	8	9	10	10	11	12	12	13	14	14	15	16	16	17	18	18	19	20
7 1/4	18%	5	6	7	8	9	10	11	12	13	14	14	15	16	17	18	19	20	21	22	23	23	24	25	26	27
7 3/8	16%	5	6	6	7	8	9	10	10	11	12	13	14	14	15	16	17	18	18	19	20	21	22	22	23	24
7 1/2	13%	4	5	5	6	7	7	8	8	9	10	10	11	12	12	13	14	14	15	16	16	17	18	18	19	20
7 5/8	9%	3	3	4	4	5	5	5	6	6	7	7	8	8	9	9	9	10	10	11	11	12	12	13	13	14
7 3/4	6%	2	2	2	3	3	3	4	4	4	5	5	5	5	6	6	6	7	7	7	8	8	8	8	9	9
7 7/8	3%	1	1	1	1	2	2	2	2	2	2	2	3	3	3	3	3	3	3	4	4	4	4	4	4	5
8	2%	1	1	1	1	1	1	1	1	1	2	2	2	2	2	2	2	2	2	2	3	3	3	3	3	3
8 1/8	1%	0	0	0	0	1	1	1	1	1	1	1	1	1	1	1	1	1	1	1	1	1	1	1	1	2
8 1/4	1%	0	0	0	0	1	1	1	1	1	1	1	1	1	1	1	1	1	1	1	1	1	1	1	1	2
8 3/8	1%	0	0	0	0	1	1	1	1	1	1	1	1	1	1	1	1	1	1	1	1	1	1	1	1	2

HELMET SIZE RANGE FOR COLLEGE AND PROS

HELMET SIZE	% OF USE	SQUAD SIZE 30	35	40	45	50	55	60	65	70	75	80	85	90	95	100	105	110	115	120	125	130	135	140	145	150
6 5/8	0%	0	0	0	0	0	0	0	0	0	0	0	0	0	0	0	0	0	0	0	0	0	0	0	0	0
6 3/4	1%	0	0	0	0	1	1	1	1	1	1	1	1	1	1	1	1	1	1	1	1	1	1	1	1	2
6 7/8	2%	1	1	1	1	1	1	1	1	1	2	2	2	2	2	2	2	2	2	2	3	3	3	3	3	3
7	6%	2	2	2	3	3	3	4	4	4	5	5	5	5	6	6	6	7	7	7	8	8	8	8	9	9
7 1/8	9%	3	3	4	4	5	5	5	6	6	7	7	8	8	9	9	9	10	10	11	11	12	12	13	13	14
7 1/4	15%	5	5	6	7	8	8	9	10	11	11	12	13	14	14	15	16	17	17	18	19	20	20	21	22	23
7 3/8	17%	5	6	7	8	9	9	10	11	12	13	14	14	5	16	17	18	19	20	20	21	22	23	24	25	28
7 1/2	14%	4	5	6	6	7	8	8	9	10	11	11	12	13	13	14	15	15	16	17	18	18	19	20	20	21
7 5/8	11%	3	4	4	5	6	6	7	7	8	8	9	9	10	10	11	12	12	13	13	14	14	15	16	16	17
7 3/4	7%	2	2	3	3	4	4	4	5	5	5	6	6	6	7	7	7	8	8	8	9	9	9	10	10	11
7 7/8	6%	2	2	2	3	3	3	4	4	4	5	5	5	5	6	6	6	7	7	7	8	8	8	8	9	9
8	5%	2	2	2	2	3	3	3	3	4	4	4	4	5	5	5	5	6	6	6	6	7	7	7	7	8
8 1/8	3%	1	1	1	1	2	2	2	2	2	2	2	3	3	3	3	3	3	3	4	4	4	4	4	4	5
8 1/4	3%	1	1	1	1	2	2	2	2	2	2	2	3	3	3	3	3	3	3	4	4	4	4	4	4	5
8 3/8	1%	0	0	0	0	1	1	1	1	1	1	1	1	1	1	1	1	1	1	1	1	1	1	1	1	2

*NOTE—The percentage of use is based on "historical sales experience" of Riddell Inc.

FOOTBALL EQUIPMENT SIZING SHEET

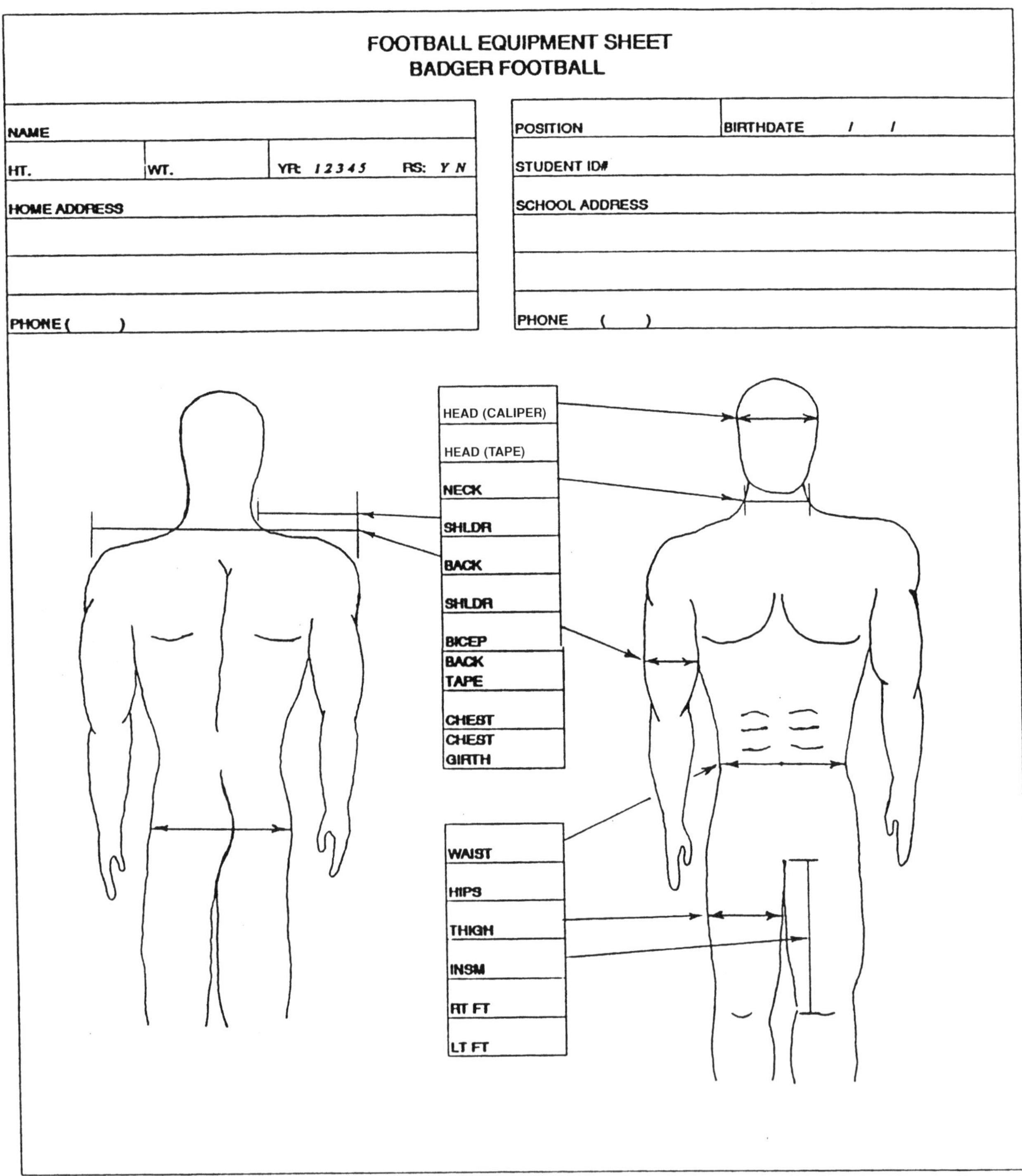

FOOTBALL EQUIPMENT SHEET
BADGER FOOTBALL

NAME

HT. | WT. | YR: 1 2 3 4 5 | RS: Y N

HOME ADDRESS

PHONE (   )

POSITION | BIRTHDATE / /

STUDENT ID#

SCHOOL ADDRESS

PHONE (   )

FOOTBALL EQUIPMENT SIZING SHEET

UNIVERSITY OF WISCONSIN

FOOTBALL EQUIPMENT SHEET

NAME

SEASON

HELMET

TYPE: *WD1 AF2 M155 VSR3 AIR/PWR PRO-AIR MAXPRO*

SHELL SIZE: *Med. Reg. Lg. Xl.* YEAR:

LINER SIZES	A	B	C	1/2"	3/4"	1"
Frnt						
Side						
Top						
Back						
Neck						

FACEMASK	THCK	THIN	DW	R	SW	XL
OPO						
NOPO						
JOP						
NJOP						
EGOP						

VISOR: *ITECH Z-LEADER* CLR: *SMKE ROSE CLR AMBR*

CHEEK PAD: *Riddell AHI Maxpro Other:*
Vinyl Foam Leather
SIZE: *XS S M L XL*

CHIN STRAP: *Riddell AHI Adams Other:*

NOTES:

SHOULDER PADS

BRAND:

STYLE:

SIZE:

NOTES:

PANTS	BRAND	SIZE	LENGTH
BELT			
R-GME			
W-GME			
PRCTC			

NOTES:

JERSEYS	BRAND	SIZE	CUT	FULL	BELT
W-GME					
R-GME					
PRCTC					

NOTES:

HIP/THIGH/KNEE PADS

	STYLE	SIZE
HIP		
THIGH		
KNEE		

NOTES:

SANITARIES	MED	LG	XL	XXL	XXXL
T-SHIRT					
SHORTS					
JOCK					
GIRDLE					

NOTES:

SHOES

	STYLE	DATE	RT.	LT.	NEW	USED
GRASS						
GRASS						
GRASS						
TURF						
TURF						
TURF						
TURF						
GAME						
GAME						
RAIN						
B-BALL						
B-BALL						

NOTES:

PROTECTIVE PADS

NECK ROLL:

BUTTERFLY: DELTOID:

ELBOWS HEELBOW VOLLEYBALL STANDARD
BIKE: *S M L* TRACER: *S M L* OTHER:

FOREARM TRACER: *MSH NYLN* J-PAD CLOTH

KNEE WRESTLING *M R L* BIKE: *M R L*

HAND BIKE: *M R L*

GLOVES

		MED	ML	LG	XL	XXL	XXXL
NEUMAN	TCKY						
	WNTR						
	LB'S						
	OL'S						
SARANAC	LTHR						
	NUBS						
	LB'S						
TUFFWEAR	OL'S						
BIKE	OL/LB						

NOTES:

APPENDIX E

FOOTBALL HELMET INSPECTION / MAINTENANCE RECORD

UNIVERSITY OF WISCONSIN FOOTBALL

HELMET RECORD

HELMET ID #____________ DATE PURCHASED____________ WARRANTY DATE____________

BRAND____________ MODEL____________ SIZE____________

USER INFORMATION

	NAME	ISSUE DATE	RETURNED
USER #1			
USER #2			
USER #3			
USER #4			
USER #5			
USER #6			

RECERTIFICATION INFORMATION

	DATE	BY		DATE	BY
Yr. 1			Yr. 4		
Yr. 2			Yr. 5		
Yr. 3			Yr. 6		

Shaded areas indicate years recertification is not necessary.

INSPECTION / MAINTENANCE RECORD

DATE	DESCRIPTION OF WORK DONE	COMPLETED BY

Continued on next page

FOOTBALL HELMET INSPECTION / MAINTENANCE RECORD

INSPECTION / MAINTENANCE RECORD

Page 2

Continued from page 1

DATE	DESCRIPTION OF WORK DONE	COMPLETED BY

If additional space is needed use another form & attach to this form.

HELMET DISPOSAL

DATE____________ BY____________________ HOW DONE______________________________

INSTRUCTIONS FOR OPERATING THE BRANNOCK SCIENTIFIC FOOT-MEASURING DEVICE

Courtesy of the Brannock Device Co., Syracuse, N.Y.

WHY HEEL-TO-BALL MEASUREMENT IS ESSENTIAL

Figure One, below, shows two feet that are the same length, but each requires different size shoes. There are different fittings for short-toed feet and long-toed feet. Proper shoe fitting incorporates not only overall length (heel-to-toe measurement) but also arch length (heel-to-ball measurement). Shoes are designed to flex at the ball of the foot. Correct fitting properly positions the ball joint in the widest part of the shoe and provides room for the toes so they are not confined.

WITHOUT UTILIZING HEEL-TO-BALL MEASUREMENT

Improperly fitted shoes (shown in Figure Two, below) can cause a variety of foot problems in addition to general discomfort and shoe breakdown. If the arch of the foot is not positioned properly in the shoe, the foot will become fatigued and uncomfortable.

THE BRANNOCK FOOT-MEASURING DEVICE ENSURES CORRECT FIT

The foot in Figure Three, below, is correctly fitted. The arch of the shoe and ball joint of the foot meet at the same point. The foot arch is correctly positioned in the shoe. The foot and shoe bend at the same location, with the arch fully supported, allowing the toes to remain straight. There is ample space in front of the toes for a proper fit. This will ensure a correct fit and a comfortable shoe that will keep its shape.

1. PREPARE THE DEVICE

Prepare the Brannock Device as shown in Figure Four on page 69. The width bar should be set to its widest position and the arch length indicator should be slid back, so the foot can be positioned easily on the device.

Note—Some devices have dual calibrations for the heel-to-toe, arch, and width measurements. Be sure to read the colored area that corresponds to the calibration you are fitting.

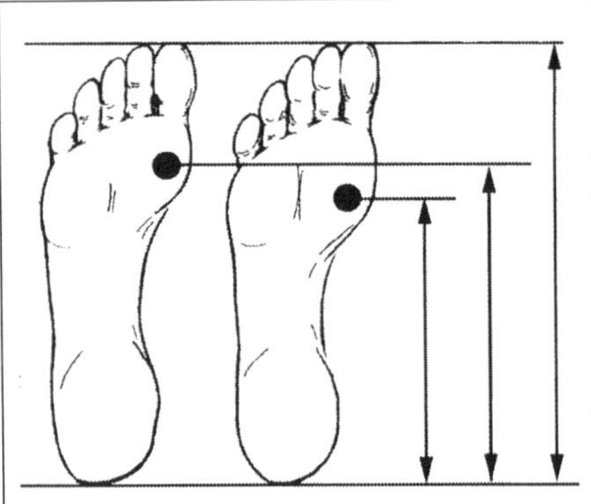

FIGURE ONE
Heel-to-ball measurement.

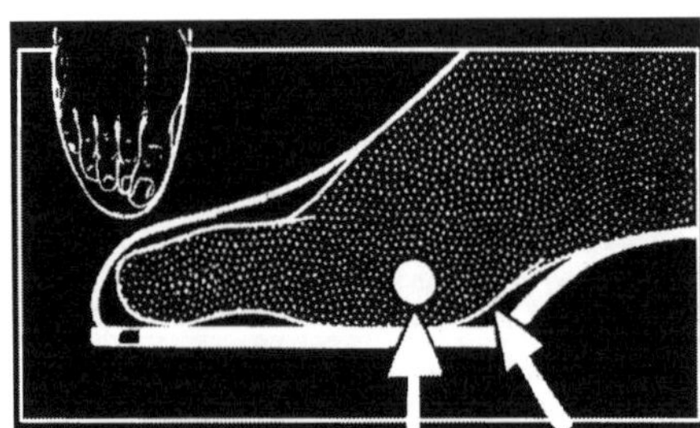

FIGURE TWO
Improperly fitted shoes.

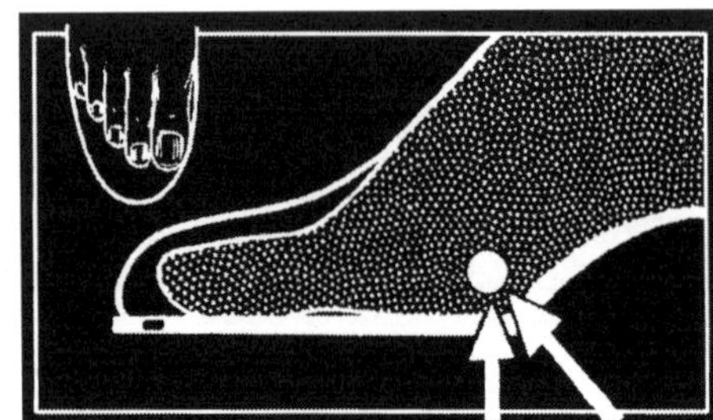

FIGURE THREE
Correctly fitted shoes.

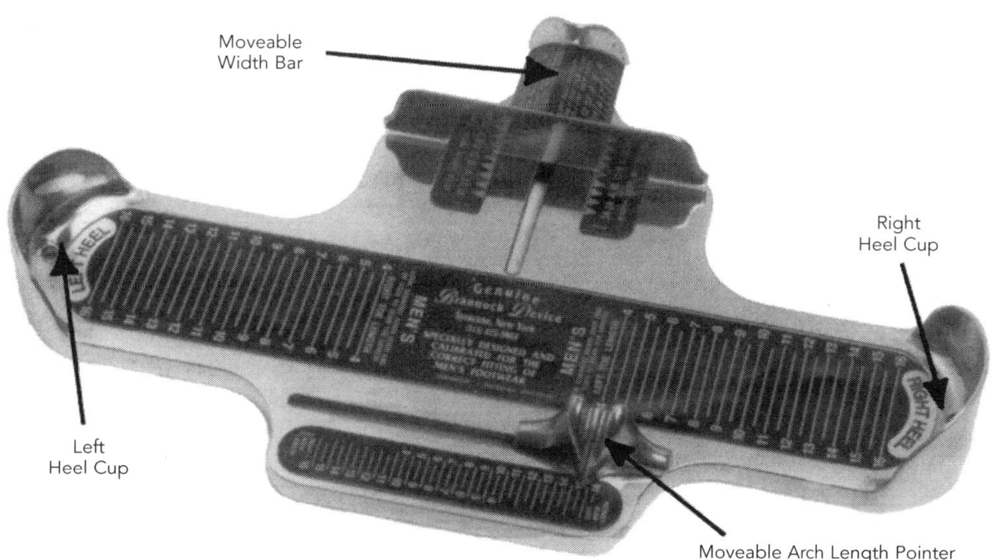

FIGURE FOUR
The parts of the Brannock Foot-Measuring Device.

2. POSITION THE FOOT

Have the customer remove their footwear and stand, placing their right heel into the right heel cup. The customer should stand with equal weight on both feet to ensure that the foot being measured has elongated and spread to its maximum size. Be sure the heel is properly located against the back of the cup by grasping the customer's ankle and the device together, as illustrated in Figure Five on page 70.

3. MEASURE LENGTHS

Heel-to-Toe Length

Press the toes flat against the base of the device and look straight down over the longest toe (not necessarily the first toe) to read toe length (see Figure Six on page 70). Make sure the customer's socks are snug against the toes (without drawing the toes back) to yield an accurate measurement.

Arch Length (Heel-to-Ball)

Place your thumb on the ball joint of the foot as shown in Figure Seven on page 70. Slide the pointer ('A' on Figure Eight on page 70) forward so the inside curve of the pointer fits the ball joint of the foot and the two high ribs come in contact with your thumb. When the pointer is properly located, the lower middle rib will be against the ball joint on the side of the foot ('B' on Figure Eight on page 70). This yields the arch measurement. The arch length represented in Figure Eight is 8 1/2.

4. FIND THE CORRECT SHOE SIZE

Compare the arch length to the heel-to-toe length and use the larger of the two measurements as the correct shoe size. If the arch length and heel-to-toe length are the same, this will be the shoe size. If the heel-to-toe length is larger than the arch length, then fit to the heel-to-toe size. If arch length is larger than heel-to-toe, then fit to arch length.

It is important that both measurements be taken and compared to find the proper shoe size. Simply using the heel-to-toe length may result in an improper fit.

5. MEASURE THE WIDTH

Slide the width bar firmly to the edge of the foot (see Figure Nine on page 70). On the sliding width bar, locate the size (determined in step four). Find the width measurement that lines up to the shoe size on the width bar. If the shoe size falls between widths, choose a wider width for a thick foot, a narrower width for a thin foot.

If the foot is extremely fleshy or has a high instep, it may be necessary to fit an extra width wider. If the foot is extremely thin, compress the foot slightly with the width bar and determine the size while holding the bar in this position.

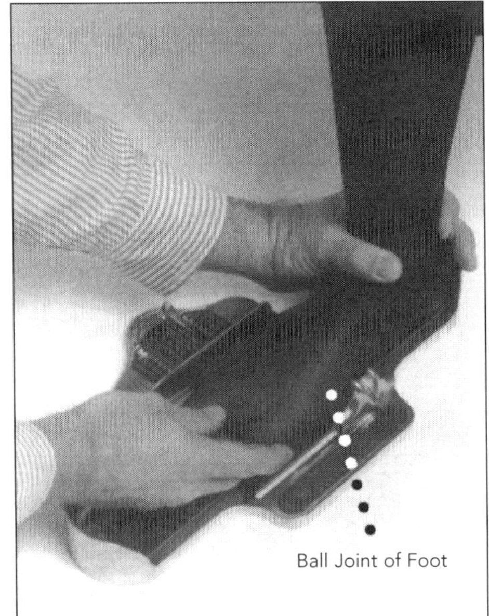

FIGURE FIVE
Placing the foot on the device.

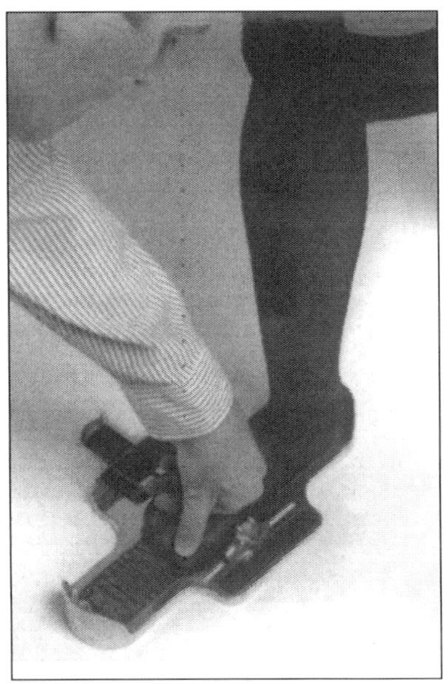

FIGURE SIX
Measuring heel-to-toe length.

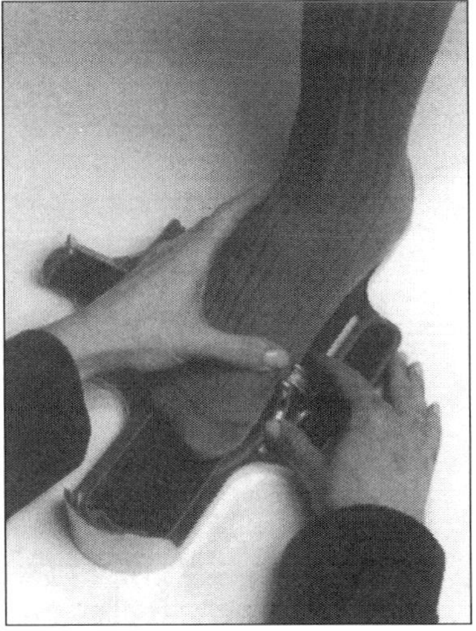

FIGURES SEVEN
Measuring arch length.

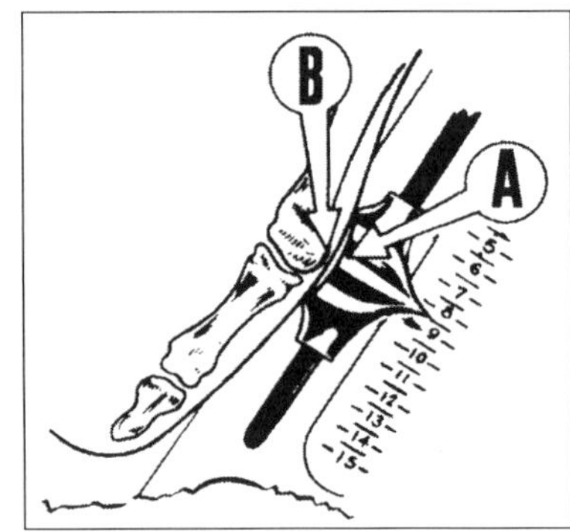

FIGURE EIGHT
Positioning the pointer to determine arch length.

6. MEASURE THE OTHER FOOT

Reverse the device end-for-end and measure the other foot following the steps described above. Be sure to measure both feet, then fit the larger foot. It is common to have feet of different sizes.

7. REMEMBER THE FITTING PROCESS

When used properly, the Brannock Foot-Measuring Device is designed to indicate the correct shoe size. This is the first step in the fitting process. Due to differences in manufacturing, styling, and other variables, it is up to each fitter to be knowledgeable of shoe styles and fit characteristics. It may be necessary to make compensations in sizing to achieve a proper fit for each individual customer. The fitting process often involves trial fittings to ensure that the proper size was selected.

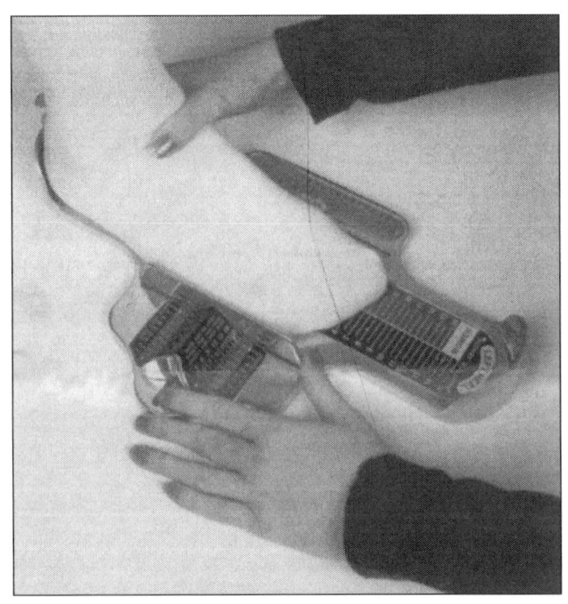

FIGURE NINE
Measuring foot width.

LACING TECHNIQUES

Most people prefer the standard crisscross method of lacing shoes. There are several additional methods of lacing shoes, however, that can be of great benefit to athletes with certain types of injuries or biomechanical problems.

Shoes with **variable-width lacing** have two sets of eyelet holes. The wider set is used by people with narrow feet, while the closer set is used by people with wide feet (see Figure One, below).

Dual lacing systems have an arrangement of three punched holes and three speed rings to give an even pull to the eye stay and speed up opening and closing. The **independent-lacing system** (also called dual lacing) uses a lace for the forefoot/front quarter and a lace for the ankle/top quarter (see Figure Two, below). This allows the laces of each area to be adjusted to the shape of that specific area.

Crisscross alternative #1 is an excellent way to help prevent heel slippage if the heel of the shoe is too wide. With this method, the lace is brought out of the next-to-last hole and is then looped through the top eyelet hole; the next step is to cross and pass the lace through the loop made on the other side (see Figure Three, below). This gives a better pull on the collar of the shoe.

Crisscross alternative #2 offers relief from a sore spot on the top of the foot or the first metatarsal ray. The shoe should be laced conventionally to just below the trouble spot. The lace is then taken straight up the same side, and crisscrossing is begun again above the problem area (see Figure Three). Missing one eyelet section is normally enough to provide relief.

Square-box lacing distributes lace pressure evenly on the top area of the foot and stops the traditional lace strain on the foot. This may help athletes with high-arched or rigid feet. The laces pass under the eyelet stay and do not crisscross over the top of the foot at all (see Figure Four, below).

The **single-lace cross** (or dress shoe) method may help athletes with blackened, sore, or tender toenails. One lace runs from the inside front eyelet to the opposite last eyelet. The other end of the lace is threaded side to side through every remaining eyelet. This method lifts the toe box off the toe area (see Figure Four).

Finally, **combination lacing** uses a different method on each foot to help solve each foot's own problems.

FIGURE ONE
Variable-width lacing—left for wide fitting, right for narrow fitting.

FIGURE TWO
Independent-lacing system using two laces.

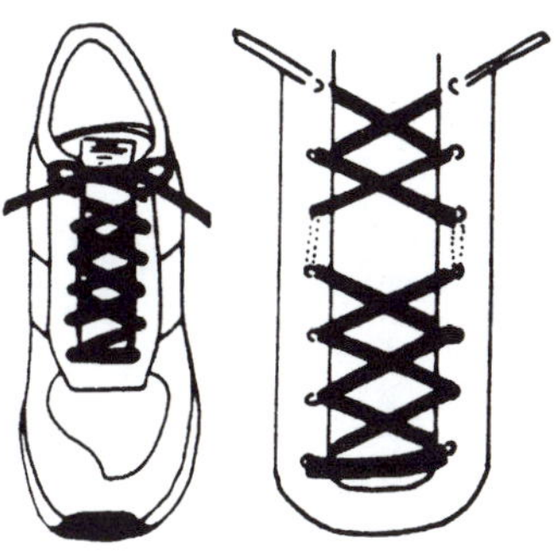

FIGURE THREE
Left: crisscross alternative #1.
Right: crisscross alternative #2.

FIGURE FOUR
Left: square-box lacing.
Right: single-lace cross.

ANATOMY AND BIOMECHANICS OF THE FOOT AND LEG

When working with athletes, it's helpful to have a basic understanding of the anatomy and biomechanics of the foot and leg. The following provides more detail than most equipment managers require. Especially when fitting athletic shoes, however, it's important to know how the foot and the various components of the shoe (discussed in Appendix J, "Parts of the Modern Athletic Shoe," on page 80) work together to protect the athlete and enable him or her to perform the movements required in his or her sport.

Anatomy

The foot is made up of 26 bones that are held together by ligaments, cartilage, tendons, and muscles. It contains nerves, arteries, and veins to carry blood to all parts of the foot, and sweat glands to keep it cool. The foot is covered with skin and nails to protect the toes. The leg is made up of four bones and is attached to the main trunk of the body at the hip joint.

Bones

The bones of the foot can be divided into three major groups: tarsus (the back group), metatarsus (the middle group), and phalanxes (the distal [farthest from the body] group) (see Figure One on page 73).

There are seven short bones in the tarsus group. The calcaneous (heel bone) carries a large part of the body's weight; the talus (ankle bone) links the foot to the lower leg, helping distribute body weight to the forepart of the foot and heel (the joint between the calcaneous and heel bone is called the subtalar joint, and it will be discussed later). The remaining bones in this group are the navicular, the cuboid, the inner cuneiform, the middle cuneiform, and the outer cuneiform.

The metatarsus group contains five long bones that make up the midfoot. The first three join to the cuneiforms, the last two (fourth and fifth) to the cuboid. The phalanxes are the 14 long bones that form the toes.

The sesamoids are two small bones that lie under the distal head of the first metatarsal. They act as fulcrum points for the muscles that pass over them.

The four bones of the leg are the femur (thigh bone), the patella (kneecap), the fibula, and the tibia. The fibula and the tibia make up the lower leg.

Joints

Joints are locations where two or more bones meet. The major joints of the leg and foot are the hip (ball-and-socket type), knee (hinge type), ankle (hinge type), and toes (gliding type).

Cartilage

Cartilage is a specialized material that covers the ends of bones and provides the surface over which bones can move against each other. Synovial fluid is the lubricant for cartilage. Because of this fluid, ball-and-socket, hinge, and gliding-type joints are called synovial joints.

Ligaments and Tendons

Ligaments connect bones to other bones. They are similar to elastic bands that strap around bones and hold them in place to prevent dislocation. Tendons connect bones to muscles.

Muscles

Muscles are fibrous tissues that run from bone to bone (the fibers of the muscles attach to tendon fibers, which attach to bones). The contraction (shortening) of the muscle causes the bones to move. Muscles work together in groups. Each muscle group has an opposing group of muscles (antagonistic) that works against it to allow continuous, fluid movements.

There are four muscle groups in the lower leg that attach to the bones of the foot through tendons. The front, or anterior, group (four muscles in front of and between the tibia and the fibula) raise the foot (dorsiflexion), turn the soles in (inversion) and out (eversion), and extend the toes up. The outside or lateral group's tendons pass behind the ankle joint and bend the foot down (plantarflexion) and turn it out (abduction). This group of muscles includes the two that join the fibula. The surface back group on the calf pass via the Achilles tendon, over the back of the ankle, and bend the foot down (plantarflexion). One of the muscles of this group is joined to the femur and the other is joined to the tibia and the fibula. The deep back or posterior group, which consists of four muscles under the calf, pass behind the ankle to flex the toes down (dorsiflexion) and turn the foot in (adduction).

The muscle groups in the foot above the skeleton extend the toes, whereas the muscles below the skeleton control the other movements of the toes.

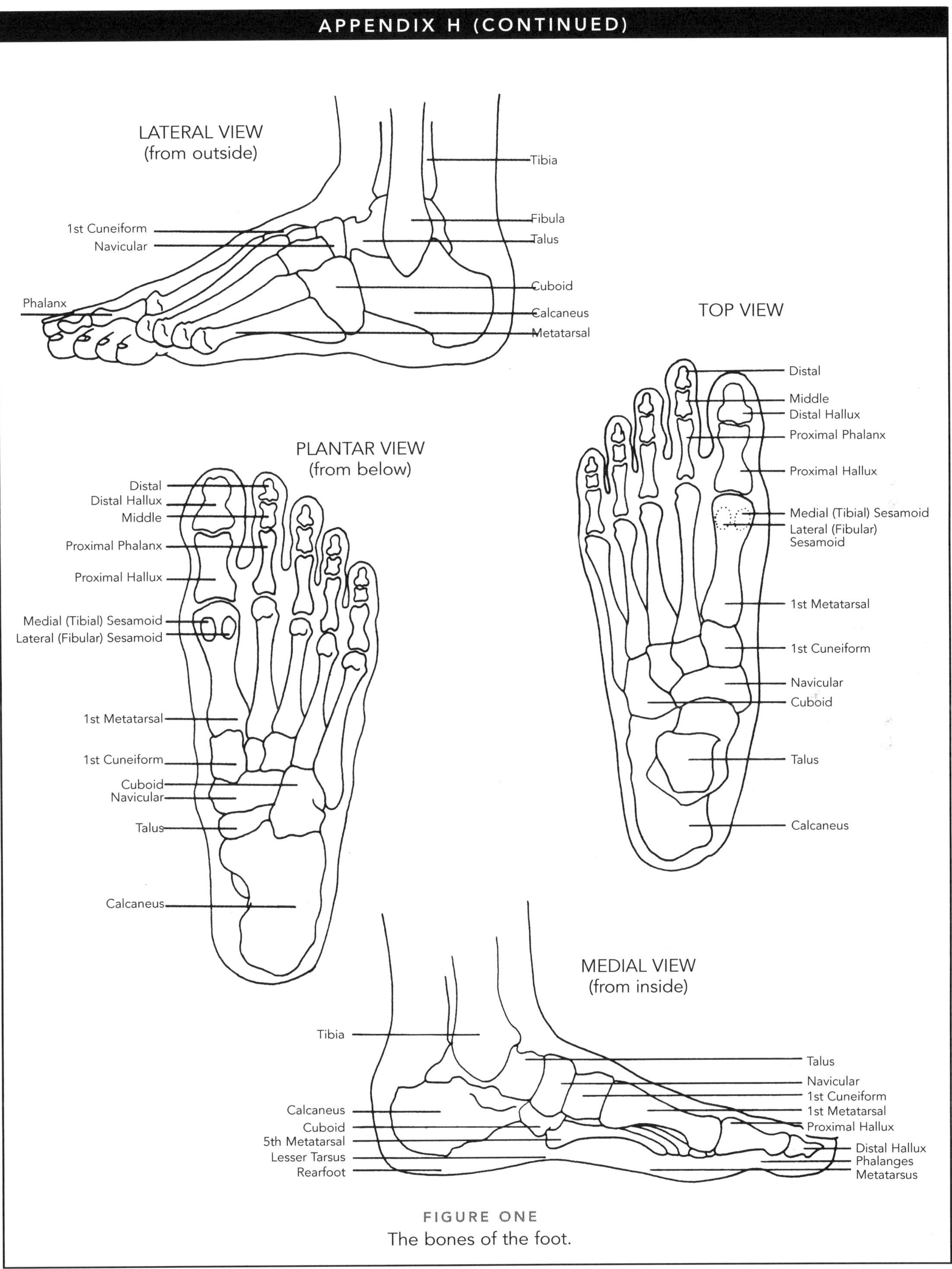

FIGURE ONE
The bones of the foot.

Nerves

Nerves cause muscles to contract, resulting in movement. Nerve stimuli to muscles may cause voluntary, involuntary, or relax actions.

Circulatory System

Blood is supplied to the foot via arteries and returned via veins. The circulatory system nourishes all tissues, removes waste, and provides repair material. The feet contain more blood than is necessary for their nourishment, which allows them to play an important part in controlling the temperature of the body.

Skin

Skin is the body's protective covering. It contains nerve endings, blood vessels, sweat glands, and hair follicles. Skin is the material that contacts the shoe, usually through a sock or socks while engaged in athletics. There are roughly 250,000 sweat glands in a pair of feet, pouring out half a pint of moisture, salt, and acids into shoes each day.

Mechanics of Foot and Leg Motion

The hip, a ball-and-socket joint, is the only joint in the lower extremity that can move in all directions. The pelvis (hip bones) passes the energy created by the feet and legs to the rest of the body. The proximal end (closer to the center of the body) of the femur acts as a ball and socket. This allows the quadriceps (the four large muscles on the front of the thigh) and the femur to rotate medially (toward the inside), laterally (toward the outside), anteriorly (forward), and posteriorly (backward). The hip allows the knee, ankle, and lower joints to retain straight-ahead positions during forward movements such as walking and running.

The knee joint is the largest joint in the body. The distal end (away from the center of the body) of the femur forms the top of the knee joint. The proximal ends of the tibia and the fibula form the bottom of the knee joint. As a hinge joint, most of its motion is flexion and extension; however, some lateral and medial rotation is also possible in the knee joint.

The distal ends of the tibia and fibula join at the ankle. The ankle joint allows dorsiflexion (upward movement) and plantarflexion (downward movement) of the foot. The ankle is most important in maintaining the body's center of gravity during forward and backward movement.

The subtalar and midtarsal joints play a major role in plantarflexion/dorsiflexion and pronation/supination. Pronation is a lowering of the medial border of the foot and elevation of the lateral border of the foot, abduction (moving away from the midline of the body), and dorsiflexion. Supination is a raising of the medial (inside) arch through three movements: inversion (elevation of the medial border and depression of the outside border of the foot), adduction (moving a part toward the midline of the body), and plantarflexion.

These two actions help absorb retrograde shock at heel strike and help the foot change from a rigid lever for propulsion to a mobile adapter during the contact phase of gait. As the subtalar joint pronates, the fibula and tibia rotate inward, causing stress at the knee (see Figure Two, right).

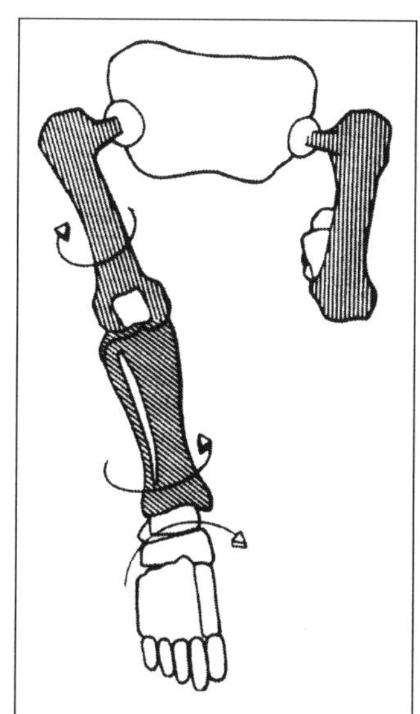

FIGURE TWO
The subtalar joint.

Metatarsal-phalangeal joints are hinge-type joints that allow plantarflexion and dorsiflexion of the toes, as well as their grasping action. Phalangeal-phalangeal joints are hinge-type joints that allow grasping of the toes.

Foot Types

The arches of the foot provide strength and support body weight. The longitudinal arch extends from the heel to the toe and gives spring to a person's walk. The transverse (mediotarsal) arch goes across the instep. Arches are grouped by three types: high, normal, and flat.

In the high-arched foot (cavus foot type), one or more of the arches is high. The forefoot and heel generally carry the predominant pressure and weight. This type of foot requires exceptional shock absorption or anatomical plantar-surface fitting, because exercise exerts tremendous force on the ball and heel of the foot.

The normal arch type distributes weight evenly on the forefoot, lateral border, and heel area. The long, inside arch area is raised.

In a flat foot the arches are collapsed or low, distributing body weight over the total foot area. This exerts extra pressure on the outside border of the foot.

Arch types can be identified by taking the wet foot test. Have the athlete wet his or her feet and stand on a smooth, dry surface. Look at the impressions that remain after the athlete steps away (see Figure Three, right).

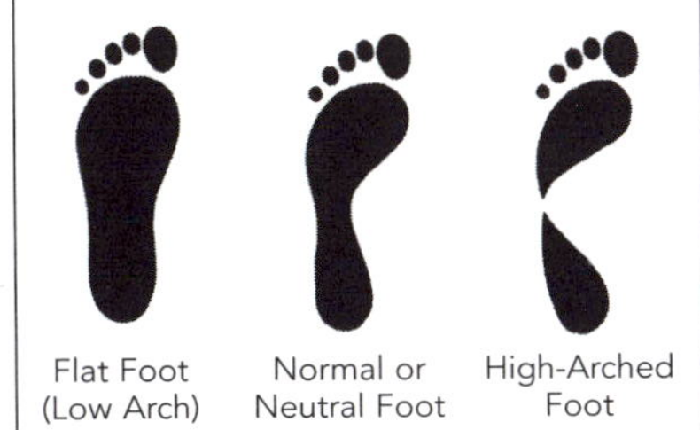

FIGURE THREE
Determining arch type with the wet foot test.

Although no two feet are identical, shoemakers do group them by common characteristics. Some studies have shown common foot characteristics among racial types; however, it's important to treat each athlete individually when fitting them. The only generalities that can be made regard certain characteristics that vary between men and women.

Anatomical Differences Between Men and Women

The physical differences between men and women cause different stresses on the foot and leg. The larger angle of the femur in females increases the chances of lateral knee injury (see Figure Four, below). This angle makes the leg less biomechanically efficient. Ligaments, tendons, and cartilage are more delicate, and there is less muscle mass, resulting in more flexibility. The result is that women tend to have less power than men but their movement is more fluid. Further, shorter and narrower foot structure in women allows them to complete the heel-to-toe gait movement quicker, but puts a greater impact on the heel area at foot strike.

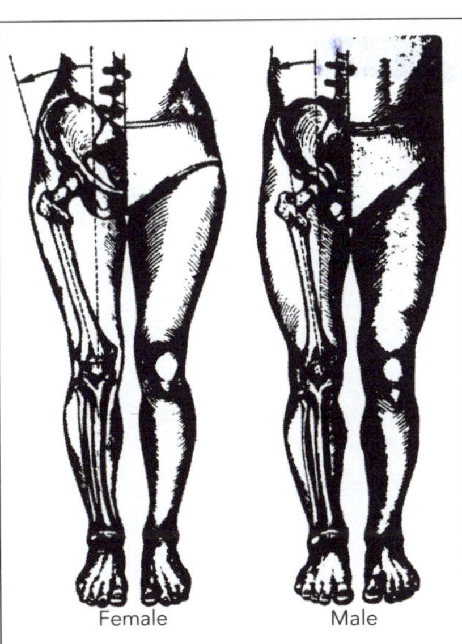

FIGURE FOUR
The angle of the femur in women and men.

Joints Out of Alignment

Problems with joint alignment in the lower extremity have been identified as one of the principal causes of injuries to runners. Two words that physicians use to describe alignment problems are varus and valgus.

Varus means turning in toward the midline of the body. Thus, rearfoot varus is a condition where the angle of the feet as seen from the ankles down toward the ground turns inward (bowlegged). Forefoot varus means the toes turn inward. Valgus means turning away from the midline of the body (knock-kneed) (see Figure Five, below).

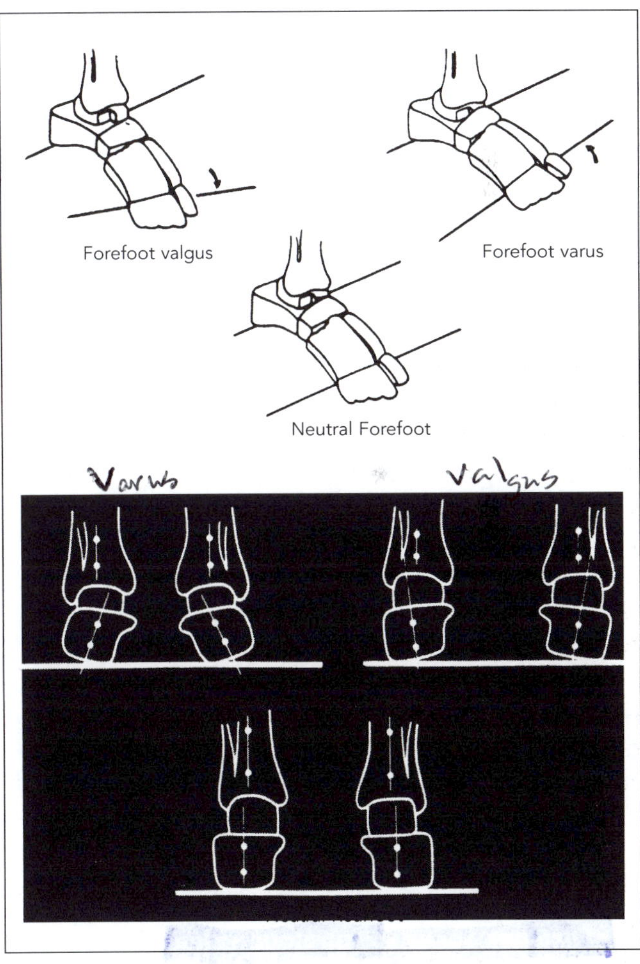

FIGURE FIVE
Alignment problems with the joints of the leg and foot.

INJURIES RELATED TO FOOTWEAR

The purpose of this appendix is to inform. Many of the injuries discussed here need the professional treatment of other members of the sports medicine field, such as the team doctor and athletic trainer.

There are two basic types of athletic injuries: acquired and inherited. An acquired injury is a direct result of being involved in an activity. A sprained ankle is an example. An inherited injury is a biomechanical abnormality that may be the cause of a sports-related injury. Subtalar varus is an example of a biomechanical abnormality that can increase an athlete's risk of injury to the ankle, knee, hip, and back. This section covers both acquired and inherited types of injuries.

The Normal Foot

The "normal" foot is the ideal, not the average. The following statements are true about the "normal" foot:

- the calcaneus is parallel with the leg and perpendicular to the supporting surface
- the plane of the forefoot (metatarsal heads) is perpendicular to the calcaneus and parallel to the supporting surface, all five metatarsal heads lie on that surface
- the ankle joint must be able to dorsiflex at least eight to 10 degrees
- there are no external forces from the leg to the foot in any three body planes causing it to dorsiflex or plantarflex, adduct or abduct, or invert or evert

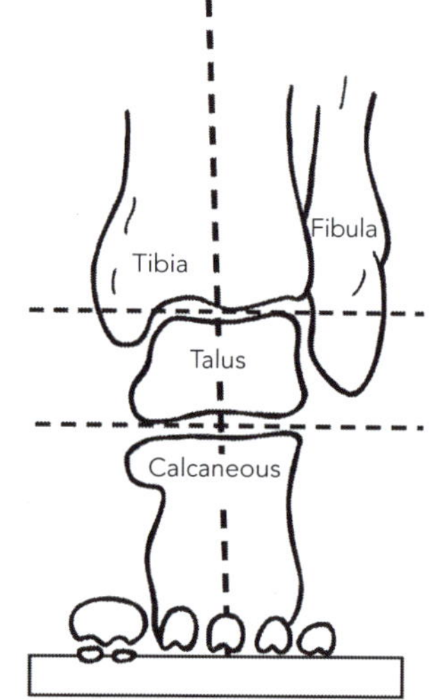

FIGURE ONE
The alignment of the "normal" foot.

Inherited Foot and Leg Abnormalities

There are several foot and leg abnormalities that are inherited that can cause sports injuries.

Metatarsus adductus is a transverse plane abnormality in which the metatarsal bones are pointed inward relative to the rearfoot, causing a C-shaped foot.

Forefoot varus or forefoot valgus is a frontal plane deformity of the forefoot in which it is inverted or everted in relation to the rearfoot.

Subtalar varus is the most common bony abnormality of the foot; **subtalar valgus** is relatively rare. In these abnormalities, the frontal plane of the subtalar joint is either inverted (varus) or everted (valgus) relative to the leg.

Equinus (commonly called talipes equinus) is a bony abnormality of the ankle in the sagittal plane that makes the ankle joint unable to allow the foot to dorsiflex on the leg at least 10 degrees. This affects the midstance phase of the gait and the midtarsal joint of the foot.

Tibial varum (bowlegs) and **tibial valgum** (knock-knees) occur in the legs, above the feet, but they affect foot function. **Leg-length discrepancies** will also affect foot function.

These inherited conditions all cause abnormal pronatory motion. With these abnormalities, the services of a podiatrist or other sports medicine professional is sometimes a necessity.

Acquired Lower-Extremity Injuries

This section describes some of the acquired injuries to the lower extremity. It is not the purpose of this section to discuss treatment for these injuries, other than to mention things that can be done to the shoe or the foot to possibly speed recovery or to help prevent these injuries from occurring. The other members of the sports medicine team can be of great help in rehabilitating these injuries.

Two of the most common toe injuries involving the nails are **ingrown nails** (onychocryptosis) and **black toenails** (subungual hematoma), which are caused by repeated trauma of the toe against the toe box or tight-fitting shoes in the toe area. A shoe built on a last more the shape of the athlete's foot; a higher, wider toe box; or a more square-toed shoe will help reduce the chance of being injured again.

Corns (heloma dura) usually form on the top side of the toes, on the joints. They are hard skin (hyperkeratosis) and are caused by the toe rubbing on the inside top of the toe box. A bigger toe box will help correct this problem. Commercial corn pads and lamb's wool can protect the area. Hammertoes will increase the likelihood that corns will form, because this condition causes the joint to become more prominent. Simple surgery can correct hammertoes. Athletes involved in contact sports need shoes with a rigid, protective toe box, but one that is roomy enough so that the toes don't rub.

Blisters are caused by friction. Some are caused by a shearing between two layers of skin; others result from constant rubbing. The fit of the athlete's shoes should be checked. Both shoes too large or too small can cause blisters. Any exposed seams or other rough areas that could cause irritation should be dealt with by trimming away excess fabric or other material within the shoe, stretching the shoe, or adding moleskin to ease the friction that was caused by the seam or rough area.

A **callus,** which is an area of thickened skin, occurs in cases of extreme pressure or friction. Abnormal pronation and poor alignment of the metatarsals are probable causes. Using a thickly padded innersole, or putting a pad doughnut under the innersole to redistribute the weight, may help. Employing the proper lacing pattern for the area may also help.

Pain in the forefoot, called **metatarsalgia** or **dancer's foot,** can be caused by overpronation, a thin foot pad, excessive pressure on the heads of the metatarsals, capsulitis (inflammation of the capsule around the joint) resulting from overuse or too much pressure, and interdigital neuromas (an outgrowth of nerve cells). An athlete's shoes must have good shock absorption qualities. Racing flats and other shoes with very little foot padding should be avoided until the pain has disappeared. In addition, the sole in the forefoot area should be flexible, and the shoe should have the proper girth in the forefoot.

Sesamoiditis is an injury to the sesamoid bones, which are located under the distal head of the first metatarsal. Their location makes them prone to injury. Landing very hard can injure them. When using cleated field shoes, an athlete should be careful not to align a cleat directly under these bones, as this can place undue pressure on them. Poor biomechanics can also cause problems. Shoes with good shock absorption in the forefoot area, use of orthotics, and careful fitting of cleated shoes can help with this injury.

Stone bruises are caused by landing on a hard object. Good shock absorption in the outsole, midsole, and insoles will help prevent this injury and aid in healing.

Tendinitis is the inflammation of a tendon. It can be aggravated by a non-protective toe box or an inflexible forefoot. A podiatrist or orthopedist should be consulted for this condition.

Compression of nerves right below the skin can be caused by wearing shoes that are too tight. This condition is very common in those who wear ice skates and ski boots. Surgery is the normal treatment for this injury.

The plantar fascia is the strong ligamentous band on the bottom (plantar) aspect of the foot that ensures the shape and integrity of the longitudinal arch (the concave portion of the medial aspect of the foot). It begins on the plantar aspect of the calcaneus and inserts into the metatarsal heads. If the plantar fascia is injured, an athlete cannot perform to his or her potential. Abnormal pronation and excessively flat feet make it easier to injure the plantar fascia. Shoes with a good shank and arch are a must. If the problem is biomechanical, a podiatrist or orthopedist should be consulted. **Plantar fasciitis** in the heel at the attachment to the calcaneus, if it lasts long enough, will cause a bone spur to develop. Some simple methods of treatment for this injury are heel cups and shoes with a sturdy, but flexible forefoot to control the stresses that pass through the plantar fascia.

In children, the calcaneus (heel bone) has at least two growth centers; **apophysites (inflamed outgrowths)** can occur in any of these locations. If a child is tender in this area when placing weight on it, the athlete/child needs rest. Shoes with a firm, shock-absorbing heel area are needed. A good heel cup will also help.

Bursitis around the Achilles tendon and the calcaneus can be caused by ill-fitting shoes, a poorly padded heel counter, or excessive heel motion. Properly fitted shoes with good Achilles tendon padding will help. Exceptionally high padding has to be monitored to make sure it does not cause problems rather than prevent them.

Achilles tendinitis usually occurs in an area centered about five centimeters above the tendon's attachment on the posterior aspect of the calcaneus. This is a triplane injury. Low heel elevation may be a factor.

Hagland's deformity is the occurrence of small, irregular bumps on the back of the heel bone, usually between the heel and the Achilles tendon. It is most common in tall people with high arches. When shoes irritate these bumps, they become sore and swollen. If they are irritated long enough, additional bone growth will occur. Shoes with a good Achilles tendon protector are a must. Heel lifts to change the position of the bumps and reduce irritation can also help.

There are two types of **ankle sprain:** those that occur when the ankle turns in relative to the leg, which is called an inversion sprain (about 75 percent of all ankle sprains are this type); and those that occur when the ankle turns out, which is called an eversion sprain. Shoes with solid heel counters are a must. High-top shoes, and flared heels in running shoes, may help.

In **tarsal tunnel syndrome,** the posterior tibial nerve is impinged and compressed, as it goes under the medial malleolus. It is more common in athletes with elongated feet. Shoes with good heel counters and other types of pronation controls such as elongated medial counters or external pronation-control devices can help athletes with this injury.

Shinsplints is a term used to describe pain in the lower leg brought on by activity. The pain is usually associated with a change in footwear (especially to an inflexible forefoot) and playing on a harder surface or engaging in more jumping than normal. The pain may be caused by inflammation of the tendons (tendinitis), muscles (myositis), and/or the bone covering (periostitis).

Overuse is a major factor in spinsplints. A sports medicine specialist in this area will be invaluable. Bowlegs (tibial varum) can also cause shinsplints. A specialist will be needed to treat bowlegs as well. Shinsplints that last more than three to four weeks could be a stress fracture and need immediate medical attention. Excessive arch scoop may be a factor in posterior shin splints. Athletic shoes with good shock absorption help prevent shinsplints. In addition, flexible forefeet reduce stress on the leg muscles (especially the anterior group).

Compartment syndrome occurs when one of the seven muscle compartments in the leg, which are tightly wrapped with fascia (tissue covering), is injured. Inflammation occurs and increases the pressure inside the compartment. Blood flow and nerve function to the compartment will be impaired. Numbness, coldness, a feeling of "pins and needles," and exquisite pain are produced. ***This is a medical emergency.*** Immediate surgery may be needed to release the pressure inside the compartment.

Many knee-related injuries can be helped by controlling abnormal foot motion. Neutralizing an abnormal foot requires a specialist. However, a few simple precautions can help. Good heel counters help prevent overpronation, which causes rotation in the knee. Excessive flare in the heel also seems to cause knee problems.

Other Foot Problems

If **foot odor** or **hot spots** are a problem, washing the feet daily, at a minimum; using absorbent, antibacterial insoles; wearing shoes that breathe; and wearing absorbent, natural-fiber socks (60/40 cotton/wool blend) all seem to help. If a hot spot occurs, activity should stop. Some athletes find that wearing two pairs of socks will help, as well as lubricating ointments and moleskin.

When wearing two pairs of socks in running sports, the outer layer provides friction protection and can be thinner than the inner layer. In winter sports, this situation is usually the opposite—a thinner layer on the inside and a thicker layer on the outside. Fitted socks (with toe and heel) usually fit better. The athlete should make sure there are no wrinkles in the socks before putting on the shoes, or hot spots might occur.

Hosiery and socks should never be worn a second time without washing them. Infection and blisters can be caused by wearing socks more than one time between washings.

There are two skin conditions that are the exact opposite of each other: **"wet feet"** (hyperhidrosis) and **"dry feet"** (anhidrosis). There are many causes of wet feet, such as metabolic disorders; hot, humid weather; even the use of poor-quality socks. Changing socks several times a day, daily alcohol rubs, wearing absorbent socks, and using foot powders all help. Medical help may be needed if these steps do not bring the condition under control. Dry feet can be caused by such conditions as allergies, blockage of sweat ducts, or diseases. Applying moisturizing creams is the usual treatment. Medical help should be sought if immediate results are not gained from the moisturizing creams.

Many **nail problems** can be prevented by cutting toenails straight across, making sure that the center of the nail is the same length as the sides. **Fungus problems** in the nails are best treated by a professional.

Athletes foot is a term used to describe several types of skin infections, usually those between the toes, especially between the fourth and fifth. A sports medicine professional can make a proper diagnosis and prescribe the correct treatment. Wearing clean cotton socks that are changed at least twice a day, dusting shoes with an antifungal foot spray, and giving shoes 24 hours to dry before wearing them again will help with this condition and prevent it from recurring.

Warts can occur on the feet, as well as on other parts of the body. They are very common during adolescence, and they are contagious. Warts on the bottom of the foot (plantar warts) are sometimes misdiagnosed as calluses. A sports medicine professional can quickly tell the difference and prescribe the proper treatment.

A **bunion** is a bump or enlargement on the medial (inside) part of the foot at the joint of the great toe. The three primary causes of bunions are pronated feet, heredity, and long-term use of ill-fitting shoes. Pronation, the most common, causes muscular imbalances in the big toe joint. Bunions will produce pain and arthritic changes in the joint, and they will make the foot look ugly. Athletes participating in kicking sports can get traumatic arthritis and bunion formation. **Early treatment by sports medicine professionals is a must if any bump or deviation is noticed on the great toe.**

A **"tailor's bunion"** is a protrusion or bump at the base of the fifth metatarsal, without deviation of the fifth toe. Wearing shoes wide enough to prevent irritation, stretching the shoe material over the bump, and placing doughnuts or half-moon pads around it to take pressure off the area are simple treatments. Professional help is the only real solution.

PARTS OF THE MODERN ATHLETIC SHOE

Athletic shoes are designed to protect athletes' feet and ankles (and, to a lesser extent, the entire kinetic chain) and provide traction during their sport activities. Figure One, below, shows the basic parts of the modern athletic shoe. The two major components are the uppers and the bottoms, both of which can vary greatly by style.

Upper

The upper of the shoe includes all of the following:

- vamp—upper covering for the forefoot
- inside and outside quarters
- featherline—where the bottom and the upper meet
- eyestays—form the throat of the shoe
- foxing—covering for the back of the shoe
- wing tip—covering to protect the front of upper
- collar—where the ankle and upper meet
- achilles tendon protector—back tab of the upper that extends up the Achilles tendon
- internal heel counter—stiffener in a pocket in the back of the shoe to control rearfoot movement
- external heel counter—attached to the outside of the shoe to help stiffen the base of the internal heel counter
- arch bandage—reinforcement sewn on the inside of the upper along the inside arch
- saddle—reinforcement sewn on the outside of the upper along midfoot

Bottom

The bottom of the shoe is basically everything under the foot. It includes the following:

- outsole—the part of the shoe that contacts the ground, usually made of a very wear-resistant material with some type of pattern to improve traction
- midsole—an essential unit in which the upper and bottom are cemented together; this provides shock absorption
- wedge—adds heel lift and provides shock absorption
- insole board—helps support the foot and connects the upper to the bottom
- sockliner and arch cookie—where the foot makes contact with the bottom of the shoe; its major purposes are support and comfort

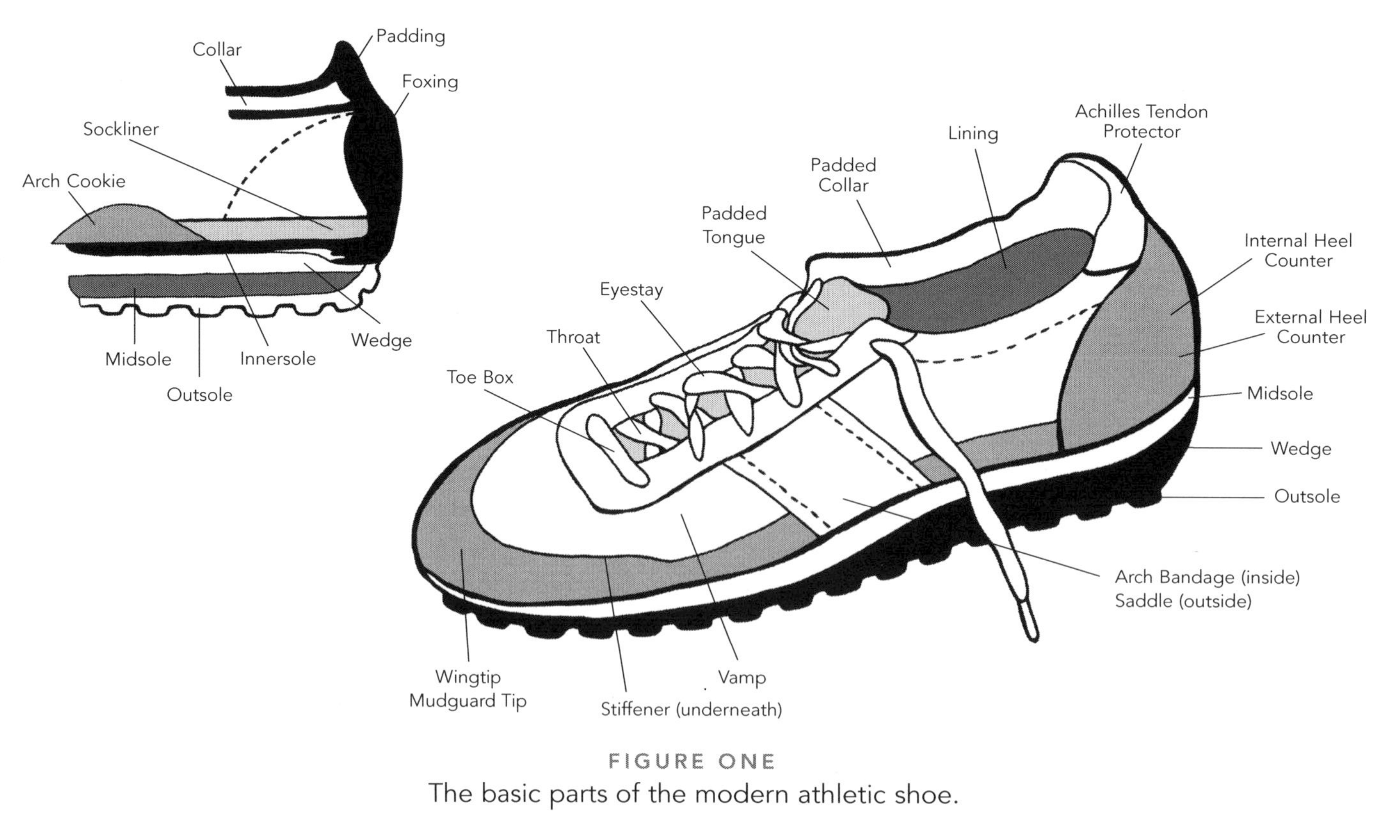

FIGURE ONE
The basic parts of the modern athletic shoe.

The Last

The last is the wood, plastic, or metal forms around which shoes, especially the uppers, are assembled. It determines the shape, size, and dimensions of the shoe, including toe spring (the vertical distance between the ground and the toe point, giving the shoe frontal pitch) and heel pitch (the amount of rise at the back of the last when it is held level). The last also sets the shape of the instep, girth, bottom curvature, and feather edge. Last variations in the girth (widest part of the forefoot) and heel width establish how tightly or loosely a shoe will fit.

When making athletic shoes, manufacturers must determine what activities the shoe will accommodate and by what segment of the population the shoe will be worn. Last makers do surveys to come up with standard measurements for the target population (people actually using the shoe), and the lasts are then made from this information.

There are four major types of last: straight, curved, anatomical, and combination.

The majority of human feet have a slight inward curve, and a last that mimics this curve (**curved last**) improves fit and comfort, especially in athletes with a high or flexible long arch. Sports shoe companies work with approximately a seven-degree curve. The greater the curve, the more the shoe is suited for underpronators.

Straight-lasted shoes provide better support to the lateral side of the foot and are a better choice for athletes with flat feet. About 30 percent of athletes find this type of shoe more appropriate.

Anatomical lasts are technical lasts with built-up bottoms that make the shoe conform better to the sole of the foot. They can be designed to accept devices such as heel cups, raised insteps, and metatarsal bridges.

Combination lasts differ in shape from standard lasts. These lasts are made for a specific use and will reflect the special needs of that sport in their shape. Combination lasts are most commonly found in shoes for track and field throwing events, such as the javelin, as well as in some baseball and softball cleats.

Athletic shoes are made all over the world, on many different types of lasts, in a process that requires a great deal of work done by hand. This means that the sizes and fit can vary greatly not only for shoes from competing companies, but even for exactly the same style of shoe from the same manufacturer. I have received seven cleated football shoes from one manufacturer in the same year that were made in Korea, the United States, and Yugoslavia. Production from this many locations creates last standardization problems for manufacturers and fitting problems for the equipment manager. Try to choose a shoe model that is consistently made in the same factory.

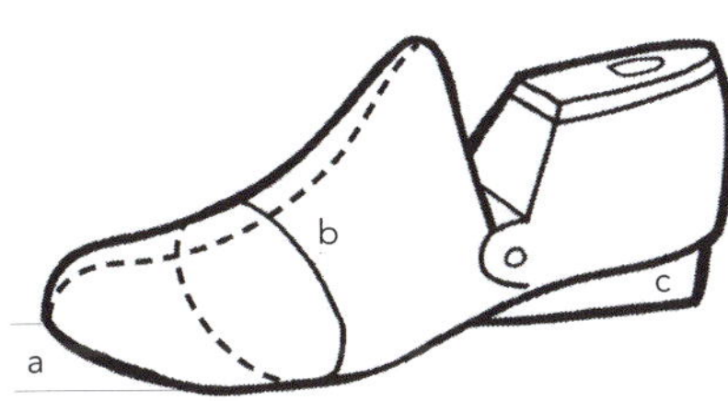

FIGURE TWO

The last: a) toe pitch, b) girth, c) heel height.

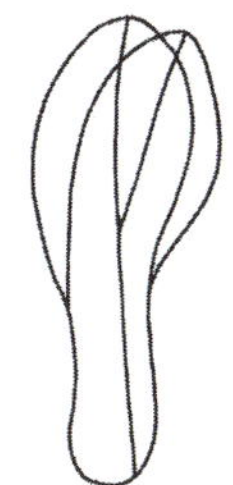

A curved last and straight last.

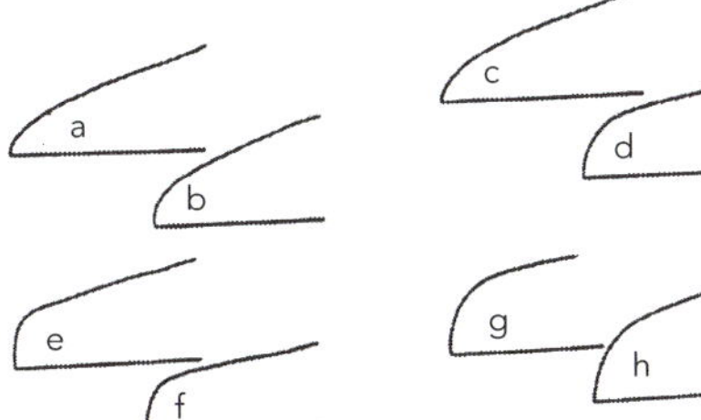

Last Shapes: a) narrow/round, b) oxford, c) oval, d) oval/round, e) natural shape, f) high/wide, g) high, h) high/round

FIGURE THREE

Types of lasts.

SELECTING ATHLETIC SHOES

The following are points to consider when you are selecting athletic shoes. This list is from Melvyn P. Cheskin's book, The Complete Handbook of Athletic Footwear (New York: Fairchild Publications, 1987).

Weight—important but not critical in training; comfort, cushioning, and support should not be sacrificed for lightness in most instances.

Fit—critical; fit depends on the shape and design of the last.

Flex Path—important on all shoes where the foot is required to bend at the metatarsal joints.

Flex Torque—important where lateral movement or plantar surface stability is needed. A shank is used on heeled shoes to support the foot between the heel of the shoe and the forepart of the sole; a wedge sole provides continuous support through the mid-part of the shoe without the need for a shank.

Heel Counter—prevents heel drift and cups the heel for protection and fit. A rigid form is best, possibly one that is elongated on the medial side. Additional outside heel stabilizers may help.

Upper Material—should be suitable for the particular sport. It can be protective and supportive or flexible and breathable.

Upper Lining—should be suited to the requirements of the sport. Most desirable characteristics include breathability, comfort, a padded ankle collar, and a padded tongue; it should be free of seams; can have or be accompanied by inside tape supports, arch supports, heel cups, and canted soles and insocks.

Soling—important for shock absorbency, durability, traction, and support. The main methods of building the soles of sports shoes are cement, built-up vulcanized, direct injection, Goodyear welt, lockstitch, and rivet.

Last Shape (curved, straight, or combination), **toe spring**, and **heel lift**—toe spring provides running ease; heel lift transfers the weight of the body onto the forefoot across the width of the forepart of the shoe.

Ankle Support—highcut designs should be selected when necessary.

Practical Design—design features include U-throat, lace to toe, derby, blucher, and adjustable width; the heel and forepart of the sole should have suitable width for stability; the toe box should fit comfortably and protect against jamming of the toes.

Traction—outsole should be made of the correct material and have the right profile (wear pattern) for the requirements of the sport. For example, court shoes should have pivot points under the ball of the foot and running shoes should have reinforced heels for running on pavement.

Shock Absorbency—in order to find the optimal amount of cushioning one must consider energy loss and transfer body weight, playing surface, and support. Underfoot cushioning materials often take a "compression set" (compaction) after several hours of use, affecting the above criteria.

AEMA CERTIFICATION MANUAL

CHAPTER 5

Equipment Maintenance and Repair

By Brian Allis

EQUIPMENT MAINTENANCE AND REPAIR

As always, today's coaches are trying to tap into everyone's maximum potential, but today's athletes are bigger and stronger than ever. That means machines and equipment used in practice drills need to be maintained more than ever.

Because of the size, speed, and strength of today's athletes, the impact this equipment absorbs is often much greater than it was originally designed for. Therefore, the wear on the equipment needs to be monitored more often. If an athlete unleashed an enormous hit into a piece of equipment, such as a sled, and if the sled collapsed or failed to absorb the blow, an injury might very well occur. So equipment managers, grounds crew, or whoever is responsible for the equipment need to be more aware of all equipment to be maintained, not just helmets and shoulder pads.

IMPORTANT EQUIPMENT ITEMS

As is the case with any professional work, when dealing with the maintenance and repair of athletic equipment, proper tools are required for quality results. A fully stocked athletic equipment facility benefits not only the equipment manager but everyone involved in the program. The following list of maintenance tools and machines should help guide an equipment manager in constructing a highly functional and versatile workplace.

Sewing Machine

According to Dorothy Cutting, who at one time did all of the athletic clothing repair at Cornell University, the best machine to purchase is a top-of-the-line household sewing machine. The only functions the machine needs to perform are zigzag and straight line. A machine with all the bells and whistles is not practical and too confusing to operate. How often are you going to need to put a rose or a tulip on a jersey?

An industrial machine is not ideal for the novice seamstress, which would include most equipment managers. They operate at a high rate of speed and can be dangerous. Industrial machines pull fabric through so fast that it can be very easy to get your fingers caught by the needle.

One important feature to look for when purchasing a sewing machine is to find one that is self lubricating. If you have to clean and oil the machine each time you use it you will soon learn how time consuming it is and how nice it would be to have a machine that doesn't require a lot of maintenance.

You will also want to purchase a machine that can be locally repaired. Check to see if replacement parts like extra bobbins and needles are available locally.

There is no need to go to great expense on a work table—an old desk works great, and what school doesn't have one lying around? The drawers work perfectly to store your sewing supplies and patching material. It should be located in a well-lit space out of any main traffic areas.

Scissors

A good pair of scissors is a must for the sewing machine operator. Dull scissors will NOT cut fabric, they will chew it. Keep good scissors in the desk and don't use them for cutting paper, cardboard, nylon, or anything with epoxy.

Seam Ripper

We all make mistakes and have to undo what we've done but there are numerous other uses for a seam ripper. For example, it works great at taking a nametag off a jersey, whereas a pair of scissors would probably ruin the jersey.

Awl

An awl is a single-needle hand-punch tool that sews with a special heavy duty wax-covered thread. It works well to make small repairs on things like shoulder pads or very heavy items that are too large or too thick to go through your machine. You will need to use your own discretion as to whether to try to fix the item yourself or send it out. You will not want to sew your entire shoulder pad inventory by hand. Awls are very hard on the hands to push through the cloth, but to fix a few stitches before they become a lot of stitches, they are great.

Fabric and Uniform Scraps

If you have an old jersey or pants that are too far gone, instead of tossing them out, cut out the good parts, including zippers, buttons, and snaps. Granted, you don't want to patch a game uniform, but these scraps may help get a little more use out of some practice jerseys and practice pants.

Elastic

Elastic can be used for replacing waist bands in pants or shorts, but more often, it is used for repairs to any equipment that uses elastic strapping, like shoulder pads, catchers' shinguards, and hockey shinguards. As the strap gets worn, torn, or stretched out, just cut another piece of elastic at the appropriate length and replace the old piece.

Rivet Gun/Hole Punch

A rivet gun can be used if the factory rivet on a pair of shoulder pads has broken—you just line the holes up and rivet it back together. Some situations might need a hole for the rivet to go through; you can create one with the hole punch.

Laundry

Perhaps the most valuable equipment available to an equipment manager are washers and dryers. Besides prolonging the life of athletic wear, a proper laundry system can save the equipment manager time, money, and inventory. Refer to the Laundry section of this Manual (Chapter 6) for a comprehensive discussion on laundry needs and practices.

Miscellaneous Equipment and Supplies

Stocking an array of tools is essential for equipment maintenance. The following is a list of basic and specialized tools that should be included in all equipment facilities. Regardless of the apparent usefulness or uselessness of an item, be assured that a need will arise for it at some point.

- regular and Phillips screwdrivers (various sizes)
- claw hammer
- regular and needle-nose pliers
- channel locks
- drill (cordless recommended) and drill bits (various sizes)
- cloth measuring tape
- 8' to 25' metal measuring tape
- 100' to 300' measuring tape
- heavy-duty metal snips
- hack saw
- utility knife
- iron
- packing tape
- rubber cement
- Shoe Goo
- glue gun
- Armor All
- Scotch Guard fabric protector or equivalent
- 32-gallon trash containers
- spray bottles
- air pumps
- WD 40
- 3-in-1 oil
- duct tape
- shoe stretchers
- belt slider
- Belgian rubber
- disinfectant spray
- snowproof reconditioner
- shoe cleats and tighteners

MAINTAINING EQUIPMENT

The following are some of the major maintenance points to consider for some of the equipment we use every day.

Football

Football Sleds

[Courtesy of Neil Gilman, Vice President of Gilman, Inc., one of the leading manufacturers of football sleds.]

1. Check the hardware. Replace any rusty bolts and be sure to tighten them. Loose bolts can cause excessive vibration of the chassis and springs.
2. Check the pads. If the cover is torn beyond repair, replace it. Sometimes, if it is the seam that has come out or ripped, it can be fixed with a hand stitcher with strong nylon thread. If, however, it is torn on the surface where the athlete makes contact, it should be replaced. If the foam padding is rotted or deteriorated due to sun exposure or moisture, it should be replaced.
3. Check the elastic straps. The elastic keeps the pads from sliding around. Keep the straps tight and replace

them if there are any signs of wear, particularly if they've lost their elasticity.
4. Check for any areas of rust. Grind off any surface rust and repaint.
5. Storage—all equipment should be stored out of the elements when not in use.

Football Dummies

1. Dummies should have a protective boot cover at the bottom, since this is the area that takes the most abuse. If the cover is torn or the handles have ripped off, replace the whole cover.
2. Check the foam. If it has deteriorated to the point where it does not stand up or bottoms out when hit, it should be replaced. Once the foam gets water-logged, it becomes twice as heavy and so hard that it could cause injury; therefore, the dummy should be dried out before being used again.

Football Shields

1. If you have air shields, check the innertube. If it is punctured, replace it with a new tube. Keep the tube inflated.
2. Check the handles, which should be made of a nylon web with plastic tube overlay. This allows the player to grip the handle better and rotate the hand if the shield is shifted, thus preventing a hand injury.

Running Ropes

1. Check the frame supporting the running rope. A frame with criss-crossing metal bars underneath the rope can lead to turned and twisted ankles. Replace the frame with one that has no underlying metal bars.
2. Check to see whether the rope has elastic mounts; the rope should bounce up if it is stepped on or fallen on. Without elastic, the athlete could receive a rope burn.

End-Zone Pylons

Check the bottom of the pylon. If it has a pointed coil spring or pitch-fork-type anchor, it should be replaced with a weighted pylon that doesn't have anything protruding from the bottom. Coil springs can cause injury when a ball carrier falls on them.

Chain Set

Check to make sure that the bottom of the stick has no points. If the end is pointed, cut it off and cap off the bottom with a rubber crutch tip.

Goal Post

Make sure the goal post is padded. If a ball carrier or receiver runs into an unpadded post, injury can result. Padding is cheap insurance and also adds to school spirit and to the beauty of the field.

Jugs™ Football Passing Machine

The Jugs™ Passing Machine is essential to most football programs. As with other pieces of equipment, maintenance is the key to ensuring that the machine performs reliably.

The following are points to check for the safe use of this machine:

1. Before using the machine, check to see whether the wheels are set and locked in place. Check the main bolts on the wheels for tightness.
2. Make sure key areas of the machine are well lubricated, including the cables, wheels, and sliding plunger.
3. Always keep the machine clean, and store it in a dry area.

Jugs also recommends checking the following areas [taken from the company's brochure and Web site, www.thejugscompany.com].

1. Most of the time people call thinking they need new tires, they don't. Tires should be replaced when a groove has worked its way into the tire to the black tire cord. Cracking and dry rot on the sides of the wheel are normal and nothing to be concerned with. With the machine off, simply clean the center of the tire with 40-grit sandpaper, which will also help the tire grip better. Maintain tire pressure at 17 p.s.i. By doing these steps you could extend the life of the existing tire for many years to come.
2. It is a myth that the machine needs to be sent back for maintenance every few years. In truth, the machines rarely have to come back to the shop for service. It can all be done by you. As long as the air pressure in the tire is checked, and the machine is kept away from water, routine maintenance is all that is needed.
3. If the machine's motor has become wet, it could cause damage to the circuit board, and may need to be replaced. If it has, you should call your service department.

Football Helmets

Proper fitting and inspection of helmets is discussed elsewhere (see Chapter 4, "Fitting Equipment and Clothing"), but here we just want to talk about basic maintenance that should be practiced on a regular basis. Ideally, each week of the season, the helmet should be inspected. This goes for all hockey, lacrosse, and all types of goalie helmets, but we will concentrate on football helmets for this discussion.

Football helmets are designed to protect athletes' heads. The helmet may be the most important piece of equipment available to the football player. It has evolved into a very sophisticated protection device that depends largely on proper fit and maintenance to ensure its efficiency. The helmet is capable of peak performance when it leaves the manufacturer; equipment personnel assume the responsibility of maintenance once the helmet is received.

Before issuing the helmet, make sure it has a warning label. As established by NOCSAE guidelines, all football helmets must have warning labels affixed to the back outside shell. The warning label is an important addition to the helmet because it directly addresses safety and, as a result, liability (see Figure One, below right).

There are three separate times when a warning sticker may be affixed to the helmet. The original sticker is put on by the manufacturer before the helmet is purchased. The second instance occurs when a certified reconditioner tests the helmet and affixes the sticker to the helmet. The third, and perhaps most important, instance when the warning sticker is affixed occurs at the equipment facility. The equipment personnel are responsible for having a legible warning sticker affixed to the helmet at all times.

The wording on the sticker may become unreadable. This can occur as a result of normal wear, particularly when the helmet repeatedly hits the ground. If at any time the warning label becomes unreadable, it must be replaced. There are two options presently available to equipment personnel regarding labels—white labels with black lettering or transparent labels with colored lettering. These labels are available from the helmet manufacturer or a certified reconditioner.

HELMET INSPECTION

The following areas should be checked regularly:

- air bladder
- inside padding
- face mask
- buckles & snaps
- chin strap
- shell

Each week, you should give the air-filled bladders a pump or two of air just to make sure air is going in and staying there. If the player often complains of lack of air, check for any slow leaks by taking the bladder out, pumping it as full as possible, and submerging it in water. If it is leaking, it should be replaced with a new bladder. At the end of each season, the bladder should be thoroughly checked again for leaks.

Then, check the inner padding. Helmets without air pads will have foam padding in place of the air bladders. The foam needs to be checked for wear or cracks. Cracked padding can cut the player's head and face and should be replaced. Also, check the jaw pads for cracks and bad snaps. The front and back sizing pads should also be checked and replaced if cracked. If the helmet has a nose bumper, check it for cracks and wear and replace it if the Velcro doesn't hold or it is cracked and worn.

The facemask needs to be checked thoroughly for bare metal and if it is bent or sprung wider than normal. Also, check it for broken or damaged hangers. If the mask is sprung, dented, or has metal showing, replace it. While you are changing damaged helmet hangers, replace any rusted or damaged T-nuts and screws, too.

Next, check the chinstrap for wear. If the strap is worn in the cup area or worn where the buckles adjust the fit, it should be discarded and replaced. Check all the hardware for rusted or damaged buckles and T-nuts and replace any faulty pieces.

Last but definitely not least is inspection of the shell. As you take the mask or padding off, you should at the same time be checking the shell. The most common place for cracks to start is under the nose bumper and anywhere there is a screw hole, which weakens the helmet in that area. So look especially closely in those areas.

HELMET CLEANING

All football helmets have the same basic maintenance procedures. Steel wool (#000 or #0000) along with one of the manufacturer's recommended cleaning solutions works best for removing old wax and dirt. A wax coat can then be applied for extra shine. Armor All is recommended to keep liners soft and supple. Glycerin is a great air-needle lubricant.

WARNING...

Do not strike an opponent with any part of this helmet or faceguard. This is a violation of football rules and may cause you and your opponent to suffer serious injury, including severe brain or neck injury, paralysis, or death.

Severe brain or neck injury may also occur accidentally while playing football.

No Helmet Can Prevent All Such Injuries. You Use This Helmet At Your Own Risk.

FIGURE ONE
The NOCSAE Football Helmet Warning Sticker.

It is important to know your helmet manufacturers' warranties and abide by their guidelines. They all have slightly different warranties, and they all stand behind their products.

Paint warnings. Substances applied to the helmet shell that are not compatible with the shell material can cause deterioration and/or breakage, thereby exposing the wearer to unnecessary risk and danger. Using non-compatible paints, polishes, and/or cleaners will make the helmet shell unsafe for further use and will void warranties. Only manufacturer-approved primers, paints, thinners, polishes, and cleaners should be used. For proper helmet painting, contact an approved NERA reconditioner.

Helmet maintenance. The helmet shell and all interior parts can be rinsed in warm water to remove normal grime. Taking the fully assembled helmet into the shower and flushing out the inside is an effective way to keep the head gear clean.

If further cleaning is required, a mild detergent should be used. Solvents or strong cleaning agents should not be applied to the helmet shell, liner, or interior parts. Any worn part is easily replaced and is available from your local dealer.

If the helmet shell still requires additional cleaning to remove old decals, etc., use a kit made especially for that purpose. Most dealers carry these types of products. The use of other chemical products may void your warranty and could adversely affect the helmet's protective capabilities.

Helmet systems that use air pads must be checked periodically to see that proper air pressure is maintained for the air liner system. Many factors could affect the helmet fit, including air temperature, altitude changes, haircuts, loss of head fat, horseplay, and damage to the air valve resulting in puncture or leakage. It is very important that proper sizer selection and liner inflation be achieved and maintained for player protection and comfort.

Worn-out parts should be replaced as soon as possible. To prevent voiding the manufacturer's warranty, use only manufacturer-approved parts for replacement. See the manual provided with each helmet for specific replacement parts and maintenance guidelines.

FACEMASK

Over the course of the season, the facemask can become worn or bent. Routine maintenance checks are recommended to analyze the wear of each player's facemask. These routine checks should coincide with your weekly helmet cleaning routines. It is better to perform maintenance in the equipment room rather than on the sidelines. As you clean the helmet, check the facemask for the following:

1. Tightness of mounts. A loose mount can cause the facemask to shift or to fall off during contact. Both may affect the athlete's vision or ability to compete. A mount that has been tightened too much could actually push the screw through the opening on the mount. This may cause the mount to pop open under contact.
2. Mount wear. Check mounts for wear or for cracking. The mount may crack or break occasionally, especially on the side. Change any mounts that appear worn or cracked.
3. Bar alignment. A quick observation will determine whether the facemask is sitting properly on the helmet. Also check to see whether the facemask has become bent or spread open because of contact. Realign the facemask if it is out of position, but any facemask that has become bent or spread open should be replaced.
4. Coating wear. Check to see whether the coating of the facemask has worn off. Steel showing through the coating could gouge the helmet shell. If the coating has worn off the facemask, the entire facemask should be replaced. Facemasks with exposed metal can harm the helmet shell of opposing players.

WARNING: Some equipment managers have begun having their facemasks re-dipped. Re-dipping any facemask voids all warrantees that accompany newly purchased facemasks. The manufacturers recommend that as a facemask loses its protective coating, it should be replaced.

EYE SHIELDS

The latest addition to protective devices for the helmet/facemask system is the eye shield. The number of professional athletes now using the eye shield is increasing, and the eye shield is being used sporadically in intercollegiate play. There are some advantages to adding eye shields as opposed to using the conventional open-air facemasks. The shield protects the face and eye area from being poked or scratched. As with all equipment, the use of the eye shield should be in compliance with NCAA rules. This could occur when an opponent's fingers invade the facemask or when pieces of debris get kicked through it.

The requirements for maintaining the shield are minimal. Cleaning is the only necessary routine; any scratches or cracks that may occur to the eye shield are un-repairable, and the shield should be replaced. To clean, rinse with clear water and wipe with a soft cloth. Do not polish or buff, as this could damage the anti-fog application. Keep eye shields away from all chemicals, abrasive products, and strong detergents. Avoid extended exposure to heat and sun. For your protection, never alter the eye shield in any way.

Shoulder Pads

Like helmets, shoulder pads should be checked on a weekly basis and then again more thoroughly at the end of each season. (See Chapter 4, "Fitting Equipment and Clothing," for more on this.) Areas to be sure to check each week are:

1. loose and worn elastic
2. damaged snaps and buckles
3. laces
4. stitching
5. neck padding
6. rivets

Each week, you should check the elastic to be sure it has elasticity and check the snaps or buckles for rust or damage, and replace any faulty parts. Check the laces for wear and broken strings. You can even string two strings at the same time to lessen the chance of the pad breaking during a game. Check the stitching to be sure it's not coming unraveled or broken. If it is, you should be able to fix it with an awl. Or you can send it out to be fixed at your local reconditioner.

Then, check the padding around the neck area for cracks. Worn, rough, or cracked neck padding can irritate or cut the player's skin, so it needs to be repaired or replaced.

The last thing to be sure to check is the rivets and fasteners. Make sure they are not damaged or loose. Be sure to check up underneath the deltoid cup. Sometimes, the rivet there is broken or worn and it is hard to tell without really checking it out thoroughly. If any rivets are loose or broken, you should be able to fix it yourself with your own rivet gun set and save on an expensive reconditioning bill.

Other Pads

Any pads like tailpads and girdle, knee, and thigh pads that have a plastic covering should only be washed with a sponge and a bucket of soapy disinfectant-type soap. You don't want to submerse the pad, because if water gets inside the plastic coating, the inner padding could rot and wear out quicker. After washing with soapy water, dry the pads with a towel and stack them together in pairs. The girdle sets can be put in plastic bags and tied so they are ready to be reissued. If the plastic covers are torn, cut, or just cracked due to wear and tear, the pads should be discarded.

Baseball/Softball

Batting Helmets

At the end of the season, batting helmets should be cleaned and, if needed, reconditioned. First, check the helmet for cracks. If it is cracked in any way, the helmet should be discarded. Then, check the inner padding for missing, worn, or loose padding. If padding is worn or missing, replace it with a new pad or the same pad from a discarded helmet if it's still in good shape. Then, glue the replacement or loose piece back to the helmet, and wipe away any excess glue.

Pine tar accumulation is a problem with baseball helmets. There are several different vendors that sell different types of cleaning agents to help take the pine tar off. Tar Off and Wureack Industrial Finish Helmet Cleaner are two that work very well. After you've removed the pine tar, you can buff and shine the helmet by hand or use a buffing wheel just as you would with your football helmets. Never use the buffing wheel to remove the pine tar or any helmet decal or glue; it will gum up the wheel and you will soon be in need of a new one.

Catchers' Protective Equipment

CATCHERS' MASKS

Check the mask carefully for any breaks or dents in the metal. Never allow a player to play with a dented or broken mask. If broken, the mask should be stripped of any reusable parts and discarded. Then, check the padding for tears and cracks, and make sure the stitching is not coming apart. Depending on the location of the cracks or tears, the pad may be repaired by using some moleskin from the athletic training room. Just cut off a piece of moleskin to cover the appropriate area and attach it firmly. Cracked chin pads will cut and irritate a player's chin and face, so if it can't be repaired, replace the pad with a new one. Finally, check the strapping and the buckles. Be sure the strapping is elastic enough for sizing adjustments to be made. Replace any rusted, bent, or damaged buckles or fasteners.

SHINGUARDS

Check the shell or the hard surface of the shinguards for cracks and loose or unraveling thread. If the shell is cracked, the shinguard should be discarded. If the stitching is fraying apart, you can use an awl to rethread it. Next, check the padding, buckles, and straps. The padding may be cracked or worn out. Use your own judgement as to whether or not to replace the padding, just discard the shinguard, or send it to your local reconditioner. Be sure to replace any stretched out or worn elastic straps and any rusted, bent, or damaged buckles.

CHEST PROTECTORS

Chest protectors can be cleaned with a variety of foam or spray cleaners. If in doubt, use a sponge and warm soapy water. Try not to get it too wet, and make sure it drip dries thoroughly before storing. Storing chest protectors wet could cause mildew to set in. Check for any missing or loose thread, and repair any necessary areas using an awl. Check the elastic strapping and buckles for stretched-out elastic and any bent, rusted, or damaged buckles, and replace them.

Gloves

OILING GLOVES

Prior to the 1950s, when ball gloves were manufactured, oil wasn't soaked into the leather, so back then, they needed lots of oil to "break the glove in." Nowadays, the leather is treated with oil so they are much softer and should not need as much oil to get them game ready.

Bob Clevan Hagen, a Rawlings representative, makes the following points for the proper care and maintenance of your gloves. (He has a video out, which can be rented through the AEMA national office.)

1. When buying a glove, look for one in which the leather is stiffer. This means it is better-quality leather. Although it will take more to break in, it should last longer.
2. Hagen suggests the best way to break in the gloves is to pour some hot water on the pocket, and then hit the pocket with the back of a wooden brush, or even pound your fist into it. Do not dunk the glove or over-water it, because this will ultimately dry it out and shorten the life of the glove.
3. After the glove has dried, apply a dab of oil and rub it in good. Do not over-oil it—this will also cause it to dry out. Hagen suggests using saddle soap or shaving cream to soften and clean the glove.
4. Once the glove has been broken in, you should only oil it at the end of each season. Oiling too often will cause it to dry out and shorten the life of the glove.
5. When working with a catcher's glove, be careful not to get it too wet. Catcher's gloves have a white polypropylene pad inside, which, if it gets wet, could ruin the glove. If you must treat it with water, use a spray bottle.

STRINGING BALL GLOVES

If you want to try your hand at restringing a glove, start with an old glove to practice on a couple of times to see what you're getting into. Nowadays, some gloves are easier to string and some shoe and leather repair stores can restring a glove for you, too. Rick Raven, Equipment Manager at the University of Illinois, has a video at the AEMA national office you can rent that will give you some insights on stringing a glove. Here are some tips from Raven's workshop:

1. Most gloves have four separate laces: a criss-cross stitch across the top of the fingers, one around the webbing, one on the palm, and another around the bottom of the glove. The first thing to go in most gloves is the lace in the finger area, usually at the index finger. The other most common place the lace breaks is in the webbing.
2. Pay close attention as you are pulling out the old broken lace to see how it was laced. There are several tools on the market for help in stringing the glove. Rawlings makes a needle similar to a knitting needle that has a hole at the end for threading the lace through. Then you can use the needle to push the lace through the holes and, finally, pliers work great at pulling it through. You can improvise with a piece of wire and a long thin-ended screwdriver or similar tool.
3. When lacing the palm, try to tighten the lace as much as possible. Leave a little slack in the fingertips, however. You can always adjust it later. The leather will stretch as it gets broken in.
4. Your laces should all be tied off on the back side of the glove to prevent the ball from popping out and also prevent hand injuries.
5. If the inner lining of your glove is torn or rotted, you can try a piece of moleskin, send it back to the manufacturer, or have a leather repair shop fix it. I would not suggest replacing it yourself, because it will never be the same. It may even be time to get a new glove.
6. Catchers' gloves are much harder to string. Raven suggests sending them back to the manufacturer or have a leather store save you the aggravation.

Caps

There are many ways to clean ball caps, but no single one that everyone can agree on. Some people take them into the shower with them to wash off or use a plastic cap holder and run them through a clothes washer or dishwasher. I question these methods, because once the brim of the hat gets wet it will never hold its shape properly again. Some people may dry clean them or send them to a reconditioner, but the costs for doing either of these would be high. Some people use cleaning agents and scrub the hat, but I'd advise against this as well. As the athlete perspires, the bleach or other cleaning agent will drip into his or her scalp and eyes. My best advice is to keep the caps as clean as possible for as long as possible and simply replace them when they get worn or dirty.

Bases

When maintaining bases, you first need to check the top part of the base itself for wear. Because of the players' metal spikes, they tend to take a beating. If they get to where they are cracked or cut and have jagged edges, they should be replaced. Players sliding in head first or feet first can get sliced up on sharp edges or divots.

Next, the bottom part of the base—the in-ground base—needs to be checked. It should have dimples that lock the top part in. If these dimples are worn, the base could pop off or rattle around, slip, and cause an injury. If this is happening, the bottom part needs to be replaced.

Hitting/Pitching Machines

Hitting/pitching machines are pretty similar to a Jugs™ Football Machine. Refer back to the maintenance procedures for the Jugs™ machine.

Track & Field Equipment

Shot

The shot is a pretty basic piece of equipment. The main damage that can happen is that, on the indoor shot, the plug can fall off, causing some of the weight to fall out. If this happens, you can fill the shot with lead to get it back to the required weight and pop the plug back in. If you've lost the plug, you can try sticking a glue gun inside the hole and fill it with glue as you pull the gun out. This would not be legal for competition but okay to practice with.

Discus

If the plate pops off the discus rim, you can unscrew it apart, pop the plate back on, and screw it back together. If it breaks or cracks, it's not worth it economically to repair, so you should just replace it.

Pole Vault Poles

The first thing to remember with pole vault poles is to never sign for a newly delivered pole until you've thoroughly inspected it. Because of the awkward size and length of poles, they often get damaged in delivery, and once you've signed for the package, it's next to impossible to get the pole replaced.

After using the pole, if the pole cracks within six inches of the top or bottom you can cut it off and recap it. Anything more than that could make the pole too short. Very small scratches are okay, but a pole that has a scratch eight inches or longer or one that is very deep, should be replaced.

While there is no proof that the poles go bad if stored in very hot or very cold locations, its best to store them in a dry, moderate-temperature area.

Pits

It's best to have a thicker vinyl cover for your pits. It will last longer if it's made of thicker material. If the pit is bottoming out when an athlete lands, you can add foam padding to extend the life of the pit a while longer. Otherwise, you need to replace it with a new pit. The foam is susceptible to damage from UV light, and will crumble if exposed too long. When this happens, it's time for new foam.

Regularly check the clips that clip the pit cover to the bottom. Make sure they are not damaged and that they are clipped properly.

Hurdles

The hurdles take a beating from runners catching their feet on them, tripping, and knocking them over. You can take boards and parts off broken hurdles or order extra boards so you can just replace the broken boards.

Hurdles have movable weights in the bottom to hold them upright. Check them regularly to make sure they are not damaged or if they need to be oiled. They should slide back and forth freely.

Starting Blocks

Starting blocks need to be checked often for broken peddles. If the peddle is broken, you must replace the whole peddle. Some manufacturers will recondition blocks for you.

Hammer

Things that need to be checked and maintained with the hammer are:

1. Broken wires. As the wire stretches, you might need to shorten it to the legal limit. According to the NCAA Track and Field/Cross Country Rule Book, the men's hammer, complete with wire from the inside grip, should be a minimum of 117.5 cm (3.85 ft) to a maximum of 121.5 cm (3.99 ft). For women, the minimum distance is 116 cm (3.81 ft). The diameter of the wire needs to be not less than 3 mm (0.118 in) for both men and women. If it becomes worn down less than that or if it becomes too short, the wire should be replaced.
2. Banged up handle. If the handle gets bent so it's jagged or the athlete cannot grip it, then it should be replaced.
3. Broken swivel. Check the swivel. If it becomes damaged or broken, replace it.
4. Weight of the hammer. For men, the minimum weight is 7.260 kg (16 lbs) and for the women it is 4 kg (8 lbs, 13 oz). If the weight is less than this, you must add weight to the hammer, or you can get a heavier handle. If a filling is used, it must be inserted

in such a manner that it is immovable. The center of gravity shall be not more than 6 mm (0.236 in) from the center of the sphere.

Javelin

Parts of the javelin that should be checked periodically are:

1. Handles. The handles can unravel from use or carelessness. You can re-grip them or send them back to the manufacturer for another grip.
2. Broken tips. Tips take a lot of abuse from hitting rocks, which cause damage and weight loss. You can replace the tip but if the javelin is more than a year old you should just replace the entire javelin. Chances are that after a year it's already slightly bent and you'd be better off replacing it.
3. Bent shaft. Javelins can get bent from use or just plain carelessness. They should land point first, but if they are thrown improperly, they can land backwards, which can damage the shaft. Or, they can be improperly transported or stored, causing damage. The javelin can become "out of balance," in which case it needs to be replaced.

Tacky Gloves

There are numerous different manufacturers of tacky gloves and many different styles. With football, there are gloves for each position. You want your receivers, running backs, and defensive backs using a glove with less padding and more grip. Your linebackers may want more padding in the palms and finger area. And, of course, the linemen want plenty of extra padding on the palms and the back of the hand.

Football isn't the only sport using tacky gloves, though. In 1998, tacky glove sales exceeded $60 million. They are also quite popular in baseball, softball, golf, racquet sports, and weight lifting.

Because some companies had an unfair advantage over others by the amount of tack they applied to gloves, the NCAA passed legislation in 1994 requiring all football gloves, unless made of "unadulterated cloth," to conform to a certain standard set by the Sporting Goods Manufacturing Association (now called SGMA International). The National Federation of High Schools (NFHS) followed suit, adopting a rule that said that gloves used in high school play must have a stamp or label attesting that they meet the NCAA standards.

In the college game, if a player is found to be wearing gloves that violate the rule, the punishment is the offending team is charged one of their timeouts. If they are out of timeouts, it's a five-yard penalty. The penalty in high school for being caught with unapproved gloves is a 15-yard unsportsmanlike conduct penalty.

For gloves to conform to the standard, they must pass the following four tests:

1. peel adhesion test
2. friction test
3. rolling adhesion test
4. material transfer test

The most important of these is the material transfer test. This test is to make sure the tack or adhesion will not be transferred to the ball. Therefore, it is not a good idea to add any oil or tackiness to your tack gloves, even after they have been worn.

The best thing to do if they get wet or muddy is to rinse the mud off and hang them to drip dry, like on a clothesline. Washing or drying them in machines will surely ruin them. Encourage your players to hang them in their lockers, away from other equipment, so they will dry properly.

Travel/Duffel Bags

There are many different types and styles of bags. Almost every sport has a bag specially designed for it. When it comes to cleaning and repairing these bags, the procedures depend on the material the bag is made of. Most bags are made of canvas, leather, plastic, nylon, or vinyl.

Canvas bags are used more for teams who have bulkier equipment, like football, hockey, and lacrosse. Always check with the manufacturer for cleaning recommendations, but most canvas bags can be washed in washing machines if you have a gentle cycle. Just make sure to use cold water, take them out before the extract cycle, and never put any bags in the dryers. After taking them out of the washer, use a clothes line to hang the bags inside-out first, and when they are dry on the inside, hang them right-side-out so they can finish drying. You might want to spray a little disinfectant on the inside before storing them. Or you can send them to a reconditioner to be cleaned, or to a dry cleaner, but you won't like the cost of these options.

Leather bags are not very practical for equipment use. You should never wash leather except with a damp cloth. Plastic, nylon, and vinyl bags could be washed in a machine with a gentle cycle, and not extracted, but you may want to do one or two first to see how they hold up. Some of these bags have a cardboard bottom covered in plastic, nylon, or vinyl. Be sure to take this cardboard piece out if you do wash them. It will never serve its purpose again if you don't. The safer way to clean these bags would be with a bucket of soapy warm water and a sponge, and just dry as you go. It'll be time consuming but your bags won't fall apart.

If the bags become ripped, you'll find that the only ones that can be patched are the canvas bags. If you can't sew it on a machine, you can always use an awl.

TURF MAINTENANCE AND REPAIR

As with every other aspect of sports, the playing surface has also evolved into a specialized entity. Each facility has characteristics that may affect the way a certain team performs on the field. Currently, there are natural-surface fields, artificial-fiber surfaces, and even Super-Omni, sand-based fields. There are also fields with crowns that slant or slope to varying degrees. As a result of this specialization it is important that an equipment manager receive some background in the care, design, and maintenance of the playing surface.

The following is a brief overview of the maintenance techniques designed by Monsanto Molendyke Inc. for their Astro Turf playing surface. This is an extremely condensed version of the Monsanto maintenance manual. To receive a copy of the maintenance manual for Astro Turf, write to Monsanto at Recreational Surfaces Dept. E3SG, 800 N. Lindbergh Blvd., St. Louis, Missouri 63166.

To get the most efficient and long-term use from an AstroTurf surface, follow these five rules:

1. Protect the surface from unnecessary mechanical damage.
2. Keep it clean.
3. Do not abuse it with vehicle traffic, heavy static leads, rally fireworks, etc.
4. Make all minor repairs promptly.
5. Call the manufacturer for help if more complicated repair or renovation work is needed.

Cleaning Artificial Turf

Be sure that litter and loose dirt is picked up promptly before it accumulates and packs. Light trash and airborne dust can be cleaned off with gasoline or electrically powered vacuum sweepers. Using a fire hose to wash the surface gives excellent results; the water stream flushes away loose dust and blasts out embedded soil. Some fire protection systems use raw rather than treated water. Raw or polluted water is not recommended for field washing or cooling. The removal of loose rubbish and surface dust should be done as needed, usually about once a week on most fields.

Washing

When heavily soiled, use an industrial-type carpet scrubber and a five percent solution of low-sudsing detergent in hot water. (Household detergents are recommended. Five percent equals about six ounces of detergent to one gallon of water.)

For light soiling, sponge mop with the same kind of detergent solution.

Following scrubbing or mopping, hose down and scrub or sponge again with a two percent solution of ammonium hydroxide in hot water.

Wet Cleaning

One of the easiest ways to move water off small areas is with rubber squeegees. These are usually available at mill supply or janitor supply houses. Some stadium owners have built large squeegee blades for use on a Jeep or on small lawn tractors. If a powered squeegee is to be used, extreme caution should be taken to avoid gouging the turf system and damaging it. DO NOT USE WOOD, METAL, OR OTHER RIGID SQUEEGEE BLADES.

To overcome the risk of damaging a field from excessive squeegee pressure, Monsanto has designed and offers for sale the Water Brush. This device is made to fit a standard three-point hitch on any farm tractor with a power take-off. It provides an effective way to move water from the center of a field to the edges without throwing up excessive spray, and can also be used to help clean a field. The equipment uses a specially built rotating brush to pick up the water and move it to either side of the machine as controlled by the operator. Operation of the brush is described in detail in the manual available to purchasers of the water brush.

If finances allow, you might also consider a machine like the Astro Zamboni Water Removal Machine. This machine was designed to meet the needs of large commercial stadiums for rapid water removal. It is designed to remove standing water from a baseball field in less than one hour. It consists of a high-capacity wet vacuum system on a self-propelled vehicle. The vacuum pickup nozzle is approximately six feet wide. Holding tanks and discharge pumps are capable of throwing the collected water approximately 40 feet to either side of the machine as controlled by the operator.

Removing Stains

Almost all stains can be removed from artificial turf with one of the following methods:

1. A warm, mild solution of granular household detergent in water (Tide/All, or any neutral, low-sudsing detergent recommended for fine fabrics). Use approximately one teaspoon to one pint of water.
2. Mineral spirits or a grease spot remover of the type sold by most variety stores and supermarkets can also be used.
3. Or, try a commercial dry cleaning fluid such as perchlorethylene (available from dry cleaning supply houses or most dry cleaners).
4. Chewing gum is a common turf stain. It can be removed by using dry cleaning fluid or by freezing. Aerosol packs of refrigerant are available from carpet cleaning suppliers for this purpose, or dry ice can be used.

Field Marking and Decoration

Permanent paints. New AstroTurf fields are normally painted with Sherwin Williams' water-based type A-100 white acrylic latex paint. This product offers a good balance between cost, availability, and durability. The same paint base is also available in other colors if needed for field designs or multi-game striping.

Temporary paints. In cooperation with Sherwin Williams, Monsanto offers "one-game" removable paints (B-42WW5) for AstroTurf surfaces in red, blue, yellow, white, and black. The availability of these primary colors makes it possible to blend almost any color needed for temporary emblems and designs.

Painting wet fields. Sometimes it is necessary to touch up the markings on a field in wet weather. If the surface is wet, Bull's Eye brand lacquers have been useful for retouching, but they wear off quickly under heavy traffic.

Minor Repairs to Artificial Turf Surfaces

Equipment personnel and groundskeepers can easily make minor repairs to artificial turf surfaces. First, make sure the surfaces are clean and dry. Lift the loose edge of the turf and remove any dirt, old adhesive, or other foreign matter from the areas to be re-bonded. Use a putty knife or brush to scrape away any old, degraded adhesive on the seam tape. Then wipe out the opening with a rag moistened with methyl ethyl ketone (MEK), toluene, or, if neither is available, mineral spirits. Note—All these solvents are highly flammable. Do not use near open flames, cigarettes, or other ignition sources. (MEK is also effective in removing traces of moisture if the fabric is slightly damp.)

Open the cartridge of adhesive as shown on its wrapper, taking care not to cut too large an opening in the tip of the delivery tube. Puncture the inner seal and insert the cartridge into a caulking gun. Lay down beads of adhesive (not more than 3/16" wide) along the seam tape, parallel to the red line. Leave approximately 1/2" space between each bead of adhesive. The last bead should be about 3/8" from the edge of the turf.

Press the fabric into the beads of adhesive. Apply firm hand pressure to the turf, pressing it to be sure that both the turf and seam tape are in close, wet contact with the adhesive. The beads of adhesive will be spread by the pressure and should be evenly distributed between the turf and tape. The adhesive should not flow out beyond the edge of the turf or soak through the fabric. If in doubt about the contact, lift the edge of the turf and look for "legs" (strings of adhesive) between the two surfaces. If there are no strings, contact is probably insufficient and either more pressure or more adhesive is needed. Note—If excessive adhesive soaks through the fabric or exudes at the seam line, it should be cleaned away promptly with a rag moistened with toluene or MEK. Use cement blocks or similar weights to hold the surfaces firmly together until the adhesive has set—at least four hours.

Keep traffic off the mended area until the adhesive has cured. The adhesive will stay flexible even when fully cured. However, it will require at least 12 hours to cure in warm weather and longer in cold or wet weather. Note—If emergency repairs are needed, the cure time can be shortened through the use of the "contact cement" techniques described on the label of the adhesive cartridge. The disadvantage of the contact method is that it requires very firm pressure for good contact and bond strength.

AEMA CERTIFICATION MANUAL

CHAPTER 6

Laundry

By Mark Litsky

LAUNDRY

Each year, millions of dollars are spent in the production and consumption of clothing designed for sport. From athletics to physical education, health clubs to personal use, we are surrounded by a multitude of suppliers saturating the market with active wear.

This section of the manual focuses on in-house laundry operations that service amateur and professional athletics, physical education departments, and fitness clubs (see Appendix F on page 139 for a comparison of in-house versus contracted laundry services). As you can imagine, these areas can cover a wide range of performance and function.

This chapter provides an overview of laundry operations, equipment, stain removal, laundry room safety, and fabric types. Any reference in this section to the "athlete" can be translated to mean any group or individual to whom laundry services are directed. For example, to physical education equipment managers, the athlete may refer to those involved in physical education classes, intramurals, or club sports. Likewise, to a fitness club owner, the athlete may be a club member or guest.

LAUNDRY OPERATION BASICS

From start to finish, there are many factors that can aid in the smooth running of a laundry room. If these steps are performed haphazardly, much time and money is wasted needlessly. Establishing sound procedures for each step of the operation is important. The flowchart on page 97 illustrates the steps involved in typical athletic laundry operations.

Careful scrutiny and attention should be given to all elements of laundry efficiency. Whether establishing, upgrading, or maintaining the washroom, these basic factors will dictate the success or failure of your laundry operations.

Soiled Laundry

Laundry procedures start with collecting soiled laundry. As straightforward as this may sound, there are many factors to consider. Taking extra care during this initial step will save valuable time later. The nature of the item being gathered, as well as your issuing procedures, will usually dictate collection procedures.

Collection

There are basically two ways to collect soiled laundry. One is to make the athletes responsible for turning in their own laundry, and the other is to have helpers collect it as soon as possible. It is usually more practical to place the burden of laundry collection on the athletes. After all, they will want clean laundry the next day, so they are sure to turn the soiled laundry in to be washed. Having workers pick up laundry off the floor or out of lockers is a great service to the athlete, but is impractical with limited labor.

Collection sites are important. The laundry drop should be very near the locker room, so it is convenient for the athletes, and as close to the laundry facility as possible to minimize delivery and transportation times. Laundry drops should also be secure to prevent pilfering or tampering with items. Laundry chutes, hampers, windows, and lockers or cubicles all are common laundry drop alternatives.

Pickup points (for athletes to pick clothing up) are also important in effective laundry operations. Many times, laundry is picked up through the equipment window. This works well if the window is always staffed, but it can cause congestion during peak issue times. An option that prevents this problem is simply to place clean laundry back in lockers or in issue cubicles. This practice eliminates having to have the issue window staffed at all times of the day, and it reduces congestion at the issue window when athletes arrive. Athletes simply go to their lockers, where their laundry has been placed before their arrival. Replacing clean laundry in lockers can be time-consuming, particularly because lockers must be unlocked, laundry sorted, laundry hung, and lockers locked. With open-bay lockers, the unlocking and locking stages are eliminated.

Probably the most efficient pickup system is one that uses issue cubicles. Small issue lockers are placed along a wall where athletes have access to their issue cubicles (on one side of the wall). On the backside of the wall, the laundry worker has access to all the lockers, so clean laundry can be placed in them. (This same principle is used in post office mailboxes.) This cubicle system allows laundry to be reissued quickly, while allowing athletes to pick up clean laundry at their convenience. Cubicles can be used as laundry drops for dirty clothing also.

BINS, BAGS, OR HAMPERS

Laundry should be gathered in some type of container, usually bins, bags, baskets, carts, or hampers. These are a necessity when handling bulk laundry.

A variety of laundry bins and hampers are available. Laundry hampers or bins are usually constructed of canvas, vinyl, or polyethylene. Originally, all you would find in a laundry room were bins constructed of metal frames and wooden bases. In some places, you will still find these dinosaurs. Most launderers prefer the poly or vinyl bins to the canvas and metal frame type. This is due to the fact that they can take more abuse and do not harbor bacteria. It is very easy to clean out a poly or vinyl cart with a hose and some disinfectant, unlike canvas and metal frame units.

There are many options available when looking for a cart for your facility. Carts come in a variety of sizes and colors as well as having permanently affixed or removable baskets, larger wheels for portability, lockable lids, and tilting capacities for easier loading and unloading.

Bags can also be used for collections. Those made of nylon, mesh, cotton, or lightweight canvas work best when supported by a portable frame so that dirty clothes can be dropped in easily. These frames support the bag, keeping it spread open. When the bag is full, it is removed so another empty bag can be attached to the frame. Bags are practical for collecting lighter loads (towels, coaches' clothing, and practice gear) that are not heavy as a result of excess water or perspiration saturation. Remember to always wash the bag you are using after each use, especially plastic bags. Bacteria will grow in these bags even if you only use them for an hour or so. In most states, the local health department requires that all bags used in the transport of dirty clothes be washed or discarded.

ISSUE AND RETRIEVAL

Even though this section deals with collection of laundry, much of the discussion of how best to collect laundry hinges on how it was issued in the first place, so some of what follows addresses both of these steps. Needs for issue and retrieval vary greatly from athletic departments to health clubs to physical education departments. In many cases, health clubs and physical education classes issue towels on a daily basis, and no other equipment. On the other hand, athletic departments issue and retrieve many clothing items for many different sports as often as three times a day. Each situation is different and therefore

FIGURE ONE
Laundry flow chart.

demands different issue and retrieval methods. Following is a discussion of some of the most common.

Exchange System. This system is the most popular when only towel service is offered. With this system, patrons turn in something of value, usually a driver's license or student identification card, in exchange for a towel or other item (thus the name). Many times, a fee is charged to help defray the cost of towel service. This fee often includes the purchase of a towel, which can be exchanged at any time.

Bag System. The bag system uses a mesh laundry bag to gather, wash, and issue laundry. With this system, one or more mesh bags is issued to each athlete, along with his or her workout gear. The bag is equipped with an identification flag with the player's number for easy recognition, and a rubber closure or metal pin is used to close the bag. After the workout, all dirty items are placed in the mesh bag, the bag is closed securely, and it is placed in the laundry drop-off area. The bag is then washed and dried, with the contents of the bag remaining inside throughout the entire process. The perforations in the bag allow water, detergent, and air to penetrate the clothing, as well as keep all items together throughout the cleaning process. The bag is then reissued to the same player, who receives exactly what was placed in the bag.

Bags can be bought in various sizes and colors. Using bags of different colors for different sports, teams, and events is a common practice called "color coding." This is particularly helpful if a central laundry room is used, where the possibility of confusing bags exists.

The bag system has many advantages. Athletes are responsible for placing their own laundry in their own bags, relieving other workers of the burden. The bags are easily identifiable, making it easy to issue them. Many items can be placed inside the mesh bag and they all remain together during the cleaning process, so no daily shortage checks are necessary.

The mesh bag system does, however, possess certain disadvantages. In the cleaning and drying process, the more surface area of clothing that is exposed, the better. This allows cleaning chemicals to penetrate fabrics better and more hot air to come in contact with the clothes. With mesh bags, particularly if they are too small, the gear tends to "wad up," limiting surface exposure, and preventing optimum cleaning and drying. If bags are sufficiently large, where the clothes have plenty of room to move inside the bag, this is less of a problem.

Another drawback of mesh bags is their closure device. Metal pins are noisy in the machines, and, if they come undone, they can damage washers and dryers and scatter the contents of the bag. Because of this drawback, rubber closures have been designed to replace the pins; they keep the bags closed just as tightly as metal pins, are much quieter in the machines, and will not damage laundry machinery. Over a period of time, however, they can wear out or break as a result of constant exposure to heat and chemicals.

The Loop System. The loop system uses a plastic loop to gather, wash, and issue laundry. With this system, one loop is issued to each athlete, along with his or her workout gear. After the workout, all dirty items are placed on the loop, the loop is closed securely, and it is placed in the laundry drop-off area. The laundry and loops are then washed and dried. The loop is then reissued to the same player, who receives exactly what was placed on the loop.

Similarly to bags, the loop is equipped with an identification tag and is numbered for easy recognition. Loops can also be bought in various sizes and colors. And using loops of different colors for different sports, teams, and events is also called "color coding." Again, this is particularly helpful if a central laundry room is used, where the possibility of confusing loops exists.

The loop system also has many advantages. Athletes are responsible for placing their own laundry on their loops, relieving other workers of the burden. The loops are easily identifiable, making it easy to issue them. Many items can be placed on the loop at any time, and they all remain together during the cleaning process, so no daily shortage checks are necessary.

Another reason that most athletic facilities are using the loop system is that they do not make the noise that pins and other devices do. They also do not damage washers and dryers. The only drawback is that the plastic loops also can wear out or break as a result of constant exposure to heat and chemicals.

Roll System. The roll system is used less frequently than other methods, although it can be used effectively under certain conditions. With this system, certain items of sized clothing, usually a T-shirt, jock, socks, and shorts, are placed inside a towel and then rolled inside the towel. This roll is placed in lockers or issued in some other manner. The athlete is then required to return the roll to be checked in when he or she has finished.

The roll system is best used for sports in which the teams or squads have small numbers of players, such as volleyball or basketball, because of the time it takes to assemble and distribute each roll. Often, athletic departments will make rolls available to staff members for workouts, with good results.

The disadvantages of the roll system outweigh the advantages. Because items are not labeled, they are often accidentally traded or taken by athletes. In addition to the time it takes to assemble and distribute rolls, checking rolls in is also time consuming, because daily records of missing items must be kept. Also, athletes are often issued items that are the wrong size. Probably the biggest problem is that it is not conducive to reducing theft or pilfering and therefore ends up costing the department money.

Combination System. Many times, a combination of the previously mentioned systems works best in accommodating laundry needs. An example might be to give athletes a loop and a bag for their laundry. Certain items (T-shirt, shorts, towel, and jock) are placed on the loop, while other items (jersey, pants, socks) are placed in a mesh bag. Other items, particularly those that are heavy (sweats, thermals) might be handed in loose or exchanged. This requires labeling such items to make it easy to reissue them. Another example might be to wash all practice gear on loops. The key to successfully controlling laundry collection and reissue is to decide which systems will work best for your situation.

Collecting Uniforms

There is little difference in the techniques for collecting uniforms as compared to other laundry; the difference comes in when you set yourself up to wash them. Game uniforms should always be separated (pants from jerseys). The best time to do this is in the locker room after the game. It is highly recommended that a bin or bucket be set aside in the locker room for the players to deposit their uniforms. Depending on the condition of the practice uniforms, you can wash them together or separately. I recommend the latter so there is no chance of colors bleeding.

Transportation

From the locker room to the laundry room, the particular method of transporting dirty laundry should suit your needs. If these facilities are near each other, rolling carts or baskets probably are the best method of transport. Hand carrying light loads is also possible, but this is usually impractical and unpleasant. If laundry is to be carried up or down stairs where there is no ramp or elevator, opt for smaller bags to ease the load of handling. When traveling between adjacent buildings, baskets or hampers with lids work well. A truck or van may be needed when traveling from the playing field to the laundry room.

When dirty clothes must sit for several hours—for example, when the team is driving them from a road game—make sure the uniforms and/or clothes are pre-sorted. This will assist you in getting your job done more efficiently when you return and will stop transfer staining from occurring. **Never—and this cannot be stressed enough—never soak your uniforms after a game.** Soaking uniforms can cause some of the dyes in the fabric to release, which will dye your uniforms.

Regardless of the transport mode, keep the following in mind:

- Do not overload carts or bags. Remember, someone may have to carry them a long way.
- Take steps to avoid spillage. This can result in laundry being dropped, dragged, or stepped on.
- Clean and sanitize transport carts regularly. Do not allow bacteria, mold, or mildew to grow, particularly with canvas baskets. The same applies when laundry chutes or lockers are used as drop sites.
- Avoid using old or damaged hampers. Broken wheels, sharp corners, or rusty parts can add to your laundry headaches.
- Repair bags as needed. Bags with holes can expose laundry to dirty floors of cars and trucks or the greasy underbellies of buses, airplanes, etc.
- Use bags with zipper closures, sturdy pins, or drawstrings to keep laundry contained and sealed.

Transportation should be as expedient as possible. Letting laundry sit overnight allows stains to set and bacteria to grow on fabric. When heavily soiled clothes sit overnight, setting also occurs; that is, moisture from the clothes on top settles to the bottom of the hamper. This causes the clothes on top to dry, which allows stains to set, while the clothes on the bottom of the hamper absorb sweat and grime from the clothes on top. This can be avoided by transporting dirty clothes to wash sites as quickly as possible.

Sorting

Whenever possible, laundry should be pre-sorted (separated before washing). Uniforms, in particular, should be sorted according to their fabric type and coloration. Three criteria determine how soiled laundry is sorted: soil (type and extent), fabric (type, weave, and color), and finishing process (drying equipment). When pre-sorting, always check clothing carefully for damage or tears. Empty pockets of coins, gum, sunflower seeds, ink pens, tissues, thigh or kneepads, as well as any other items that will damage clothing or machinery. Laundry should also be post-sorted (sorted before drying) to avoid setting stains that may have been overlooked when pre-sorting.

When using a programmable washer, one should not worry about pre-sorting the uniforms per soil type, since most wash cycles are set to remove various soil types during the wash program. A good laundry tech will make sure that the wash cycle is sufficient to clean several types of soils.

SOIL

Sorting laundry by the amount of soil it contains ensures that cleaning is more effective. Heavily soiled clothes demand stronger cleaning formulas than lightly or medium-soiled clothes. Detergent strength, the length of the washing cycle, and water temperature all vary in wash load formulas. Lightly or medium-stained clothes can therefore be separated, washed with milder detergents, and washed on shorter cycles, saving both time, energy, and chemicals. Clothes with heavy stains may also require a soak or flush stage before they are washed. Why waste detergent washing off caked mud when plain water will eliminate much of the soil? It makes sense to pre-wash rather than to toss clothes caked with mud in the washer and end up washing them three or four times, when a flush and a wash will produce the same result without wasting detergent or time.

Further, different stains require different cleaning formulas. For example, oil-based stains are removed with different chemicals from those used to remove organic or water-based stains (see "Stain Removal" on page 118 for more on this). Therefore, similarly stained clothes should be separated and washed accordingly.

FABRIC

Different fabrics have different characteristics, depending on the fibers from which they are made. This means they need different chemicals and wash times to clean them (see Appendix C, "Fibers and Textiles," for more on this). Clothes made of tightly woven, strong fibers are durable and will withstand more rigorous wash formulas than more delicate garments normally composed of loosely woven, gentle fibers, which must be treated with gentler wash techniques. Fabrics that have been treated during their manufacturing (rubberized, waterproofed, permanent press, etc.) also have special wash needs. So, separating by fabric type will also make the wash more effective.

COLOR

With few exceptions, separation of colors is the most important reason for sorting soiled laundry. Improper care of colors can yield disastrous results. It is critical that colored clothes be separated into similar color groups; for example, solid colors (blues with blues, greens with greens, etc.), multiple colors (striped, spotted, patterned, etc.), and light colors (whites, grays, pastels, etc.) should always be carefully sorted and separated. Colors are usually washed in cold or warm water with mild detergents. Separate dirty colored items quickly—allowing dirty colors to sit in hampers can cause fading, bleeding, or spotting.

Washing colors and whites together can ruin both, especially if they are washed in hot water or in an elongated wash cycle. This causes the colored pigments to run off the colored clothes and be absorbed by the white clothes. Once a fabric does bleed it is nearly impossible to remove the color from the affected areas. The most important thing a launderer can do to prevent this from occurring is to add a pound of salt to a cold-water wash formula that's run before the first time they're handed out to the players or staff. This wash should go for no less than 10 minutes, and should be followed up with a five-minute rinse. This assures that the colors, for the most part, are set and will not bleed.

Also, remember to use a detergent that activates in cold water. Many detergents will not actively remove soil unless they reach a certain water temperature; therefore, these detergents should not be used to wash colored items (see "Laundry Products and Chemistry" on page 110). Never use chlorine bleach on colored items.

POST-SORTING

Sorting of clothing by soil, fabric, and color is usually done before the wash stage, hence the term pre-sorting. This ensures that similar fabrics receive similar cleaning care.

Some items can be sorted after the wash stage, which is termed post-sorting. Post-sorting may be performed to separate heavy and light clothes that are washed together, but need to be dried in separate dryers. Drying at temperatures that are too high can be as harmful as harsh chemicals to certain clothes (see "Finishing" on page 103).

Post-sorting can also be effective when washing uniforms. After the initial wash, sort through clean uniforms and look for stains. If only a few of the uniforms retain stains, dry the clean uniforms and rewash or treat only the items that need special attention. By post-sorting you do not wear out your uniforms in the washing machine. In other words, the less you expose the uniforms to harsh chemicals, temperatures, and high-speed extracts, the longer they will last.

Washing

Obviously, the most important part of the cleaning process is the wash stage. The sidebar "Elements of Cleaning Efficiency" (page 101) discusses the five elements of cleaning efficiency that must come together to produce clean laundry. Many of the particulars concerning this stage are discussed in detail in "Basic Laundry Products and Chemistry" on page 110. To avoid redundancy, they will not be mentioned now, but here are a few brief facts to remember about washing:

- Wash soiled laundry as soon as possible.
- Check clothing labels for proper care instructions.
- Follow cleaning directions on detergents, bleaches, softeners, and all chemicals exactly as they are printed.
- Use common sense when purchasing, using, and maintaining washroom equipment and supplies.
- Learn all you can about laundry practices and inform laundry personnel of proper methods and practices.
- Use dry cleaners only when absolutely necessary, and choose them carefully. The worst thing any equipment manager can do is send uniforms to an inexperienced dry cleaner. Most if not all uni-

form manufacturers state that uniforms should never be dry cleaned. The chemicals used in dry cleaning will damage the nylon and Lycra. They will turn white uniforms gray or give them a brown tint. Also, the chemicals used are not only harsh, most of them are extremely toxic.

It is highly recommended that all uniforms be washed in cool to warm water. The water should not exceed 124 degrees F, especially when washing colors. Most dyes get released after the water exceeds 125 degrees F, though this can depend on the color of the dye (blues and greens release faster than most other dyes). Red is historically the worst color to have on a uniform, but it's also the most sought after. Red dyes will generally bleed out at a temperature of as low as 112 degrees F, whereas blues and greens will hold until at least 118 degrees F.

Before washing most laundry, you should consider putting it through two steps: pre-wash and soak. These two stages can greatly enhance the wash, yielding better results and ultimately saving time and resources.

PRE-WASH

Prior to washing any garment it is advisable to pre-wash. This is usually the first cycle on a fixed-cycle washing machine. If you are lucky enough to have a programmable machine, have your chemical company program a flush or pre-soak prior to the main wash. This allows the water (the best-known cleaning chemical) to remove the loose granules that sit on the fabric. This also helps to temper the fabric for the coming wash and chemicals.

The two things that you always want to do is temper the water for the fabric and allow the fabric to absorb as much fluid as possible prior to the addition of chemicals. The reason to temper the water is so that the fabric does not go into shock. When a fabric goes into shock, it tightens up. This has been known to happen with hot water as well as cold. Therefore, what we like to see is a warm mix of water used up front, prior to the wash, to prepare the fabric for the coming onslaught of hotter water and chemicals. This process also allows the fabric to absorb water. This is important because you do not want the fabric to absorb your chemical and hold the chemical in its webbing. When chemical is injected into dry clothes, the clothes absorb the water and chemical. This means that the chemical is now *in* the fabric rather than *on* the fabric working on the stains and dirt.

The pre-wash cycle should be no less than two minutes in length (fixed-cycle washers are set at three minutes) and no more than five minutes in length unless you propose to add a chemical agent such as an enzyme to assist the cleaning process prior to the main wash. Ideally, you would not wish to add any chemical in the prewash,

Elements of Cleaning Efficiency

Cleaning laundry involves removing foreign matter from the fibers that make up the materials of the items being washed. For this process to work optimally, five elements must come together: water, action, temperature, chemical, and heat (known as WATCH). Each of these works together in concert. Once one of these areas is imposed upon, another area must pick up the slack.

Water. Basically, this refers to whether the water is hard or soft (the amount of minerals in it). Hard water is any water with a concentration of grains above five parts per million; soft water is water with a concentration of grains below five parts per million. The harder the water, the tougher it will be to get the results you want without increasing one of the components of WATCH. Minerals in the water will affect the way your chemical works (see Appendix E, "Water").

Action. This refers to the agitation, pounding, or dropping of laundry in the washing machine cylinder. Proper loading and water levels ensure correct mechanical action. It is accepted and recommended industry practice to optimize mechanical action by using low water levels in the 5"-7" range. As well as providing effective mechanical action, these low levels also minimize consumption of water, energy, and chemical supplies.

Time. This refers to contact time between laundry and chemicals, wash, flush, and spin cycles, and total wash formula, including the total number of steps programmed into the wash cycle.

Chemical. Interaction of fabrics and soils with the various types and concentrations of chemicals used in the wash wheel constitutes chemical action.

Heat. This term refers to the temperature range for optimum performance based on types of soil, types of fabric, chemicals used, and energy-saving requirements. Water temperatures between 130 degrees F and 150 degrees F are best for medium to heavily soiled garments; 100 degrees F to 125 degrees F for light soil; and 80 degrees F to 90 degrees F for rinse and flush cycles are recommended. Higher temperatures accelerate the chemical reactions necessary for soil removal, which is why temperature-reduced energy formulas are rarely used for heavily soiled linen. The exception to this is when washing colored linens and uniforms, which can bleed at temperatures above 112 degrees F.

Another area that must be considered is procedures. Procedures are the combining of all the elements of cleaning efficiency (WATCH) with proper handling procedures (collection, transfer, etc.). If any one (or more) of these factors is significantly out of balance, you're not likely to achieve optimum cleaning. To some extent, a deficiency in one area can be compensated for by adjusting one or more of the other factors—for example, if mechanical action (the action of lifting and dropping of garments) is poor (due to overloading), increased time, temperature, or chemical action may help somewhat. However, you'll never achieve the same degree of efficient cleaning compared to if the washer is properly loaded.

yet you may have a machine that has limited program space, if any at all.

SOAK

Soaking of uniforms is advantageous when you can do it under controlled conditions. Placing uniforms in drums after a game or overnight has one or two pros, yet many more cons. The best way to soak any article of clothing is in a controlled environment, such as a washing machine. Most washing machines allow you to soak. The problem is that machines known as fixed-cycle soakers or hold soakers do not give the fabric any motor action. This means that if a garment is not fully submerged it dries and thus does not get any benefit from the soak.

Programmable washers allow you to soak for the time you set and will turn every few minutes. This motor action allows the garment to get the full benefit of being in the watery solution. I say watery solution because you should always add a mild detergent with emulsifier into the soak bath. This will give you the best results. Water is the universal solvent but chemical makes it that much better. You could soak in water for 10 hours without chemical and still get staining after you wash, whereas with chemical added to the soak you will not get as much staining, and you could even cut the soak time down.

I do not recommend soaking uniforms in drums on the way home from any game. The reason, as stated above, is that it is not a controlled environment. Also, it requires the use of heavy-duty drums or buckets. These drums or buckets have to be unloaded and can be very heavy. Heavy drums can lead to many physical problems as well as liabilities few wish to confront. The best that any equipment manager can do after a road game is to collect and sort the uniforms then place them in their own trunk or bag for when they return home. The few hours in this position will not cause harm to any fabric. The worst-case scenario is that you happen to get a minor transfer stain. This should and has always been an easy stain to remove in a pre-wash or main wash. This type of staining is usually on the uppermost part of the fabric and washes away cleanly.

Whether or not to soak comes down to a personal decision. Here are some pros and cons:

Pros:

- Soaking with cleaners or emulsifiers can help remove stains prior to the wash stage.
- Soaking may be preferred to scrubbing or spot-cleaning individual stains.
- Soaking heavily soiled laundry can often save many hours of scrubbing.

Cons:

- Improperly soaked clothing can be damaged or ruined.
- Soaking can cause bleeding in some fabrics after a sustained period in water.
- Soaking can transfer stains in the water to other garments.
- There is no agitation in a drum or tub, which means that the chemicals, if you added any, sit at the bottom of the container.
- The water will chill fairly quickly and could actually set the stains that you are trying to remove.
- Soaking after games requires large drums or tubs, which take up space.

WASH

The basic steps of washing laundry (after items have been sorted) are as follows:

Loading. Basically, this term refers to loading the proper amount of clothing into the wash wheel. This is discussed in more detail later.

Flush. Normally the first step in a washing cycle, the flush is used to rinse away any soils before detergent is introduced. In essence, a flush is actually a rinsing stage that prepares clothing for the break or rinse stages. Flushes help prevent stains from setting and prepare garments for chemical exposure by bringing them to the proper temperature.

Break. Break refers to the washing machine cycle during which detergents are added and most cleaning occurs. Also termed the "wash" cycle, it is the most important step in the washing process; therefore, it is normally longer than the other cycles. Many machines automatically adjust the length of break cycles according to the setting that is selected (light soil, medium soil, etc.).

Rinsing. Rinsing refers to the stage in which water enters the wash wheel with no detergents present. Rinsing rids the wash wheel of suspended soil and detergent. More than one rinse is generally used. In most 50- to 100-pound washers, three rinses are used. The first two perform the previously stated functions, while the third is used to add softeners and sours, as well as to bring clothes to a temperature where it can be handled when laundering has been completed.

Souring. Sours are entered into the final rinse stage. Souring neutralizes any residual alkalinity that may be present in clothing. Along with sours, fabric softeners, bacteria fighters, and brighteners are often added in the sour stage.

Extraction. During extract cycles, the wash wheel spins at a high speed, causing water to be extracted from clothing. Intermediate extract cycles are used following certain wash and rinse cycles, usually at reduced speeds and times. Final extraction occurs after the final rinse (or sour) stage and is the fastest and longest extract cycle. Extraction of clothing significantly reduces drying time, because it rids clothing of most of its moisture. No chemicals are introduced during the extract cycle, as the centrifugal force would cause chemicals to set in clothes, particularly during the final high-speed extract.

Most washing machines are equipped with a spin/extract cycle with one or more speeds, although separate extractors can be purchased. Many football reconditioners use extractors extensively to help remove moisture from shoulder pads, shoes, and other items that are air-dried. Industrial clothing extractors are also available in all sizes. Extractors are practical when laundry rooms have a limited number of dryers or when drying items that cannot be heat dried. On the other hand, many delicate fabrics cannot withstand the high-speed extraction capabilities of some machines and should not be spun. Note that allowing clothes to remain in extractors too long can wrinkle them, as well as waste electricity. Extractors are also very dangerous and should only be used by highly trained personnel.

Finishing

Finishing consists of drying (heat or air), pressing, or ironing. This stage ensures complete removal of moisture from clothing. Rarely in athletics are clothes pressed or ironed. With the onset of permanent press and superior fabric blends, pressing and ironing can be left to professional dry cleaners. Even 100% cotton shirts, if pulled from the dryer immediately and hung or folded, do not require pressing or ironing.

Care labels on garments also include drying directions. Follow them closely to avoid problems such as shrinkage or discoloration.

Dryers vary in size and function and can be purchased to fit particular needs (see "Dryers" on page 109). Tumble-drying is the most common way to bulk-dry laundry. Tumble-drying with heat is effective on bulk goods such as towels, jocks, socks, and T-shirts. Lower heat levels should be used on uniforms and coaches' apparel. Items that include Spandex, rubber, elastic, or delicate fabric should be dried in short, cool dryer cycles or hung so that they dry naturally. Drying these items in a medium or high heat will degrade their elasticity. The best way to dry these items is on low or medium-low heat for five to 10 minutes with a no-air cool-down for five minutes. This will dry the garments without over-drying them. This will also allow the fibers of the fabric to stretch and contract naturally, thus preventing the loss of elasticity.

Proper drying of uniforms varies from fabric to fabric and type of lettering and/or inlays on the uniform. The most important thing to remember about drying uniforms is not to allow them to burn. This can occur very easily, especially with older dryers and excessive chemical. The worst chemical one could use on uniforms is softener. Softener coats the uniforms and doesn't allow them to breath. Also, if too much is added to the wash wheel and is allowed to stay on the uniform prior to drying, you will get a yellowing effect. This yellowing is the softener burning. This will occur on all types of fabrics regardless of whether they are nylon, poly, or cotton.

When drying nylon or poly uniforms, it is recommended that one dries them on a five and five cycle. This means that you dry them at low (100 degrees) or medium (110 degrees) temp for no more than five minutes followed by a five-minute cool down. This will allow the material to dry without wrinkles and will leave two to three percent moisture in the material so that if a stain was missed it can be removed at a later date. When drying a uniform too much you can actually set the stain you missed. The other reason for the five and five is to protect your heat transfers. These are the letters or numbers that are on the uniforms. These transfers are very easily destroyed in high heat, especially since it takes high heat to set them on the fabric.

The other type of lettering that appears on uniforms is tackle twill. Tackle twill, for the most part, is similar in composition to burlap, yet is a much tighter weave. This product is usually color-set. This means that it usually does not bleed. There have been instances of poorer quality tackle twill bleeding and, therefore, it is recommended that all fabric, regardless of composition, be color-set prior to wearing or doing a standard wash. Tackle twill will not burn per se but will stay as is when dried. The main concern with tackle twill is not its shrinking but the shrinking of the garment that it is on. When this occurs, you will have a bunching at the sides of the twill by the under fabric. The best way to avoid this would be to adhere to a strict five and five dry.

You can see that a five and five dry is highly recommended for most garments. The place where that changes is when you are drying cottons. Cottons can be dried at various temperatures depending on the use of the garment. Cotton uniforms are very fickle and must be washed and dried very carefully. When washing these garments, one must use a wash cycle that slowly raises the water temperature then lowers it toward the end. The same goes with drying. One must slowly increase the temperature then bring it down just as slowly. Bringing the water temperature or drying temperature up or down too dramatically will cause a "shocking" effect, causing the fibers to pull into themselves and the garment to shrink dramatically and hold this size. Once this occurs, the garment is ruined beyond repair. Make sure your chemical supplier knows what type of fabric you are employing so as not to ruin your uniforms or personal clothing. A good chemical supplier will see what you use prior to trying or setting up any wash formulas.

Folding vs. Hanging

Folding or hanging finished laundry serves three basic purposes: preparation for storage, preservation of superior aesthetics, and final inspection. Laundry room personnel perform these steps manually, although folding machines are often used for large amounts of linens (sheets, tablecloths, etc.) in large laundries.

Preparing clothing for storage is important. The decision to fold or hang uniforms depends on storage and issue facilities. Folding clothes for storage may be more space-saving, but it usually leaves creases where they are overlapped. Hanging clothes eliminates creases, but requires more closet space. Learn to fold clothes to fit storage spaces and to leave size tags or numbers exposed for ease of issue or inventory. Folding clothes correctly the first time will definitely save time later.

There really is no set rule in regards to hanging or folding uniforms. Basically, one would want to keep the uniforms that need to be in pristine condition hanging when possible and when in-season. The uniforms that are the most likely to wrinkle and need the most attention are and always will be the baseball and football uniforms. These uniforms are bulky and get the most abuse in regards to wear than those of most other sports. Therefore, it is highly recommended that these get hung up when possible and not folded.

Baseball and football practice uniforms can be folded since they do not need to be in perfect condition at all times. Most other uniforms can and should be folded and put in a well-ventilated area. The area chosen should always have airflow so as not to promote any mildewing. A ventilated area can be either a shelf, closet with airflow rack, or basket with side and bottom airflow. There is no bad way to store uniforms as long as there is airflow. One suggestion would be not to store any uniforms on the floor of any facility even if in baskets. This is due to the fact that any moisture or water leak will potentially ruin the garments.

Preservation of superior aesthetics simply means keeping uniforms looking good. Folding or hanging eliminates wrinkling and helps provide an excellent appearance for coaches and teams.

Usually, the person who does the folding or hanging also acts as a final inspector. Checks are made for stains, tears, or any other problems that can be remedied. A final inspection when folding or hanging can definitely add to the life of the garment, as well as prevent embarrassment to you and the athletes.

When dealing with large amounts of bulk laundry used by athletes, folding or hanging is often eliminated. Particularly in bag, pin, or loop systems, laundry goes directly from the dryer to the athlete. Bags, pins, or loops are stored in individual lockers, issue cubicles, or pick-up areas for immediate issue and use by the athletes. Folding workout clothes for 200 to 300 athletes every day is simply not possible in most cases, and certainly not practical.

Storage

Storage of laundry is the next step in the laundry flowchart. Laundry that does not go into storage goes directly into use. Allow ample and secure storage areas for uniforms and clothing. Storage closets, shelves, baskets, and racks are all viable methods of storage. Open shelves are advantageous for often-issued items such as towels, T-shirts, jocks, and socks, and they allow ample airflow and ventilation. Closets or closed shelving offer secure, dust-free, dark areas for uniforms or other items not used daily. Always provide ventilation to prevent mildew or mold.

Storage areas for clean clothes should be separated from areas used to store dirty clothes. This helps avoid inadvertent mixing of clothes and helps keep storage areas sanitary.

Transfer of Clean Laundry to Destination

In daily laundry operations, use laundry hampers or carts for short-distance delivery. Keep carts clean, especially if the same ones are used to transfer dirty laundry.

When transferring game clothing to event sites or road games, heavy-duty portable trunks are advantageous. These trunks can withstand heavy road travel, where laundry carts may tear or break. Heavy-duty trunks also offer security. Remember to clean and maintain trunks in the same manner as hampers. As previously stated, in most if not all states, the local health department requires that all reused transport vehicles (carts, trunks, bags, or nets) must be washed. There cannot be cross-contamination between dirty and clean vehicles. Trunks can be cleaned on a regular basis with an antiseptic germicide and odor mitigator.

Use of Laundry

Use of laundry may seem obvious, but it is important to use the right item for the right function. All too often, towels end up being used as cleaning rags, uniforms as floor mats, and socks as sandals. Athletes use their laundry to wipe up any mess they make. Soft drinks, tobacco, blood, mucus—all may be deposited on clothing after the garment has served its purpose.

You and your laundry personnel cannot control all of these situations. This problem can be reduced, however, with the use of strategically placed wastebaskets and easily accessible laundry drops. Posting signs for the athlete's information near public access areas may also help to deter misuse of laundry.

Laundry use is the last step of athletic laundry operations. From here, all steps are repeated.

LAUNDRY WASHROOM EQUIPMENT

Washing Machines (Washer-Extractors)

The primary function of washing machines in any laundry operation is to provide the mechanical action necessary to remove soil and stains. Modern washing machines are available in a vast array of sizes and capacities, with an equal diversity of functions and capabilities.

Most washers consist of a stationary tub or tank that accepts, holds, and flushes water. A cylindrical-shaped, perforated wash wheel is housed inside the tank, where laundry is placed. Hinged or sliding doors allow access to the wash wheel. Tubs and wash wheels are placed on mounting brackets and framework, along with all the plumbing, mechanical, and electrical necessities. All moving parts are then housed in an exterior shell constructed of stainless steel or metals that inhibit corrosion. The outer shells provide protection and desirable aesthetics.

Institutional and industrial washers are equipped with one of three wash wheel types: open-pocket; split-pocket, also called Pullman; and Y-pocket (see Figure Two, below). Split-pocket and Y-pocket wash wheels are used primarily by commercial laundries that handle extremely large workloads. These styles are generally not practical for athletic departments, which most commonly use open-pocket-style washers. Open-style washers are generally equipped with high-speed extract cycles and are therefore technically termed washer-extractors. For our purposes, any reference to a washing machine will imply a washer-extractor.

Washer-extractor-type machines are advantageous for the following reasons:

1. The need for a separate extractor is eliminated. This reduces requirements for both floor space and labor handling.
2. The weight of the load is markedly reduced.
3. The rise of intermediate extractions during washing can reduce time, energy, and water requirements. An intermediate extract between a cold or warm flush and hot suds reduces the energy requirements necessary to raise the temperature. An intermediate extract during rinsing operations can eliminate one rinse.

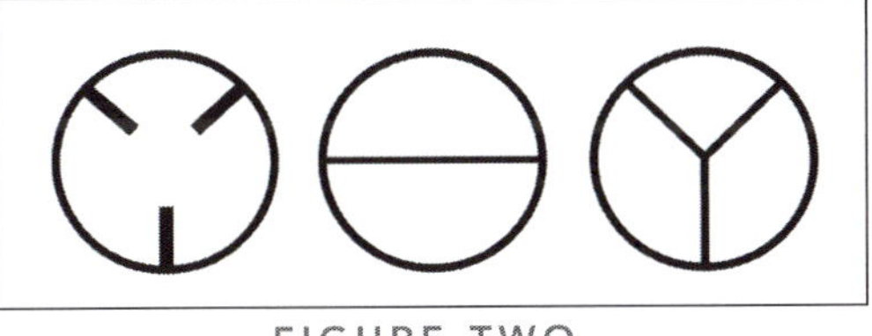

FIGURE TWO
Common wash wheel types.

Open-pocket wash wheels are equipped with perforated walls to allow a controlled flow of water within the wash wheel. Mounted on the inside of the wash wheel are baffles or lifters. These lifters are designed to raise the clothing from the bottom of the wash wheel to the top, where the clothing then drops down into the cleaning solution. The rotation speed of the wash wheel is of utmost importance. "If rotation is too slow, there is no lifting action, if rotation is too fast, the load will not fall. This continuous lift and fall provides the necessary mechanical action for cleaning."[1]

Different cylinder speeds are used for the different functions of wash, rinse, and extract. Generally, these machines are equipped with three-phase electrical motors that drive the cylinders with a system of pulleys and belts. They also reverse wash wheel direction, as well as speed, several times during each operation step to reduce tangling of the load.

Loading Guidelines

It is generally accepted among machine manufacturers that a loading weight of 5.2 to 5.3 pounds per cubic foot of wash wheel space be used as a guideline for loading washing machines. This figure evolved from the general industrial practice of loading 42-inch-by-84-inch wash wheels with 350 pounds of linen. Cylinder volume is derived from the following equation: *dxdxl*/2200=cylinder volume (in cubic feet), with *d* being diameter and *l* being length. Therefore, 42x42x84/2200=67.35 cubic feet. So, 5.25 pounds/cubic foot x 67.35 cubic feet=353.5 pounds.

This formula can also be applied to the typical machines found in athletic washrooms (usually between 35 and 75 pounds). A machine with a wash wheel measuring 30 inches by 22 inches yields a loading weight of 45 to 50 pounds. Here's how to compute it: *d*=30 inches, *l*=22 inches, so 30x30x22/2200=9; then, 9x5.25=47.25 pounds. From this, it is evident that a machine with a wash wheel size of 30 inches by 22 inches should be loaded with about 45 to 50 pounds of laundry. Table One on page 106 illustrates recommended load weights for commonly used machines.

Establishing and enforcing correct load weights is a vital part of washing efficiency. It is important not to overload washers, because it hinders laundry performance. As discussed previously, the constant lifting and dropping of clothing in the wash wheel provides the mechanical action necessary for effective cleaning. Packing the cylinder tightly with laundry restricts this motion, thus impeding optimum soil removal. Additional washing or rinse cycles are often necessary to achieve desired results.

[1] Charles L. Riggs. *Textile Laundering Technology.* Hallandale, Florida: Linen Supply Association, 1979.

Overloading a machine can also cause problems in the spin and extract cycles. Overloaded machines become unbalanced, causing excessive shaking. This shaking can be so violent that if the machine is not firmly affixed to the floor or base, it can actually tear away from the floor. To prevent this disaster, most machines are now equipped with a sensor that will automatically shut off the power or disengage the high-speed extract, reducing the spin to a slow, safe level.

Overloading a machine will also cause chemical spotting on garments. This occurs because the clothes are so tight to the outer rim that the chemical drops or washes up against the same area over and over, thus causing one area to have a high absorbency of chemical product. This spotting can look like anything from a grease spot to a full discoloration. When caustic soda is introduced into the wash and spotting occurs, you get a hard white area. This is the caustic soda hardening and drying in place. Most spotting can be reversed, yet this depends on the type of garment and spotting that has occurred.

Overloading a machine also gets you a "log roll" effect in cleaning. This means that the outer garments are wet and cleaned while the inner, packed garments are semi-dry and still dirty.

The other area that is affected by overloading a washer is the longevity of the unit. Most units when continually overloaded will fail more times than a properly loaded unit. An overloaded unit will also need to be replaced three to five years earlier than a properly loaded and cared for washer.

The best way to stop overloading from occurring is to put your hand into the drum after you have loaded it. If you can put your arm in the washer, where half your arm goes in with some resistance, you have loaded it properly. What you want to see when the wash is wet and the unit is running, is the linen "dropping" from 11 o'clock to 4:30 in a clockwise fashion and 1 o'clock to 7:30 in a counter-clockwise fashion.

Underloading a machine is just as dangerous as overloading it and is much more wasteful. An underloaded machine will nearly always be unbalanced when it goes into its extract. This will cause the machine to "buck" side to side. This occurs because the weight is in one area in the drum, which makes the drum oblong rather than round. Therefore, when the unit goes into extract, the weight in the drum is being thrown right to left rather than concentrically.

Underloading is also very wasteful in that the chemicals being used are geared for a full load. When there is a half to a quarter load and you are injecting (when a peristaltic pump is in use) or adding chemical for that machine, the amount used is usually too much for that load. This is not only wasteful but means that you will not have enough rinses to get all the excess chemical out of the garments, which will cause garment deterioration as well as potentially giving your players rashes when their sweat rewets the garment. The sweat is warm off the body and actually activates the chemical. Also, chemical when introduced into a dryer will actually reactivate as if it was in the wash wheel. Therefore, you are causing the chemical to work without the water to dilute it and carry it away. Clothing dried with chemical still embedded will turn yellow and brown very quickly, and the chemical will deteriorate the fabric.

The other areas that become wasteful is in the use of water and electricity. You still use the same amount of water and electricity to run the machine whether or not you overload, underload, or correctly load a washer.

If your machines only accept detergents manually, using smaller doses of chemicals for smaller loads can reduce drying your clothing with chemical still embedded, yet you will be wasting many gallons of water as well as electricity. If you do have a chemical injector and it cannot be dosed lower for small loads, you will be floating the fabric in a chemical bath.

This is why it is highly recommended that any institution doing varied loads have more than one size washer at its disposal (see Appendix F, "In-House vs. Contracted Laundry," for more on calculating washing machine requirements). A small university should have a washer capable of handling the maximum load it may have and a "pony" machine for small, quick loads.

TABLE ONE

LOAD WEIGHTS FOR FRONT-LOADING WASHER-EXTRACTORS

(all figures are for clean, dry cotton textiles)

Cylinder Size *dxl* (inches)	Free Space* (cubic feet)	Suggested Load Weight@5.25 lb/ft³	Manufacturers' Suggested Range (lb/ft³)
30x15	6.1	30	35
30x16	6.5	35	35
30x20	8.2	45	50
36x18	10.6	55	50-60
36x21	12.4	65	65-75
36x26	15.3	80	75
37x34	21.1	110	130
40x36	26.2	135	135
42x24	19.2	100	125
42x31	24.9	130	135
42x44	35.3	185	200

**Cylinder volume = dxdxl/2200: where d is diameter in inches, and l is length in inches. Volume is expressed in cubic feet.*

Variables

WATER LEVELS

Controlling water levels in washing machines is imperative for efficient cleaning. Usually, two different water levels are used for two different functions, one for washing and one for rinsing.

If water levels are too low in the wash cycle, the concentration of the chemicals remains too high, which can harm clothing. Poor saturation of clothing also results. If water levels are too high, chemicals become too diluted by the water, weakening the chemical effectiveness. Excessive water also impairs the mechanical action of the machine. When water levels become too high, the lift-and-fall action is eliminated, because the water acts as a barrier to the falling clothes. Again, when laundering clothes, you want to see the linen fall from 11 o'clock to 4:30 in a clockwise motion and from 1 o'clock to 7:30 in a counterclockwise fashion. If you do not get this falling action, you have overloaded or underloaded the washer.

If water levels are too low in the rinse cycle, detergents are not flushed properly from the clothing. The reason for high level here is also to dilute the remaining chemical so that it is rendered harmless and carried to the sewer. Excess chemical in the rinse stage can add to the deterioration of fabrics. Excessively high rinse levels, on the other hand, inhibit mechanical action by eliminating the necessary lift-and-fall action. This is what is commonly known as "floating the linen." The wheel is turning and the clothes are in the middle, not moving much. There is no mechanical action. Think of how pioneers cleaned their garments. They beat them against rocks in water. The same principle applies here. The difference is that you are using the metal fins or lifters of the machine as rocks.

Water levels can be governed manually or automatically. Manual water levels are controlled by measuring the amount of water pumped into the machine or by observing level indicators. This method is used primarily on commercial machines that handle extremely large wash loads.

Machines used by athletic washrooms are equipped with automatic water level controls. These controls allow water to flow into the machine until the desired level is achieved, then the water is cut off automatically. Different levels are used for wash and rinse cycles. There are two types of water level controls—pressure switch and float switch. Pressure switches use water or air pressure to govern water levels. Normally, a small tube coming from the back of the wash tank is connected to a sensor on a diaphragm. Water or air pressure causes the diaphragm to rise, triggering sensors that cut off the water flow. Float switches use a floating device for water control. Usually, an L-shaped pipe is attached to the wash tank, so tank levels and pipe levels are the same. The float rises simultaneously with the tank level, switching water off when the float makes contact with the sensor.

Generally speaking, desired water levels in machines between the 35-pound and 75-pound range are six inches for wash cycles and 10 to 12 inches for rinse cycles. For precise information, read the machine instructional repair or maintenance manual.

TEMPERATURE CONTROL

Temperature control means adjusting the amount of hot or cold water pumped into the washing machine. Most machines use domestic hot water or hot water from the heater/boiler for regulating and controlling wash wheel temperature (some use steam). Although some washing machines require manual temperature adjustments (opening and closing hot and cold water valves by hand), most machines today offer temperature settings that control water input automatically.

Common settings on fixed-cycle and home-style machines include hot, medium, and cold permanent press. Each setting adjusts water temperature as needed for the cycle function. For example, a hot setting may use hot water for the two wash cycles, but it may rinse with warm water. Permanent press usually washes and rinses in warm water, except for the final rinse, which uses cold water. Most, if not all, programmable washers allow for hot, warm, and cold water, as well as dial-in settings. Dial-in settings are settings you control. Water temperature is discussed in more detail in "Laundering Formulas" on page 114.

CYCLE CONTROL

Cycle control is the selection and performance of the number of cycles and length of each cycle required to clean the laundry. There are five basic types of cycle controls: fixed, manual timer, push-button, card, and programmable microcomputer. All cycle controls provide the common function of choosing and using the number of cycles performed, and the length of each individual cycle.

The most common style is the fixed-cycle washer. This is also the worst type of washer an institution can have for cleaning uniforms. This unit will do only what it has been set to do. The standard unit allows the wash to have a two- to three-minute pre-wash, five- to six-minute wash, three three-minute rinses, and a five-minute extract. There are some fixed-cycle washers that allow a minor variation of the times stated and a select few offer a bleach bath, but, all in all, these units are great for laundromats and are horrific for facilities that need to clean ground-in dirt and stains such as those from sports.

Manual-control timers are set by hand before using the machine. These used to be the most common in industrial machines and are rarely used in athletic laundry rooms or many other places at this time.

Push-button controls use buttons rather than dials as the triggering device. Cycle variations are selected by pushing buttons, which tell the machine which function to perform. A start button is used to initiate the process. Stop buttons or switches are included to allow for emergency stops.

Card-control machines use plastic or paper cards for cycle control. These cards are designed to allow programming of cycle amounts and lengths for different purposes. Cards have a series of notches or holes that can be punched out or notched out to set desired times. These cards, when completely programmed, are then labeled, each providing proper control for various washing needs. The card is inserted into a slot, where the control device reads the card, and the machine advances through its cycles as it reads that particular card. The problem with card readers is that you are limited in the amount of wash time on any particular card. Usually, the longest a formula can be with a card is 60 minutes.

Programmable microcomputer controls make use of the latest technological advances. This control system uses memory storage to set different machine variables. Time, water, temperature, and number of cycles can be set, altered, or erased by adjusting the memory setting, which is easily controlled using a control panel. This system offers an almost infinite number of cycle settings. This is definitely the most versatile control system. It should be programmed and operated only by authorized personnel who have been properly trained.

CHEMICAL CONTROL

Chemical control is the measurement and administration of each chemical agent or product as it is needed throughout the wash cycles. Adding the correct amount of detergent for the wash and softener for the rinse are examples. Controlling chemical usage is accomplished manually (measured and dispensed by hand) or automatically (measured and dispensed by machine). Both types of controllers allow changing chemical doses as well as, with many newer programmable machines, having different, multiple doses in the same formula.

Manual administration of chemicals should only be done by knowledgeable personnel. Putting the wrong additives in the washer can be potentially disastrous; clothing and machinery can both be damaged by chemical misuse. A front-loading washer is equipped with a small compartment, or dispenser, on the top or the side of the machine. These dispensers accept liquid and powder chemicals, which are released into the wash wheel at the desired times. These dispensers are of various shapes and designs, but they all provide the common function of releasing chemicals into the cylinder. Normally, a small stream of water is pumped into these dispensers, allowing the chemicals to enter through a controlled opening.

Automatic control of chemicals offers consistent, precise, and unmonitored dispersal. Liquid chemicals are used for this system. They are pumped into the machine by separate controls that are wired in conjunction with the washing machine controls. Chemical dispensers are also used with this system, except that the compartments do not hold the chemicals until the desired release time. Instead, the chemicals are pumped in at the exact time that the dispensers are flushed.

Selection of manual or automatic chemical control is strictly a matter of choice. There are advantages and disadvantages to both systems. Here is a brief comparison of the two systems:

Manual-control advantages:

- allows freedom to use powdered or liquid chemicals
- makes it easy to add special agents
- makes it easy to adjust washing formula
- eliminates the need for dispenser space

Manual-control disadvantages:

- produces irregular or inconsistent measurements
- makes it necessary to monitor machines to add agents during later cycles
- makes it necessary to measure and dispense chemicals for every load, adding time
- increased chance of spillage and waste

Automatic-control advantages:

- ensures consistent measurements of chemical with every load
- eliminates spillage and waste
- eliminates time required for personnel to measure and dispense chemicals
- no charge usually required for installing and maintaining injection equipment
- can be modified quickly

Automatic-control disadvantages:

- generally limits choice to liquid chemicals being used without supervision
- requires initial time to set up injection system machinery
- requires space for injection machines and hoses
- requires knowledge of injection equipment

Extractors

Because most washing machines incorporate extraction capabilities, separate extractors are somewhat uncommon in athletic washrooms. However, they can be beneficial, particularly if there are limited numbers of dryers. The extraction function is simple. It reduces the moisture content of the fabric, thus enhancing drying.

There are three basic types of extractors: pressure, hydraulic, and centrifuge. The first uses rollers to squeeze moisture from garments. This type of extractor is usually used with very small (hand-cranked rollers) or extremely large (commercial types with heavy, machine-driven rollers) wash loads.

Hydraulic types extract moisture by a different method. Laundry is placed in a tub and sealed with a perforated lid. A bladder on the bottom of the machine is then filled with water, exerting pressure on the clothes from below. This forces the water to heat up, where it exits through the perforated lid.

Centrifuge-type extractors are the most common. They remove water by using high-speed spinning. Laundry is placed inside a perforated drum housed inside a tank. The drum spins at a high speed, forcing water outward into the tank, where it drains immediately. Balancing clothing inside the extractor drum is necessary to create a balanced spinning action.

Few institutions use extractors; not even many commercial launderers use them nowadays. This has to do with the amount of floor space they have as well as the labor involved. There is also the ever-present danger of losing a limb or one's life when these units are not properly used or maintained. The last reason that these units are going the way of the dinosaur is that the newer washers have great extract cycles built in. The newer units can extract at speeds close to 4Gs (four times the Earth's gravitational pull) or 690 rpm.

Dryers

The function of tumble-type dryers (sometimes called tumblers) is to remove all moisture from cleaned clothing. Dryers are available with a wide variety of capacities, but for the most part, they all perform their function by using a perforated, rotating drum that allows heated air to pass through it. The drum rotates in one direction (a few models have both forward and reverse) at approximately 40 to 50 revolutions per minute. As the drum rotates, three or four baffles mounted inside lift wet clothing and then allow it to drop.

The air in the drier is heated in one of three ways: with gas, electricity, or steam. Because steam-heated dryers require the presence of a boiler, they are rarely, if ever, used in athletic laundries. Gas and electric dryers are by far the most widely used. Gas dryers require a gas line and electrical outlet to each dryer, and electric dryers require heavier electrical wiring than that needed for normal household outlets. Gas dryers tend to be less expensive to run, depending on current utility rates. Electric dryers also take much more time to dry articles than a steam or gas dryer. This makes electric dryers less preferred over gas or even steam.

In gas dryers, burning natural or propane gas generates heat. A burner is ignited via a pilot light or automatic igniter. Electrical dryers use electrically heated coils for this purpose. Both dryer types are almost identical in outward appearance and, except for the heat-producing elements, are almost the same internally as well.

Most dryer models have heat controls. Higher temperatures are used for heavy, durable textiles, lower temperatures for lighter, delicate clothing. Cool cycles are used to provide no-heat tumbling and cool-down cycles.

Most new dryers also have two great features that should be looked into when purchasing new equipment: automatic moisture retention and continual cool down. The first feature will sense when the moisture level in the garment is at the right level. You ideally want the moisture level in the uniform to be at three percent. This ensures that the garment is not "over-cooked" and that any missed stains are not set. The other feature allows the dryer to spin every five minutes for one minute after the cycle is complete. This ensures that the uniforms do not wrinkle and/or stick together.

Timers are used on dryers to adjust cycle length, although some machines require that this be done manually. Timers are practical when dryers are not constantly monitored, as the machines will simply cease operation when timers shut off. Most electricians can easily install timers on a manual machine.

Dryers are generally front-loading, with doors providing automatic shutoff when they are opened. As is the case with washers, perforated tumblers rotate, lifting and dropping clothes. Thermostats housed near the tumbler turn heat sources off when desired temperatures are reached, and back on when temperatures begin to drop below desired levels. These thermostats are usually housed below the tumbler drum in the lint area. Lint traps eliminate lint and dust from exhaust pipes and require regular cleaning.

All dryers function best when proper airflow through the machine is maintained (see Figure Three on page 110). Any blockage of airways, exhausts, exchanges, or lint traps minimizes drying efficiency. Dryers should always be kept clean and lint-free to prevent airflow problems. A good equipment manager will also make periodic checks of his or her ductwork going from the dryer to the exterior of the facility to ensure that the air is flowing and optimum drying is occurring.

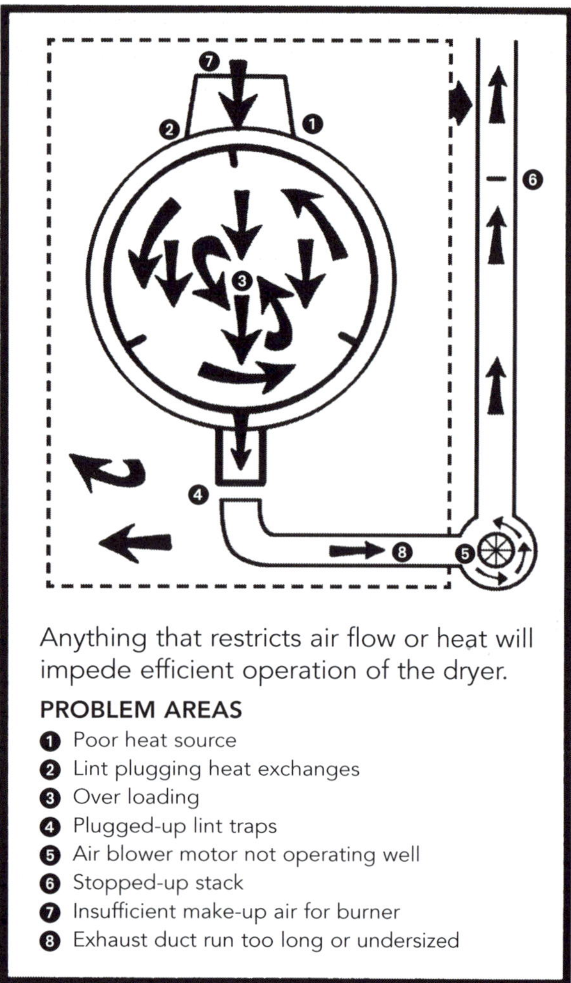

FIGURE THREE

Cutaway view showing airflow through a typical tumbler dryer.

Dryers of all sizes are available. Those in the 35- to 100-pound range are best for athletic washrooms, with 50-, 75-, and 100-pound models used most often. When setting up a laundry system a general rule of thumb is to allow for twice the drying capacity of the washing capacity. For example, if there are two 50-pound washers, it is best to have four 50-pound dryers or two 100-pound dryers. This, of course, is not always feasible, so do the best you can in your situation.

The latest dryers come with many bells and whistles. The best dryer for athletic institutions would be a unit with a microprocessor, reversing capability, moisture sensor, and intermittent cool down when the cycle is complete. These features do not add much to the cost of a basic unit and can be no charge when purchasing several units at once.

Commercial Laundry Equipment

A variety of automatic laundry equipment exists in industrial and commercial washrooms, but it is seldom used in on-premise laundry rooms. Therefore, being familiar with these machines is not necessary, although an awareness of them is beneficial. The following briefly explains these machines and their functions:

- **Spreader**—spreads and loosens tightly packed laundry for easier handling by personnel
- **Folder**—folds towels, linens, sheets, etc. quickly and uniformly
- **Press**—irons shirts, work uniforms, pants, etc. to eliminate wrinkles
- **Steamer**—removes wrinkles from clothing that cannot be pressed
- **Flat work ironer**—irons flatwork (sheets, tablecloths, etc.) through automation
- **Dry cleaner**—cleans delicate fibers and animal hides usually labeled Dry Clean Only

BASIC LAUNDRY PRODUCTS AND CHEMISTRY

There is an immense amount of information and research on the subject of laundry chemistry, products, and their interaction. Because of the complexity and vastness of the subject, this section presents only very basic laundry principles and chemistry and the products involved in the cleaning process. All chemicals have the potential to cause harm to people and garments. Care should always be taken when handling chemicals (see "Safety and First Aid" on page 117).

Detergency Function

Laundry equipment, procedures, and chemicals must combine to accomplish effective cleaning action. In order to understand laundry formulas, in addition to having an understanding of washing machine function, as previously discussed, it is necessary to become familiar with detergency function as well.

Eight processes are frequently used in describing the function of detergents.

1. **Wetting.** The penetration of water into the individual textile fibers. Wetting is enhanced by the presence of surfactants and high temperature.
2. **Neutralization.** Most soils are acidic in nature. The action of alkalis renders these acids inactive.
3. **Dissolving.** Soils that are soluble are removed by the solvent action of water. The solubility of many soils is increased by high temperature and high pH.
4. **Saponification.** Organic fats and oils can react with alkalis used in washing. This reaction, called saponi-

fication, forms soaps, which are more soluble in water than fats and oils. The soaps formed by saponification also aid in the removal of other soils from the textiles.

5. **Emulsification.** Mineral oils and grease cannot be saponified. They must be removed through the action of the alkali and surfactant, which break apart the globules of mineral oil into very small particles that can be dispersed in the water and removed.
6. **Deflocculation.** Solid soil such as carbon, dirt, earth, and clay is particularly difficult to remove. Solid clusters of soil must be broken down into smaller particles (deflocculated or peptized), dispersed, and removed. Surfactants shorten the amount of time necessary to achieve removal of solid soil by deflocculation.
7. **Suspension and prevention of re-depositing.** Once soils are removed and dispersed, they must remain dispersed until they are rinsed away. Alkali and surfactant keeps the soil dispersed in the water (suspended). Poor suspension allows the soil to become re-attached to the textiles (re-deposited), which frequently results in overall graying or specks.
8. **Dilution.** The removal of suspended soil from the wash wheel by rinsing is accomplished by lowering the concentration of the soil in the wash water (dilution). As the water from each cycle is dumped from the wash wheel, soil is removed so that the water added for the next cycle has to suspend less soil and eventually the concentration of soil in the water approaches zero.

As mentioned at the beginning of this chapter, the effectiveness of these eight processes can vary with five factors: water, mechanical action, time, chemicals, and heat (WATCH). Each of these can either hinder or enhance the overall detergency function and results.

Alkalinity/Acidity

All laundry chemicals are unique in their chemical and molecular structures. Each possesses and exhibits characteristics, abilities, and traits that make it useful for certain functions. All chemical compounds can be divided into the categories of acids and bases. When bases and acids mix in equal quantities and strengths, they neutralize each other, or become chemically inactive. Chemicals used in the laundry process fall into three categories: acids, alkalis (bases), and neutrals. It is the careful use of acids and alkalis that make modern laundering techniques so effective.

Acidity and alkalinity can be measured to determine the nature of cleaning elements such as water, detergents, and sours, by the use of a pH scale. The pH scale is calibrated between 0 and 14. A rating of 0 represents maximum acidity, and a rating of 14 represents maximum alkalinity. A pH value of 7 signifies a neutral state; therefore, a rating below 7 signifies acids, and a rating above 7 signifies alkalis. In laundry operations, pH levels can be determined by contacting chemical or water service representatives in the area. Alkalis and acids can be extremely harsh and caustic. Because of this, it is important to be careful when handling these chemicals (see "Safety and First Aid" on page 117).

In addition to knowing the pH of your laundry chemicals, it's important to know the alkalinity or acidity of your water, because it allows you to adjust your wash formula or the required chemicals and amounts that will be used in the cleaning stage. Water should be slightly alkaline for best results. (See Appendix E, "Water," for more on this topic.)

Surfactants

Soil is removed from clothing by loosening and lifting stains from the fiber to which it is attached and holding the stain suspended in water until it can be properly rinsed or flushed away. "The compound primarily responsible for soil suspension (although it also plays a key role in soil loosening) is the surface active agent, also referred to as the detergent or the surfactant. Surfactants are so named because they are active on the surface levels, involved in the loosening and suspension of soil. They, by their peculiar chemical structures, are compounds which concentrate themselves at all of the surfaces in the washing zone (solution surface, fiber surfaces, and interior surfaces of the washing machine)."[1]

When clothes are in use, soil attaches to their surfaces. The cohesive forces that make soil cling to fabric are strong. Because mechanical action and water alone cannot dissipate these clinging forces and allow soil to break away, penetrating agents must be used to separate soil from the surface to which it is attached. Detergents, or surfactants, then, serve the purpose of penetrating the particles and reducing these cohesive forces that bind soil to fabric.

The reduction of this soil-fabric bond is called wetting. "If our goal is to remove soil, then a necessary first step is to bring the detergent solution into contact with the soil. To do this requires that the surface tension of the water be reduced to make it 'wetter' and better able to contact the soil surface. Because surfactants improve the wetting ability of water they are commonly referred to as wetting agents. Wetting agents are necessary to provide penetration of the fabric and soil, emulsification of oily soils, and assistance in soil suspension."[1] Wetting, then, helps the detergent perform its role of removing foreign substances from fibers, or its detergency.

[1] Charles L. Riggs. *Textile Laundering Technology.* Hallandale, Florida: Linen Supply Association, 1979.

There are three types of surfactants: cationic, anionic, and nonionic.

Cationic Surfactants. These are commonly used as fabric softeners and bacteria fighters. They are ineffective as detergents.

Anionic Surfactants. Soap is the oldest and historically most widely used anionic surfactant. It is a completely natural element, and it works best when cleaning natural fibers such as wool or cotton. With today's laundry demands, soap is not practical because of the abundance of synthetic fibers.

Eventually, synthetic anionic surfactants were developed and became popular in the 1940s for this purpose. Anionic surfactants, both natural and synthetic, are high-sudsing detergents that are excellent wetting agents. Synthetic anionic surfactants also work best on natural fibers and at high temperatures. "With the modern-day emphasis on blended fabrics and reduced-temperature laundering, the use of anionics has been much reduced. In addition, anionics generally have very high foam properties. Excessive foaming reduces mechanical action and hinders the soil removal process. Consequently, anionic surfactants have limited use in institutional laundry detergents."[1]

Nonionic Surfactants. Nonionic surfactants were developed to meet the cleaning needs of synthetic fibers such as polyester, nylon, and rayon, as well as synthetic/natural blends. These surfactants also meet the needs of low-temperature mechanical washing, because they are active at both low and high temperatures. Mechanical action is also enhanced because nonionic surfactants are controlled, or low sudsing. The combination of these attributes makes nonionic surfactants the most versatile and practical in meeting the varied needs of today's laundry formulas. Yet, even as advanced and widespread as nonionic surfactants are, they still have shortcomings. Using surfactant auxiliaries compensates for these shortcomings.

Surfactant Auxiliaries. "In many applications, surfactants require additional agents to achieve optimum performance. The role of soap and synthetic detergent in the laundering process is wetting, penetration, deflocculating, and suspension. Soap possesses all of these characteristics but is a particularly effective soil-suspending agent. Synthetic detergents also possess these same properties, but, by themselves, do not suspend soil as well as soap."[1] To assist in the soil suspension of detergents, *sodium carboxymethylcellulose* (CMC) is added to most laundry detergents. CMC has the unique ability to enhance the soil-suspending power of all synthetic detergents.

Phosphates are phosphorous derivatives that enhance surfactant efficiency by sequestering. Sequestering can be described as a process of tying up calcium and magnesium ions (water-hardening components that inhibit detergents), making them unavailable for reaction. Because phosphates have harmful effects on the environment, their pollutive side effects have caused them to be restricted or banned in some parts of the country. As a result, synthetic sequestering agents, termed *chelates,* have been developed. They serve as phosphate substitutes, performing sequestering functions with equal effectiveness.

Antibacterials are used in laundry procedures to eliminate bacteria, fungi, and other potentially health-endangering organisms. Although most bacteria are destroyed during normal laundry wash loads, because of the presence of bacteria in locker rooms and gyms, on wrestling mats, in training rooms, etc., it is good practice to incorporate antibacterials in daily laundry wash loads.

Antibacterials can be divided into bactericides and bacteriostats. "Chemical compounds are described as bactericides if they are capable of killing all microorganisms present on textiles. Chemical compounds are described as bacteriostats if they are able to disrupt the reproduction of bacteria present on textiles treated with them and prevent rapid increase in numbers. While there are relatively few bactericides, there are a number of quite effective bacteriostats currently available to laundry operators."[1]

Optical brighteners are used to counteract the residual graying or yellowing of fabrics being washed with synthetic detergents. As stated previously, synthetic detergents do not have strong soil-suspension characteristics; therefore, redepositing of soil occurs. Optical brighteners are actually colorless dyes, which alter the "wavelength" of the invisible ultraviolet component of light, emitting it in the visible light range. The result of this is to give a visual impression of whiter and brighter linen. Optical brighteners have no actual cleaning function. They are not sold as a separate chemical, but rather are included in virtually all washroom compounds, such as detergents, softeners, sours, and alkalis.

Bluing of clothing, which was performed to obtain the same results as optical brighteners, is now outdated. While optical brighteners are invisible dyes, blues are visible (blue) dyes that were added to white clothing to enhance brightness. Because of the popularity of optical brighteners, today, blues are rarely used in laundry procedures.

Enzymes are complex protein molecules that are derived from living organisms. They act as catalysts, speeding up the decomposition of protein-based stains such as blood and grass. Although they are sometimes added to wash cycles, enzymes are much more effective as soaks, because they work best at slow rates in moderate water temperatures. Enzymes in industrial laundry are

[1] Charles L. Riggs. *Textile Laundering Technology.* Hallandale, Florida: Linen Supply Association, 1979.

usually limited to specialty detergents, but they may be used at times in athletic laundry to help eliminate blood and grass through soaking.

Alkalis

As previously mentioned, alkalis are inorganic chemicals that have a pH of less than 7 and therefore neutralize acids. They are derived almost entirely from the compounds that make up the earth's crust. Chemically, alkalis provide hydroxide ions (OH-) when mixed with water. These hydroxide ions are part of the chemical structure of base metal groups. Therefore, alkalis are also sometimes called bases. Alkalis and alkaline salts are added to detergents and other surfactants to enhance cleaning. Alkalis are caustic in nature, and so can be harmful to skin and fabrics. They should be handled carefully (see "Safety and First Aid" on page 117).

Alkaline Salts

In the context of laundry usage, most chemicals termed alkalis are not truly alkalis. Rather, they are alkaline salts that result from mixing a low dosage of an acid with a high dosage of an alkali. But, because these alkaline salts exhibit the same traits as true alkalis, they are still called alkalis in the laundry industry. For all practical purposes, there are really only three alkaline salts of detergent interest: sodium hydroxide, potassium hydroxide, and ammonium hydroxide. These three hydroxides are really the only alkalis that have any application, directly or indirectly, in the laundry industry.

Alkaline salts are advantageous over pure alkalis for many reasons. When mishandled by workers, pure alkalis, or caustic soda (the most widely used form of pure alkali in the laundry room), are hazardous. Spills can result in skin burns, as well as clothing burns. Caustic soda is also easily misused when entered in the wash wheel. If not measured precisely and entered at the correct time in the wash cycle, pure alkalis can damage clothes beyond repair.

Alkaline Silicates

Today, most alkaline agents contain not only alkaline salts, but also laundry-enhancing agents such as carbonates and phosphates. These are called alkaline silicates and display all the advantages of alkaline action, yet they eliminate most of the disadvantages of using caustic soda. While examples of detergent processes conducted in an acid medium may be cited, practically speaking, textile cleansing occurs normally in an alkaline medium. The same appears to be true with synthetic detergents, especially in a heavy soil medium. While the detergent generally is considered as the principal agent in soil suspension, studies have revealed that alkalis assist soaps and detergents in this role. This is especially true for the alkaline silicates, which exhibit marked soil-suspending power and work hand in hand with detergents in this respect.

Because each type of silicate is derived from a different alkaline source, they display different traits. (For the most part, silicates used in the laundry industry are derived from sodium.) For example, orthosilicate is commonly used on stains that contain a large amount of animal fats. Industrial laundries use metasilicate, as it tends to be more effective in removing oil-based stains, commonly found on items such as uniforms and rags. Alkaline silicates are available in both solid and liquid forms, each of which exhibit slightly different qualities.

Alkaline Soap Builders/Alkaline Detergents

Alkaline soap builders and alkaline detergents are separate agents that perform similar functions. Alkaline builders aid soap in the detergency function by suspending soil, maintaining stable pH levels, keeping soap dissolved, softening water, and offering efficient buffering. Alkaline detergents also aid in soil suspension and saponification, maintain pH levels, soften water, and provide buffering qualities. The primary difference is that detergents are used instead of soaps as the main ingredients. Alkaline detergents also exhibit what is termed colloidal activity. Very tiny colloid particles, in their constant, energetic, back-and-forth movement, maintain a highly effective bombardment against soil deposits. They thus assist substantially in breaking down agglomerates of soil into smaller and smaller soil particles, so that ultimately the nearly microscopic-sized soil particles can be very easily suspended, even though they cannot always be fully emulsified or dissolved.

As mentioned previously, detergency is best accomplished in an alkaline medium. This holds true because most soil deposits are usually acidic, and an alkaline substance neutralizes and suspends these soil deposits. In today's laundry industry, most alkali detergents or soaps also incorporate all the ingredients necessary to handle a wide variety of stains and fabrics. This is done to simplify cleaning procedures and eliminate purchasing several ingredients needed for effective cleaning. These proprietary products usually consist of a surfactant or stabilizer, soil-suspending agents, and brighteners.

Chlorine Bleaches

Should you decide to include a bleach step in your wash formula, the selection of either powdered or liquid bleach should fit your particular circumstances. In general, powder is best with hand dispensing and liquid with automatic dispensing. Always exercise great care when using bleaches, regardless of their form. It is highly unadvisable to use bleach in the chlorinated form at any time with athletic laundry, because chlorine bleach can be very damaging to fabrics, as well as harmful to equipment personnel (see "Safety and First Aid" on page 117).

Chlorine bleaches perform best on white cotton garments at slightly high water temperatures (140 degrees F to 153 degrees F). As the water temperature and the length of the cycle increase, so does the activity of the chlorine bleach. Lengthened exposure of a garment to chorine bleach under these conditions can lead to a significant loss of a fabric's tensile strength. Therefore, it is important to carefully monitor the time, temperature, and concentration of bleach in the wash cycle. This will ensure optimal stain removal, while keeping loss of tensile strength to a minimum.

Chlorine bleaches do not perform as admirably on synthetics such as polyester or nylon. Bleach can sometimes be used on such fabrics, but continued, regular use will cause dingy colors and yellowing of whites. This is due to the fact that the natural color of nylon is not white. White is a dye that is added to the nylon. Non-chlorine bleaches work best on synthetics.

In athletics, the use of chlorine bleach is usually limited to towels and other high-cotton-content articles. At times, bleach can be added to wash cycles to prevent spreading bacteria and common viruses such as jock itch, athlete's foot, impetigo, or herpes.

Note that chlorine bleach is not compatible with certain detergents and fabric types. Always read care labels before adding chlorine bleach to the wash cycle.

Non-Chlorine Bleaches

Non-chlorine bleaches are commonly referred to as oxygen or color-safe bleaches. No chlorides are present in oxygen bleaches; therefore, they are less potent, particularly in sterilizing fabrics. They are, however, also less likely to damage or discolor fabrics. Though oxygen bleaches are less effective in overall stain removal than chlorine bleaches, they are more effective on several specific stain types (cocoa, tea, and coffee).

For the most part, oxygen bleaches perform similarly to chlorine bleaches in regard to temperature, cycle time, and concentration. As time and temperature increase, so does the bleaching activity, although tensile strength is affected less markedly. Using oxygen bleaches also does not result in adverse yellowing of synthetics such as polyester and nylon. They are also more compatible with various detergent types, although it is still recommended that all labels be read before combining such chemicals.

Oxygen bleaches are probably more desirable for use in the athletic washroom. Even though they are weaker than chlorine bleaches, similar whitening and brightening effects can be maintained, without the ill effects of chlorine. Oxygen bleaches can be used on most fabric blends commonly found in athletic garments, with little fear of discoloration or pin holing.

Sours

Sours are acids that are dispensed in the last rinse stage before the final extraction of the washing machine. They serve two purposes: to neutralize the alkalinity of the solution that's left on the clothes; and to control minerals in the water, particularly iron and other hardness minerals, that can discolor clothes.

Sours are available in both liquid and powdered forms, each using a variety of acids. Liquid sours most commonly use citric, phosphoric, or hydroflousilicic acid; powdered sours use sodium silicofluoride and ammonium silicofluoride. Stronger acids such as sulfuric and hydrochloric are not used because they are potentially hazardous.

In addition to sours containing one or more acids, many manufacturers add other agents. These additives, which can include brighteners and perfumes, add little to the expense of the sour and enhance the overall appearance of the garment. Many sours also include chemicals that inhibit mildew and prevent static electricity.

Textile Softeners

As discussed in previous sections of this chapter, textile or fabric softeners are cationic surfactants. Cationic surfactants contain positively charged ions, which cause softening agents to bond to fabric surfaces. Including softeners in the wash formula is easy and inexpensive.

Fabric softeners are added to the final rinse stage of the wash cycle. Their primary functions are to soften clothing and prevent static electricity. Other benefits of softening include quicker water extraction, improved "hand" or feel, easier garment handling, and extended fabric life.

Chemically, textile softeners are considered textile lubricants, because they add substances with lubricating qualities to the surfaces. Most fabric softeners are liquid, although some powdered detergents include textile softeners.

Most softeners are not added in the wash cycle because they reduce the effectiveness of detergents. Softeners perform best in warm or cool water and are absorbed very rapidly. Also available today are softeners that are used in dryers. Although these are much easier to use, they are not considered as effective as liquid softeners.

Note that softeners should not be used on uniforms. Softeners will seal a uniform and not only impede the path of sweat from the individual, but will harm the poly or nylon when dried.

Laundering Formulas

Many factors are involved when determining laundry formulas. Because the number of most washing cycles, the cycles themselves, and the temperatures are pre-set, selecting chemicals is the only remaining job. If you decide to install automatic injection systems, the field representative will normally analyze your laundry needs and conditions and provide the correct laundry formula. If you are responsible for the wash formula, follow the directions included on the packages of the products you use. If further help is needed, contact the local distributor of the product for advice. Normally, there is someone nearby in the laundry business who can provide guidance in selecting chemicals and establishing wash formulas.

Wash formulas vary as a result of soil content. Adjusting formulas is simpler when hand dispensing than when using automatic injection systems. Liquid-injection-system wash formulas operate on the premise that most wash loads are similar from day to day and that each load operates on a wash wheel filled to near capacity. It is sometimes difficult or impossible to adjust injection systems to obtain different formulas from load to load, unless the machine is equipped with programming capabilities. Being able to program the machine allows the operator to adjust formulas according to the desired amount and temperature of water, additives, and time. If your injection system is not programmable, you may decide to disconnect the injection system from time to time to adjust formulas by hand, without interfering with the automatic injection system. This can usually be done by simply unplugging the automatic injection pumps that feed additives to the machine.

Designing wash formulas, regardless of chemical makeup, should include the same basic steps. Table Two, below, provides one example of how laundry service personnel or field representatives might establish a washing formula. By monitoring the stages and lengths of each

TABLE TWO

A SAMPLE WASH FORMULA

The following is a sample of a quick wash formula for items such as towels or personals.

OPERATION	WATER LEVEL	TEMP	TIME (min)	SUPPLIES	PURPOSE
Flush	High	90°F to100°F	3 to 5	None	Reduces soil removable by water alone
Break (Suds Wash)	Low	100°F to 160°F depending on fabric	6 to 10	Alkalis, detergents	Provides suspension and dispersal of garments
First Rinse	High	Depends on fabric	2 to 3	None	Reduces alkalinity for addition of bleach or soil dilution of residual soil or chemical
Bleach Bath	Low	As high as can be achieved—no more than 150°F depending on fabric	5 to 7	Chlorine / non-chlorine bleach	Whitens and sanitizes linen
Intermediate Extract	––	––	0.5 to 1	None	Assists in gassing off remainder of chlorine in clothing & reduces water content
Second Rinse	High	100°F to 130°F	2 to 3	None	Reduces soil and chemical content in clothing
Intermediate Extract	––	––	0.5 to 1	None	Reduces water content in clothing
Third Rinse	High	90°F to 105°F	2 to 3	None	Reduces soil and chemical content in clothing & tempers clothes for sour/softener
Sour/Fabric Softener	Low	32°F to 40°F	4 to 5	Sour Fabric softener	First conditioning of clothing, eliminates static electricity, residual alkalinity, and cools down garments)
*** * * NEVER USE FABRIC SOFTENER IN FORMULAS FOR UNIFORMS * * ***					
Extract	––	––	1 to 5	None	Removes final water from clothing

machine cycle, they can arrive at the proper formula for a specific machine. Altering cycle lengths requires an authorized laundry technician because it involves tampering with timer parts housed inside the machine.

Machines with programmable cards or buttons make it easier to alter wash cycles and lengths. Simply changing cards or pushing buttons can change any or all settings, including cycle lengths and temperature.

Remember that laundry formulas should vary slightly according to soil content and/or fabric types. Whether adjusting by hand or automatically, sufficient chemicals should be added to do the job properly, without using too much.

Safety and First Aid

Laundry room safety is an area no one seems to want to talk about, yet it seems to come up at the worst times. A chemical spill or the inadvertent splash of chemical on one's skin or clothes can cause anything from a minor to a serious consequence. All contact with chemicals, however, should be treated as serious. (See Table Three on page 117 for a list of precautions and first aid for exposure to common laundry chemicals.)

Laundry room personnel should be trained in the proper handling of laundry chemicals, and only trained professionals should handle certain chemicals. When dealing with an exposure to hazardous chemicals, one must act quickly. Seconds become very important, especially when the eyes have been affected. Training personnel and regularly reviewing safety and first aid procedures can make the difference between exposure to a chemical causing some discomfort or leading to blindness.

Measures should always be taken to ensure that chemicals do not have a chance to get on a person or an article of clothes. When handling any potentially hazardous products it is important to wear heavy neoprene gloves and protective eyewear. When dealing with chemicals, one must be prepared for the worst that can happen. Whenever any chemical gets on clothes, one should immediately remove that article of clothing, if possible, or flush it with water. There should always be chemical eyewash available as well as a sink or container of water to neutralize the effects of chemicals. These should be in an open area where they are easily accessible if a chemical emergency occurs. The telephone number of the nearest poison control center should be posted.

The basic laundry room chemicals, as previously described, are detergents (mild as well as "built"), caustic soda (commonly referred to as alkali or booster), bleach or color-safe bleach, sour, and softener. The difference between a detergent and a built detergent is the pH of the product. A built detergent usually has a pH in the range of 9 to 11, which is fairly caustic, whereas a standard detergent is around 7 on the pH scale, which is neutral (neither caustic nor acidic). A built detergent is a product that has caustic soda already in its makeup. This type of product is what we call a "hot" product—it will cause serious burns when it comes in contact with skin. A built detergent is just as dangerous as caustic soda or alkali, even though caustic soda usually has a higher pH and is therefore even hotter and more likely to cause burns. When a person comes in contact with a built detergent or caustic soda, one must immediately flush the area with water. The higher the pH, the more water it will take to neutralize the area. The best way to avoid the hazards of coming into direct contact with these and any other products is to wear safety gloves that reach the elbows, rubber boots, and a neoprene coat or front wrap.

Bleach and color-safe bleaches are in the alkali family and can be mixed with detergents and caustic sodas. Bleach is hazardous in and of itself. Bleach is a sanitizer and will also cause certain types of contact burns. These are minimal compared to those caused by an alkali or caustic soda, yet they must be dealt with immediately. Home-style bleaches are not very potent and do not cause the damage that is associated with commercial bleaches. Commercial bleaches have been known to eat through steel and wood within hours. While color-safe bleach is potent, it will not do as much harm to materials as it will cause a "tingling" sensation to the affected area, as well as turning the area a hard, pure white.

Color-safe bleach is also commonly referred to as hydrogen peroxide. Many people use hydrogen peroxide in its lesser form of two to three percent for sanitizing cuts. Commercial hydrogen peroxide is usually in the 37 percent range. This makes it very potent and allows the user to use a lesser amount in the wash wheel to get the concentration required without "floating" the garments. Both types of bleaches need to be flushed off when they come in contact with either skin or clothes. The difference between the bleaches is that the color-safe bleach will not destroy fabric when it comes in contact with it, whereas standard bleach will. It is highly recommended that an athletic facility do whatever is necessary NOT to use bleach and stay with color-safe bleach. Besides its hazardous nature to humans, bleach will do major harm to your uniforms.

Chemical burn is not the only area that care must be taken to avoid. The other thing, which happens more often than it should, is the accidental mixing of chemicals. Many chemicals should not be mixed. This is the area that can and will cause severe and long-term health effects. Certain products when mixed will cause dangerous gases to be formed, such as chlorine gas and what is commonly referred to as sour gas. Both of these can be lethal. Chlorine gas has been known to burn the lobes of the lungs within minutes of inhalation, while sour gas closes the esophagus and forces your eyes to tear and dry all at once. The long-term effects are serious. You should, therefore, avoid mixing any chemicals unless you are absolutely sure it is safe to do so. Whenever possible, have a trained chemical technician take care of the exchange of products from one container to another.

An example of common laundry room chemicals that should not be mixed is any type of sour with bleaches and caustic sodas. Sours, alkalis, and color-safe bleach should always be kept apart, especially when the sour is in its powder form. Sour in its powder form will combust when alkali or color-safe bleach has been introduced. Sours are acidic, and are commonly used when minerals are present in the water and a high pH is required to wash the garments. The main purpose for sour is to bring the pH down to a normal level so as to prevent rashes from occurring to a person's skin from contact with the garment. Sours need to be washed with water when they come in contact with skin. Sours will not harm garments immediately but over time they will cause a hard spot where they contacted the garment. Any garment or area of skin that has come in contact with sours should be flushed with plenty of water.

The last product usually found in a washroom is softener. As discussed previously, softener is a product that coats and adds a scent to fabrics. It has no cleaning or sanitizing properties. This is a non-caustic product that will not cause any harm to skin or fabric when inadvertently splashed. However, softener will cause burning to the eyes. If softener gets in the eyes, they should be flushed imme-

TABLE THREE

FIRST AID FOR EXPOSURE TO COMMON WASHROOM CHEMICALS

CLASS	EXPOSURE	TREATMENT
ALKALIS Sodium hydroxide (caustic soda) Sodium carbonate (soda ash) Sodium silicates (mets, sesqui, ortho) Sodium phosphates (TSP, STPP, hexamets) Potassium carbonates (potash) Potassium silicates (ortho)	Skin	Flush immediately with continuous stream of water for at least five minutes. If desired, a wash of vinegar or 1% acetic acid may be used after water flush. If skin is burned, do not apply ointment.
	Eyes	Flush immediately with a forced-water eyewash for at least 10 minutes. Do not use any neutralizing solution in the eyes. All except the most trivial exposure should be referred to an ophthalmologist.
DETERGENTS Synthetic detergents (liquids) Built detergents (usually contain alkali)	Skin	Flush with water in all cases. For proprietary products, consult container or technical data sheets for their recommended safety and first aid procedures.
	Eyes	Flush immediately with forced-water eyewash for at least 10 minutes. Follow product safety procedures. See an ophthalmologist as soon as possible.
BLEACHES Sodium hypochlorite Calcium hypochlorite Trichloroisocyanurates Hydrogen peroxide Sodium perborate Dimethyl hydantoin	Skin	Flush immediately with water for at least 10 minutes. Reddening of the skin is usually evident even with short exposures. After flushing, dress the affected area as for a thermal burn. Burns are often slow healing.
	Eyes	Flood eyes immediately with water for at least 10 minutes by using a forced-water eyewash. Do not use neutralizing solutions. Consult an ophthalmologist even when no burning sensation persists.
SOURS Ammonium silicofluoride Sodium silicofluoride Acetic acid Oxalic acid Acid fluorides	Skin	Flush immediately with water and wash with 1% sodium bicarbonate (baking soda) solution and then with soap.
	Eyes	Flood eyes immediately and continuously for at least 10 minutes. Do not use any neutralizing solution. Consult an ophthalmologist.
OTHER Antichlors Mildicides Softeners Bacteriostats Brighteners Solvents	Skin	Flush with water in all cases. For proprietary products, consult container or technical data sheets for their recommended safety and first aid procedures.
	Eyes	Flush immediately with a forced-water eyewash for at least 10 minutes. Do not use any neutralizing solution in the eyes. Some exposures, even if not painful or burning, should be examined by an ophthalmologist.

Adapted from Cohen, H. and Linton, GC. Chemistry and Textiles for the Laundry Industry. *New York: Textile Book Publishers, 1961.*

diately with water. Softener should only be used for towels or personal clothes and NEVER on uniforms.

A trained individual with the proper safety garments is the only person who should change laundry products or come in contact with them. The chemical lines should be checked for leaks at least every four to six months and changed every year or so. This should be done only by a trained individual. Chemical lines and chemicals should be placed in an area close enough to the washing machines yet far enough so that washroom personnel don't come into casual contact with them.

Chemical drums should be disposed of in one of two ways. First, they should be emptied as far as possible through use. Then, the product left, if usable, should be dumped into the next container by the chemical company representative. The chemical representative should then remove the drum from the premises. The other way is to use the product to its fullest, then fully wash out the drum in an open area that drains into a sewer. The proper way to do this is to run water in the area, and then clean out the drum of its residual product. In some cases, this is not permitted—check with your chemical representative prior to disposal. Once the drum is thoroughly washed, it can be disposed of through normal channels.

STAIN REMOVAL

Stains are best removed from athletic clothing immediately after they occur. Allowing a stain to remain on a fabric untreated allows the stain to set deeper into the clothing fibers, therefore making it more difficult to remove. Always launder the garment first, since most affected areas will come clean through normal washing. If the stain remains, try using a stain remover.

Stain removal differs from laundering in that each stain receives individual attention and remedy. Selecting the right stain remover for the correct stain is sometimes difficult, but certain guidelines will help.

There are many different types of stain removers. Solvents, enzymes, emulsifiers, bleaches, strippers, wetting agents, and detergents are all commonly used. Some stain removers work quickly, whereas others require long exposure. Some work best as soaks or pre-treatments; others must be scrubbed in or sprayed on each individual stain. Selecting the right stain remover is done by two primary criteria: identifying the stain's source and the fabric type.

Federal law requires that all manufactured garments, with few exceptions, include a tag sewn in the garment that gives proper fabric care. These tags should always be consulted before any stain remover is applied. Applying improper chemical stain removers can damage many garments.

Before adding a stain remover to clothing, experiment with it to see if it will damage the fabric. By putting the stain remover on an unseen area of garment (inside seam, hem, etc.), the color fastness or possible damage that the stain remover may cause can be determined. Chemicals should always be applied on a clean working surface. Painted or colored tabletops should be avoided, as many stain removers will damage the surfaces on which you are working.

In athletic laundry rooms, many of the same principles of laundering apply to removing stains. Similar colors and similar stains should be separated to ensure consistent results. It is best to look for stains after washing but before drying clothes, as heat will cause stains to set even deeper, often making them impossible to remove.

Many stains that occur in athletics are fairly unique. Grass, clay, eye black, sideline drinks, pine tar, helmet paint, blood, adhesive tape, tobacco, shoe polish, and perspiration are just a few of the stains that might grace uniforms or practice clothing. Because of the vast array of potential stains, establishing stain removal treatment priorities is beneficial.

When first trying to remove a stain, apply a mild solvent or detergent with a cloth or sponge. Use common sense when determining the concentration of these solvents. It is always best to begin with weak doses, adding more solvent or detergent as necessary.

If one solvent or detergent has no effect on the stain, rinse the garment thoroughly and try another stain remover, or increase the concentration of the original solvent. Stain removers should never be mixed without knowing how they react. Also, always rinse the fabric thoroughly between applications of different stain removers. If the second application of solvent or detergent doesn't do the job, proceed to using more active stain removers such as enzymes, emulsifiers, or other solubilizers. Alternatively, try lightly scrubbing the area to see if this action will help lift the stain.

In most cases, when using a programmable washer, there is no need to scrub fabrics. Most programmable washers are programmed with at least one pre-rinse cycle to remove loose or dried dirt prior to the main wash. In some cases, two or three rinse cycles may be required. It is highly recommended that a pre-rinse program be installed when possible. The pre-rinse does not have to exceed two minutes per wash.

When a programmable washer is not available, scrubbing and soaking may be required. The major problems with scrubbing and soaking are that scrubbing will damage the fabric over time and soaking could potentially allow the colors to bleed. Scrubbing and soaking will also add many hours of labor. Actually, the term "scrubbing" is misleading. It is never appropriate to "scrub" laundry. Scrubbing laundry puts undue stress on the material and will cause wear zones. These areas will pill and get thinner from the abrasiveness of scrubbing, even when done with a clean rag.

When presented with a stain that requires additional work or a stain that needs to have a chemical set into the fabric, the first step is to always set a clean white cloth or towel down, then lay the uniform over it. This will ensure that the uniform does not collect any debris from the work surface. Then, with another clean white towel, gently rub over the area of the stain with little pressure on the garment. Do not use a brush, as this could cause irreparable harm to the fabric. What one is trying to do is to get the chemical to absorb into the fabric rather than cleaning the fabric with the chemical at that time. Most chemicals used in this fashion require a setting time of one-half to one hour at the minimum. The garment is then washed in an abbreviated wash to remove the chemical and wash out the stain from the garment.

Most athletic clothing manufacturers do not recommend using bleaches and strippers—they should be used only as a last resort, and only with great care. Successful stain removal implies removing stains with little or no fabric damage, and bleaches and strippers can often cause more fabric damage than the stain itself. Even so, if used properly, bleaches or strippers are at times functional in removing certain stains.

Many stain removal guides or charts are available. Table Four on page 120 lists a few common athletic stains and their remedies, compiled from several sources. For

TABLE FOUR

SOME COMMON STAINS AND THEIR TREATMENTS

STAIN	TREATMENT
Adhesive Tape, Chewing Gum, Cement	First, dry for three minutes at low heat, then dab the affected area with duct tape. If this doesn't work, apply ice or cold water to harden the area and scrape with a dull knife. Saturate the area with cleaning fluid, rinse, then launder.
AstroTurf and Cleat Stains	Generally, these stains are not removable because they are burned into fabric through friction. Treatment with solvent or oxygen bleach may lighten stain somewhat.
Athletic Tape or Carpet Tape	Treat the same as adhesive tape. Tape remover solvent may be used, but can damage certain types of printing or lettering on uniforms.
Beverages (coffee, tea, soft drinks, etc.)	Sponge or soak the stain in cool water. Then, pretreat the area with pre-wash stain remover, liquid laundry detergent, or paste of a granular laundry product and water. Launder using chlorine bleach, if safe for fabric, or color-safe (oxygen) bleach. Older stains are more difficult to remove, but may respond to soaking in a product containing enzymes, then laundering.
Betadine	Launder. Betadine washes out readily, and generally is not a source of stains. Never apply chlorine bleach to betadine; it will react, causing severe fabric damage.
Eye Black/Grease	Treat with a stain remover with a high alkali content and a rubber emulsifier.
Mildew	Badly mildewed fabrics may be damaged beyond repair. Launder stained items using chlorine bleach, if safe for fabric, or soak in oxygen bleach and hot water, then launder.
Mud	When dry, brush off as much as possible. Launder as usual, yet make sure that you have at least a three- to four-minute pre-soak on your wash cycle. This will allow the removable and soluble particles to wash away prior to using detergents.
Paint	Water-based: Rinse fabric in warm water while stains are still wet, then launder with high alkali wash ±4000 ppm. This will dissolve most paints. This should be tested on older fabrics prior to using on new uniforms, to test their color fastness. Once paint is dry, it can rarely be removed. Oil-based and varnish: Use the same solvent as the label on the can advises for a thinner. If label is not available, use turpentine in an unseen area to test. Rinse and launder.
Perspiration	Use a pre-wash stain remover or rub with bar soap. If perspiration has changed the color of the fabric, apply ammonia to fresh stains, white vinegar to old stains, and rinse. Launder using hottest water safe for fabric. Stubborn stains may respond to washing in a product containing enzymes or oxygen bleach in hottest water safe for fabric.
Pine Resin	Sponge cleaning fluid into the stain; let dry. Mix liquid laundry detergent and ammonia; soak stain in the solution. Launder using liquid laundry detergent.
Pine Tar	Treat the same as pine resin.
Red Clay	Clay is a dye and thus must be treated with a dye remover. The best product is one with titanium sulfate as a major ingredient.
Scorch	Treat as for mildew. Launder using chlorine bleach, if safe for fabric. Or soak in oxygen bleach and hot water, then launder.
Shoe Polish	Liquid: Pre-treat with a paste of granular detergent and water; launder. Paste: Scrape residue from the fabric with a dull knife. Pre-treat with a pre-wash stain remover or cleaning fluid. Rinse. Rub detergent into dampened area. Launder using chlorine bleach, if safe for fabric, or oxygen bleach.
Sideline Drinks	Treat the same as beverages.
Tobacco	Dampen stain and rub with bar soap. Rinse. Soak in a product containing enzymes, then launder. If stain remains, launder again using chlorine bleach, if safe for fabric.
Urine, Vomit, Mucous, or Feces	Soak in a product containing enzymes. Launder using chlorine bleach, if safe for fabric, or use oxygen bleach.
Blood	Most standard detergents take out blood. Launder at temperatures above 110°F.

APPENDIX A

GLOSSARY

Abrasion Resistance—Degree to which a fabric is able to withstand surface wear and rubbing.

Absorption—Ability of a porous solid to hold, within its body, gases or liquids.

Acid Dye—A type of dye requiring acid environment during application, used for dyeing animal fibers.

Acid Number (Acid Value)—The measure of the amount of free acid in a substance, expressed as the number of milligrams of potassium hydroxide required to neutralize one gram of substance.

Activated Carbon—Carbon specially treated to give it the property of attracting and holding dissolved substances in dry cleaning solvent.

Adsorption—Taking up of a substance by a solid or liquid surface.

Affinity—The attraction of one substance for another, as a textile fiber for a dye.

Agglomerate—To coagulate or bunch particles into larger masses.

Air Permeability—Ability of a fabric to allow air to pass through it as determined by its porosity. Air permeability is a factor in the warmth of blankets, etc.

Amine—A compound that may be regarded as a derivative of NH_3 (ammonia) in which one or more of the hydrogen atoms have been replaced by hydrocarbon radicals.

Anhydrous—Free from water, as in anhydrous metasilicate.

Aniline Dye—A type of dye derived chemically from aniline or other coal tar derivatives.

Antimycotic—Having the property to minimize the growth of mold or mildew.

Antiseptic—A substance that is generally applied to living tissue that prevents or arrests the growth of microorganisms either by inhibiting their activity or destroying them.

Antistatic—Able to disperse electrostatic charges on a fabric and prevent buildup of static electricity.

Aseptic—Free of microorganisms capable of causing infection.

Aspergillus Niger—A type of fungi responsible for the development of mildew in fabrics.

Atmospheric Fading (Gas or Fume Fading)—Fading of some dyestuffs through exposure to certain gases given off during the burning of fuels.

Basic Dye—A type of dye capable of coloring silk and wool directly but requiring an assistant on cotton. Though they produce a very bright color, such dyes are little used because of their poor color fastness.

Bentonite—A colloidal clay capable of absorbing large quantities of an oily soil.

Bichloride of Mercury—Sometimes referred to as "bichloride" or "corrosive sublimate." A poisonous, corrosive salt of mercury used chiefly in pharmaceuticals and antiseptics. It frequently attacks and tenders cottons and linens, and the damage does not appear until the textiles are laundered.

Biodegradable—Capable of being decomposed by natural biological processes.

Bleach Bath (Bleach Suds)—Addition of bleach in a washing formula.

Bleaching in Clear—Bleaching under conditions where minimal amounts of soil, chemicals, etc., remain in solution.

Bleaching Intensity—The quantity, concentration, time, and temperature of bleaching.

Bleed—To lose dye from a colored fabric during laundering or dry cleaning; can be caused by improper cleaning methods, dye application, or excess surface dye.

Body—The compact, solid, or firm feel of a fabric.

Boiling Point—The temperature at which a substance passes from the liquid to the vapor state.

Bolt—A roll of length of fabric.

Bonding—A process of pressing fibers into thin sheets of webs held together by adhesive chemicals.

Borax—A weak and sparingly soluble alkali, known chemically as sodium tetraborate.

Break—First addition of alkali in a washing formula.

Break Compound—Any washroom supply used in the break or initial operation in the washing formula.

Broadcloth—A fine, rich looking, closely woven cotton fabric, usually mercerized. Most dress shirts are broadcloth.

Brownian Movement—A ceaseless movement of ultra-microscopic particles of colloidal nature, first observed by an investigator named Brown. This movement is important in detergent processes and is exhibited by soap and other colloidal substances.

Brush—To finish knitted or woven fabrics by raising a nap on them with circular brushes.

Buffer—Substance or mixture of substances that in solution maintain a constant hydrogen ion concentration despite addition of comparatively large amounts of acid or alkali.

Building—The use of an alkali to enhance the detergent efficiency of a soap/detergent solution.

Bursting Strength—The pressure required to rupture a fabric.

Calico—A coarse printed cotton fabric, usually made from low-grade cotton and heavily sized.

Carbonate—An alkaline chemical salt in which carbonic acid is the neutralized acid.

Carboxymethylcellulose $[C_6H_7O_2(OH)_2OCH_2COOH]_n$—Used as a surface active agent.

Carboy—A container, often encased in a protective covering and usually used to hold from five to 15 gallons of a corrosive liquid.

Carryover (Carryover Suds)—A cleaning step in a laundry formula in which no supplies are added, but supplies previously added are retained for use.

Catalyst—A substance capable of speeding up a chemical reaction. It can be recovered practically unchanged at the end of the reaction.

Causticity—The amount of free alkali or hydroxyl ion liberated when alkaline salts are dissolved in water.

Caustic Potash—See Potassium Hydroxide.

Caustic Soda—See Sodium Hydroxide.

Celsius—A temperature scale in which the freezing point and boiling point of water, under standard pressure conditions, are designated as 0 degrees and 100 degrees, respectfully. Indicated by the letter C after the stated temperature. Conversions from Celsius to Fahrenheit can be conducted with the following equation: $C=5/9(F-32)$, so that 0 degrees C corresponds to 32 degrees F and 100 degrees C to 212 degrees F.

Centigrade—See Celsius.

Centrifugal Force—The force that tends to propel a thing or its parts outward from a center of rotation.

Chaetomium Globosum—A microorganism responsible for the development of mildew in textile fabrics.

Charge—To incorporate cleaning or other supplies into dry cleaning solvent.

Charged System—A method of cleaning, employing dry cleaning solvent to which has been added a quantity of detergent for improved cleaning.

Chelate—To tie up or render certain substances inactive.

Chelating Agent—A substance that has the ability to tie up and render certain substances, such as hardness salts, iron, etc., inactive in water.

Chino—A particular type of all-cotton khaki (colored army twill made of combed two-ply cotton yarns).

Chintz—Pertaining to a glazed cotton fabric often printed with gay figures and large lower designs.

Chloride of Lime—A low grade of calcium hypochlorite assaying 35 percent available chlorine.

Chlorite—The bleaching agent sodium chlorite.

Chrome Dye—A type of dye that uses a chromium compound as a mordant or assistant.

Clarify—To remove foreign matter and soluble impurities from a solvent, usually by distillation or filtration.

Classify—To separate goods according to degree of soil and resistance of fabric and color to physical and chemical attack.

Cleaning Cycle—The total time from the beginning to the end of a complete round of cleaning operations.

Clearing Agent—A material added to lower the cloud point of a liquid detergent product.

Cloud Point—The temperature at which a nonionic detergent or wetting agent, in solution, tends to become cloudy with consequent decreased solubility and effectiveness.

CMC—See Carboxymethylcellulose.

Coagulate—To clot or consolidate into a mass. The solidification of egg white by boiling is an example.

Coalesce—The tendency for smaller droplets of a liquid to form one larger drop. In a good emulsion, coalescence does not occur.

Colloidal—State of subdivision of matter in which particles of 100mu are dispersed in a continuous medium.

Color Buildup—Accumulation of loose or non-fast dyes and other coloring matter from fabrics in a cleaning solvent.

Colorimeter—An optical instrument for measuring color intensity used to evaluate and standardize a colored solution.

Combed Yarn—A cotton yarn that has been subjected to a special combing operation to further remove short fibers and remaining impurities after the carding operation. This added process produces finer, smoother, and stronger yarns.

Compatible—Capable of being used in conjunction with other materials without loss of essential properties.

Condensate—The purified substance, usually water or solvent, formed as a result of a condensing or distilling action.

Condense—To reduce from one state to another and denser form, as steam to water. Also, to compress or compact.

Condition—To prepare goods for ironing or pressing by running in a tumbler until desired moisture retention is reached.

Construction—The number of yarns per inch in warp and filling in a fabric; e.g., 60 x 52 means 60 yarns per inch of warp and 52 yarns per inch of filling.

Contact Stain—A stain acquired by a textile touching a staining surface or another textile and picking up color.

Corduroy—A coarse, durable fabric having a piled surface raised in cords, ridges, or ribs.

Count—See Yarn Count.

Coupling Agent—A substance soluble in both water and in material to be emulsified that improves the stability of an emulsion.

Crease Resistant—A fabric with high resistance to wrinkling or creasing and good recovery from wrinkling. Often obtained by chemical finishing as in durable press.

Cretonne—A drapery or slip cover fabric, usually printed, similar to chintz, but without the glaze.

CRF—Abbreviation for crease resistant finish.

Crimp—To apply a wavy appearance to a fiber of yarn by means of a twist or mechanical application.

Crock—To rub off loose dye from a fabric onto another in contact with it. May also be a container for chemicals.

Cross-Infection—An infection that is acquired from a contaminated environment.

Crowsfeet—Indistinct wrinkles in a fabric.

Crystal—A physical shape or form of matter that conforms to a definite geometric pattern.

Crystalline—Being in the form of crystals. A material that is not crystalline is amorphous.

Culture—A growth of microorganisms on a nutrient medium; to grow microorganisms on such a medium.

Cure—To set a resin finish in treated fabric by converting it to the insoluble form by heat.

Cut Pile—Fabrics such as velvets, plush, or corduroy where pile surface is produced by cutting yarns, either warp or filling, that were originally woven in loop form.

Damask—A type of fabric usually in cotton or linen, in which the figures are formed by contrast between warp and filling yarns. The figures appear reversed on the "wrong" side.

Decompose—To break up into simpler component parts by heat or chemical action; for example, the decomposition by heat of sodium bicarbonate into soda ash and carbonic acid.

Degrease—To remove greases and oils from garments prior to laundering or dry cleaning with detergent and water.

Deleterious—Harmful or destructive, as in the action of strong acids on fabrics.

Deliquesce—The act of a solid turning to a liquid due to the absorption of atmospheric moisture.

Denier—The weight in grams of 9,000 meters of fiber or yarn. The lower the denier number, the finer the yarn.

Density—The weight of a substance per unit of volume. With dry products, it is generally expressed as pounds per cubic foot; in liquids, as pounds per gallon.

Deodorize—To destroy or mask odor.

Deposit—To settle upon, as lime soap on a wash-wheel.

Desiccate—To remove moisture, to dry.

Desize—To remove the sizing from textile fabric.

Desizing Agent—A compound that has the capability of removing sizing from textile fabric. Some enzymes are excellent desizing agents.

Diatomaceous Earth—Dirt made up of the hard skeletal remains of microscopic plants called diatoms. Commonly used in filter powder.

Diffuse—To spread or penetrate rapidly throughout.

Dimensional Stability—Ability of a fabric to retain its shape and size after being subjected to wear, washing, and dry cleaning.

Direct Dye—A type of dye used primarily to dye cotton and rayon, for which it has good affinity.

Dirt—Foreign matter out of place, such as soil or stains on fabric.

Disinfect—To free from infection; usually with a chemical agent that destroys disease germs or other harmful microorganisms.

Disinfectant-Detergent—A chemical compound formulated to disinfect while it cleans.

Disperse—To scatter finely divided particles in such a manner that the individual particles are not visible to the naked eye.

Distill—To purify a liquid, such as one contaminated dry cleaning solvent, by boiling, condensing, and collecting its vapors.

D.P.—Abbreviation for durable press.

Drill—A stout-twilled cotton fabric.

Drip Dry—See Wash-and-Wear.

Dry Side—Pertaining to cleaning or spotting agents that will dissolve in dry cleaning solvents but not in water.

Duck—A dense, heavy cotton fabric usually having two warp yarns woven as one. Lighter weights are used for service coats and uniforms; heavier weights for tents, awnings, tarpaulins, aprons, and wherever unusual strength is required.

Durable Press—A long-lasting finish applied to textile fabrics to improve their crease and wrinkle resistance. Synthetic resins are normally used for this purpose and are usually applied to cotton fabrics or blends of cotton and polyester.

Dye (Dyestuff)—Complex chemical coloring matter having an affinity for textile fibers.

Elasticity—The ability of fibers, yarns, woven, and knit fabrics to return to their original shape after being stretched.

Electrolysis—A decomposition caused by an electrical current.

Electrolyte—A solution that will easily conduct electricity.

Elongation—Lengthening or stretching of a textile fiber, yarn, or thread by a force applied to it. It is expressed as a percentage of the original length.

Emulsification—Method of dispersing one immiscible liquid in another.

Enzymatic Action—The splitting up of fats, oils, proteins, and sugars by enzymes.

Enzyme—A complex protein formed by living organisms that is capable of increasing the speed of some decomposition reactions.

Esterification—A process of producing an ester by reaction of an alcohol with an acid.

Eutrophication—The process by which a body of water, as a lake, becomes rich in dissolved nutrients with consequent oxygen deficiency. Eutrophication may occur by natural means or by artificial means such as contamination by fertilizers.

Extensibility—Length gained by stretching a fiber, yarn, or thread to the breaking point. It is expressed as a percentage of the original length.

Fabric—A system of textile fibers produced first by building yarns and then weaving or knitting them.

Fade-ometer—A standard laboratory device for testing the fastness of a colored fabric to sunlight.

Fahrenheit—A temperature scale on which the freezing point and boiling point of water, under standard pressure conditions, are designated as 32 degrees and 212 degrees, respectively. Indicated by the letter F after the stated temperature. Conversions from Fahrenheit to Celsius can be conducted with the following equation: $F=9/5C+32$, so that 32 degrees F corresponds to 0 degrees C and 212 degrees F to 100 degrees C.

Fast color—A color that when applied to a fiber will not fade or change shade by exposure to sunlight, washing processes, or body wastes.

Felt—To shrink wool fabrics with accompanying interlocking of the fibers.

Filament—A fine, continuous fiber, such as silk, rayon, polyesters, or nylon.

Filler—A material added to soap or other detergent that does not improve its effectiveness under the conditions of use.

Film—A thin coating, layer, or membrane. Colloidal films play an important role in emulsification and absorption.

Flame Retardant (Flame Resistant)—Pertaining to fabric treated or impregnated to resist burning. Also, a chemical compound capable of imparting flame resistance to fabrics.

Flammable—Capable of being easily ignited and burned.

Flash Point—The lowest temperature at which the vapors of a liquid decompose to a gaseous mixture that can be ignited.

Flatwork Ironer Rolling—The rolling that occurs, under certain conditions, to the edges of flatwork when they pass through a chest-type ironer.

Fluorocarbon—A class of highly volatile solvents similar to perchloroethylene, except that they contain fluorine atoms in place of chlorine in their chemical make-up.

Foam/Foaming Agent—A colloidal phenomena involving an air-liquid colloidal system. A material that increases the stability of this colloidal phenomenon.

Fray—To wear out due to rubbing or friction.

Fugitive (Color)—A color that has poor affinity for the fiber to which it is applied and has a tendency to bleed, run, or be washed away entirely.

Fused Fabric—A resilient two-layer collar or cuff bonded together by an intervening solid film or binder.

Gas Fade—To fade or change color because of contact with gas fumes in the air.

Germicide—Anything that destroys germs (microorganisms); usually used in reference to agents that kill disease germs.

Gingham—A yarn-dyed cotton fabric usually woven in checks or stripes.

Globule—A small drop of a liquid or particle of solid.

Glyceride—A chemical compound composed of fatty acids and glycerine. When reacted with strong, hot caustic, it forms soap and glycerine.

Go-Back—An improperly laundered or dry cleaned piece sent back for re-cleaning.

Gravity (Specific)—The relative weight of a certain volume of a solid or liquid compared with the weight of the same volume of water.

Gray—Dull appearance of fabric color due to re-deposition of soil or dye from wash water or solvent.

Grease—A general name for oily solids.

Greige (Grey)—Pertaining to fabric as produced by weaving or knitting prior to dyeing, bleaching, or finishing. It usually contains sizing or other finishes that are subsequently removed.

Greige Goods—Unbleached fabric, such as unbleached muslin or sheeting.

Gum—A sticky, viscous, water-soluble substance exuded from various trees and plants. The substance hardens on exposure to air.

Hemoglobin—The pigment of blood. It contains 0-4 percent iron and is a common source of staining.

Hand—The feel of fabrics such as "soft," "harsh," or "boardy."

Heat-Set—Pertaining to the stabilization of synthetic fabrics to ensure no change in size or shape.

High Light—A lustrous or shiny area appearing on the surface of a starched fabric.

High Tenacity—Referring to yarn of high strength.

Humidity—The amount of moisture in the atmosphere.

Humidity (Relative)—The percentage of moisture in the air as compared with the total amount of moisture that the air can hold at the same temperature.

Hydrate—To combine with water. Also, a chemical compound formed by the union of water with some other substance.

Hydrogen—A colorless, odorless, tasteless gas that is flammable and lighter than most other known substances.

Hydrogenation—A process in which hydrogen is added to the unsaturated portion of fats or oils to make them more solid and resistant to oxidation.

Hydrotrope—Hydrotropes act as solubilizers and coupling agents for otherwise incompatible materials. They help overcome turbidity or stratification in aqueous solutions containing a sparingly soluble oil or solid. They also act as cloud point depressors for light-duty liquids. Examples would be sodium or potassium toluene sulfonate.

Hygienic—Pertaining to the preservation of health. It requires sanitary conditions.

Hygroscopic—Capable of absorbing atmospheric moisture readily.

Hymolal Salt—A term used to designate the sulfated fatty alcohols that are derived from the higher-chain alcohols and have soap-like properties.

Industrial Clothing (Fabrics)—Clothing for wear in industry rather than for apparel and household use.

Infection—Invasion by pathogenic organisms, which multiply and cause disease.

Infection-Control Chemicals—Any chemicals that are used to prevent cross-infection.

Infectious—Having the ability to transmit disease.

Insoluble—Incapable of being dissolved.

Interfacial Tension—The surface tension existing between two liquids or a solid and liquid that keeps the liquids form mixing or a liquid from spreading on a solid. Soap lowers the interfacial tension between water and some soils and thus allows the soil to be flushed away.

In Vitro—Referring to the testing of antibacterial properties "in glass," as in test tubes, with no interfering material present.

In Vivo—Testing of antibacterial properties "in life" usage where practical contaminants and denaturants are present.

Iridescent—Pertaining to fabrics that have contrasting colored warp and filling yarns.

Keratin—Principal constituent of cuticle, hair, hoofs, and feathers. Very rich in sulfur.

Kier—A mechanical device in which cotton fiber or fabrics are boiled out to remove the natural impurities.

Kier Boil—A treatment for the removal of deep-seated stains. The fabrics are boiled in a solution of alkaline detergent and soap in an open tank, preferably provided with a steam injector for continuous circulation.

Laminated—Pertaining to fabrics composed of layers of cloth joined together with resin.

Latent Alkalinity—Alkalinity present in the water supply.

Lecithin—An organic fatty material containing nitrogen and phosphorus found in practically all animal tissues and in some vegetable matter, chiefly the seeds of plants.

Level—The height of the water or solvent inside the cylinder of the wash wheel when the machine is loaded and in motion.

Liberate—To set free, as in to liberate chlorine or oxygen in bleaching.

Lime—Calcium oxide or hydroxide.

Lint—Short fiber produced and loosened by mechanical action or the action of chemicals in the cleaning process.

Lipase—A fat-splitting enzyme.

Luster—The shine occurring on or imparted to fibers, yarns, or finished fabrics.

Mercerizing—A process wherein cotton yarns are held under tension while being passed through a caustic soda solution. The resulting yarn is strong and lustrous.

Micelle—A special grouping of a number of molecules of a chemical substance, such as a detergent, held loosely together by chemical bonds.

Mill—A unit equal to 1/1,000 inch that is used for measuring the diameter of textile fibers.

Mild Charge—Low concentration of detergent in dry cleaning solvent; usually one-half to 2 percent.

Mileage (Solvent)—The number of pounds of clothing that can be cleaned with one gallon of solvent.

Mineral Spirits—Petroleum solvents.

Moire—Pertaining to fabric having a grain or wood effect produced during finishing.

Moisture Retention—Amount of moisture, usually expressed as percent of textile dry weight, that a load of laundry retains after washing and extraction.

Monofilament—A single filament yarn.

Mordant—A chemical agent applied to a textile fiber to improve the affinity of a certain dye for the fiber and make the color fast.

Mote—A small impurity that may occur in cotton yarn, such as a speck of cotton seed or other impurity from the cotton plant.

Moth Repellent—A substance that has been chemically treated to resist moth damage. Also, a chemical compound for treating fabric, usually wool, to render it moth repellent.

Muck (Filter)—The combination of insoluble soil, used solvent, and filter powder that is removed from the bags, screens, or tubes of a filter. Also called sludge.

Muriatic Acid—The commercial name for hydrochloric acid.

Muslin—A firm, plain, white cotton fabric used largely for sheeting.

Nap—Fiber ends lifted from the body of a fabric to produce a soft, downy surface.

Net—A porous bag, usually constructed of cotton or nylon, to contain garments during the cleaning process.

Nonpathogenic—Not capable of producing disease.

Nontoxic—Not poisonous; not capable of producing illness or disease.

Nonwoven—A fabric produced directly from fibers matted together instead of being spun or woven.

Nutrient—A nutritious chemical element or compound; for example, phosphate or nitrate absorbed by plants to promote growth.

One-Bath System—A dry cleaning procedure employing a low concentration of detergent where garments receive a single wash with no rinse. This is also referred to as a single-bath system.

One-Shot—A built soap or built synthetic detergent that is added to the wash wheel, usually in a single dosage.

Opacifier—A substance that imparts a white, uniform creaminess or lotion effect to a liquid detergent mixture.

Ozone—A highly active form of oxygen containing three atoms of oxygen per molecule instead of the usual two. It is usually formed by a silent electrical discharge in air and is used as an oxidizing and deodorizing agent in the purification of water.

Package Dye—To dye yarn wound on perforated spools or tubes placed in a special dyeing machine containing the dye liquor. Also, a small container of concentrated dye.

Package Plant—A plant doing a complete cleaning service with all work done on the premises.

Pad—To impregnate fabric with dye liquor or other liquid by squeezing between rolls. Also, to impregnate with liquid for a special purpose, as to pad mops, etc., with a dust-control oil.

Pad Dye—To dye fabric by first passing through a trough containing the dye and then squeezing between rollers to remove the excess.

Pastel—Pertaining to light shades of color.

Pearl Ash—Common name for potassium carbonate, an alkali that absorbs moisture from the air readily and has approximately 77 percent of the neutralizing power of soda ash, which it resembles.

Penetrate/Penetrating Agent—To wet out a fiber completely. A surfactant can be considered a penetrating agent.

Percale—A closely woven fabric, either white or colored, principally used for dresses, shirts, and sheets.

Perchloroethylene (Tetrachloroethylene)—Popular dry cleaning agent.

Permanent Finish—A finish applied to fabric that will retain its specific properties throughout the normal period of wear and maintenance.

Permanganate (Potassium)—A strong oxidizing agent. It is frequently used in stain removal.

Permeable—Able to be penetrated by fluids or gases.

Perspiration—A body excretion containing salt, albumin, fatty acids, and other constituents. It may be acid or alkaline depending on varying conditions.

Petri Dish—A round glass or plastic dish with a cover employed for growing bacteria.

Petroleum Solvent—Flammable dry cleaning solvent derived from petroleum products. Two main types are in use: one that burns at 140 degrees F and Stoddard solvent, which has a flash point of at least 100 degrees F.

Pharmaceutical—Pertaining to drug or medicinal uses. A pharmaceutical grade of chemical is one that is suited to pharmaceutical use.

Photomenter—An optical instrument for measuring the light reflectancy of surfaces. Used in determining whiteness, soil removal, and color fading for laboratory control of cleaning formulas.

Physical—Pertaining to any properties or forces not chemical.

Pick—Term used for one filling thread on the loom or in the finished fabric.

Pigment—Coloring matter that, in general, has no affinity for a surface. For example, the pigments in paint have no affinity for wood, but they have an affinity for oil, so the pigments have to be dissolved in oil for the paint to work properly. Dyes, on the other hand, do have an affinity for fibers.

Pile—A pile fabric is a fabric made with yarns or fibers that stand upright from the main body of the material, such as velvet. These may be looped as in terry.

Pill—A small ball of fibers on the surface of a fabric caused by abrasion and wear.

Pine Oil—A by-product of the steam distillation of pine stumps in the manufacture of turpentine and rosin. It is used as a solvent and deodorant.

Ply—Yarn formed by twisting together two or more single strands of threads.

Polyethylene—Polymerized ethylene produced by polymerization at high pressure, resulting in a plastic film of high molecular weight. It is translucent, the lightest of all plastics, and remains tough and flexible even at low temperatures.

Polymer—The molecular chain-like structure from which resins and synthetic fibers are produced by the linking together of molecular units called monomers.

Polymerize—To link molecules together to form a polymer.

Pony Washer—Any small wash wheel. Usually used for special pieces or small lots needing careful treatment.

Poplin—A ribbed fabric, usually cotton.

Pore—The opening or space between yarns in a fabric that produces "breathing" properties. Also may refer to spaces between fibers in yarns.

Porous (Porosity)—Having minute openings that permit the passage of air or liquid through a material.

Post-Cure—The application of heat to set permanent press resins after the garment has been completely manufactured.

Potash—Common term for potassium and its compounds.

Potassium Hydroxide (KOH)—A strongly alkaline chemical used chiefly for making soap and as a reagent in chemical titrations.

Precipitate—To separate, as a solid from a liquid. Also refers to a solid substance separated from a liquid.

Pre-Shrunk—Term used to describe fabrics or garments that have been subjected to a shrinking process before being placed on the market.

APPENDIX A (CONTINUED)

Pre-Spot—To apply a cleaning or spotting compound to fabric spots or stains before cleaning.

Pressure (Detergent or Alkaline)—The total amount of alkali present for detergent use.

Primary Treatment—First stage of sewage treatment, which involves setting out of larger suspended solids by screening and sedimentation before discharge for further treatment.

Print—A general term for fabric with designs from dyes applied by engraved rollers, wood blocks, or screens.

Pure Finish—A finish in which no sizing or treatment is added to the fabric.

Quality Control—Testing and inspection of materials during manufacture of processing to assure conformance to set quality standards.

Quat (abbreviation for Quaternary Ammonium Compound)—Derivative of ammonium hydroxide or its salts, in which nitrogen is bound to four replaceable groups (usually organic radicals).

Reagent—Any substance used in a chemical reaction to detect, measure, examine, or produce other substances.

Reclaim—To recover for further use, as stained fabrics in a laundry. Also, to recover solvent from dry cleaned garments by condensing the vapors driven off during drying. Also, recovering wash water for treatment and/or subsequent reuse.

Relative Humidity (Solvent)—The amount of moisture present in dry cleaning solvent expressed as a percentage of the maximum amount that the solvent could contain at the same temperature and pressure.

Repel—To force away from, or prevent from mixing with or adhering to, as a chemical agent repels soil from fabrics.

Repellent—A chemical or substance that repels.

Residue—The nondistillable matter remaining behind after solvent distillation.

Resilient—Referring to the ability of fabrics to withstand crushing or creasing without objectionable change in appearance or shape.

Rinse Solvent—Solvent used for rinsing garments.

Rosin—An acidic material obtained from coniferous or pine trees; sometimes used to extend soap.

Rosin Soap—A soap made from rosin-containing material.

Salt—Chemically, the product of the reaction between an acid and a base. Also, sodium chloride (common table salt, brine).

Sanforizing—The trademark for a patented process for preshrinking cotton fabrics by controlled compression during manufacture. Articles made from properly sanforized cloth are not subject to appreciable shrinkage.

Saponification—Alkaline hydrolysis of an oil or fat, or the neutralization of a fatty acid to form a soap.

Saturate—To charge or furnish with something to the point where no more can be absorbed, dissolved, or retained.

Scour—To clean fibers or fabric for removal of impurities, sizing, oil, dirt, etc. in preparation for dyeing or bleaching.

Secondary Infection—A superimposed infection occurring in a host who is already suffering from an earlier infection.

Secondary Treatment—The biological treatment of sewage wastes that follows primary treatment by sedimentation.

Selvage—The natural edge of a woven fabric finished so that it will not unravel. It always runs parallel to the warp threads.

Semicolloid—A particle having only partial colloidal characteristics.

Sepsis—Poisoning caused by absorption into the blood of pathogenic microorganisms.

Septic—Causing sepsis or putrefaction; infective.

Shakeout—To straighten out cleaned goods prior to finishing.

Shrinkage—The contraction and increase in density of fibers and yarns causing a change in shape and size of textile fabric. Moisture, sudden temperature changes, fabric design, and mechanical and chemical actions promote shrinkage.

Silica—A substance known chemically as silicon dioxide. Sand is representative of silica.

Silt—A very fine suspension of mineral matter, usually found in water.

Silver Nitrate—A corrosive chemical that causes black silver stains on textiles.

Slippage—A form of textile damage that results when one set of threads slips over the opposite set. Smooth natural fibers, yarns possessing little twist, fancy weaves (floats), and wear are common causes of slippage.

Slub—A thick place in a yarn that produces an irregularity in the fabric. Filling yarns are sometimes slubbed purposely to give an irregular ribbed effect to the fabric.

Sludge (see Muck)—Concentrate in the form of semi-liquid mass deposited as a result of the treatment of sewage and industrial wastes.

Snap—The quality of a finished fabric when it possesses luster, uniformity, and unimpaired whiteness.

Sodium Hydroxide ($NaOH$)—A strongly alkaline compound used in making soaps and alkaline builders.

Soil Release—A finish applied to textiles that provides easier removal of subsequently applied soils.

Soil Repellent—See Soil Retardant.

Soil Retardant—Something that has been treated to resist soiling. Also, a chemical substance which, when applied to fabric, will enable it to resist soiling.

Soluble—Capable of being dissolved in water or solvent.

Solvent—A substance, usually a liquid, capable of dissolving other substances. It is the name usually given to the liquid used for dry cleaning garments.

Solvent (140 degrees F)—See Petroleum Solvent.

Solvent Retention—Amount of solvent that a load of dry cleaning retains after cleaning and extraction.

Specific Gravity—The ratio of the weight of a definite volume of a given substance to the weight of an equal volume of water. Temperature must be specified.

Split Rinse—A rinse of moderate temperature obtained by completely opening both hot and cold water supply valves at the same time.

Spot—To treat by hand a spot or stain with a chemical for the purpose of removing it. To position a wash wheel for opening/loading.

Squeeze Rolls—A mechanical device for applying pressure to squeeze out liquid.

Staple—The average length of a raw textile fiber that is twisted into a yarn. It may vary from one-half inch, in the case of cheaper cottons, to many miles in length as in the case of rayon filaments. In general, when comparing natural fibers of the same type, the longer the staple, the higher the quality and the strength.

Starch Lubricant—An oily or waxy material added to starch to increase flexibility.

Static (Electricity)—An electrical charge generated by rubbing unlike bodies together.

Steam Sweep—The injection of wet steam to the still, just above the liquid solvent level, to help flush out the solvent vapors.

Stearine—A glyceride composed of a stearic acid and glycerine. When tallow cools from a melted condition, stearine is the first material to solidify.

Sterile—Free of living organisms.

Stock Solution—A solution of laundry or dry cleaning supplies prepared in concentrated form for later convenient usage.

Stop Spot—To spray, splash, or pour a soil-spotting compound upon apparently heavy or tenacious soil stains prior to cleaning.

Straight Soap—Commercially pure soap containing at least 88 percent anhydrous soap.

Streak—A stain taking the form of a line on a dry cleaned garment caused by the non-volatile residue in highly contaminated solvent.

Strength Breaking—The force required to cause fabric breakage (see also Tensile Strength).

Strip—To remove dyes or stains from fabric by use of a chemical reducing agent.

Stripper—The agent used to strip dyes or stains from fabrics.

Stripping Agent—See Stripper.

Strong Charge—High concentration of detergent in dry cleaning solvent; usually about four percent.

Substantive—Self-combining or adhering tenaciously; as a dye substantive to cotton.

Suds—Addition of soap/detergent in a washing formula.

Sulfur Black—A black dye that is fast to washing but very sensitive to chlorine bleach.

Sulfur Dioxide—An irritating, gaseous compound of sulfur found frequently in the atmosphere. It is capable of causing dye fading and fabric tendering when in contact with moisture.

Sulfur Dye—A type of dye having sulfur in its basic structure with poor bleach resistance.

Sunfast—Pertaining to fabrics colored with dyes that will not fade under normal exposure to sunlight.

Supersaturate—To cause to contain more dissolved matter in a solution than is normally possible. Such solutions are unstable and readily return to the saturated state.

Surface Tension—The property of all liquids in which the exposed surface tends to contract to the smallest possible area, namely a sphere. This tendency is greatly reduced by detergents, which aid in the wetting and removal of soil from fabrics.

Surfactant (Surface-Active Agent)—A substance that alters energy relationships at interfaces, such as wetting agents, foaming agents, etc.

Swale—A stain that exhibits a wavy outline.

Syndet—Shortened form of synthetic detergent.

Synthetic Detergent—A surface active material made from synthetic organic compounds that has cleansing action similar to soap. These detergents may be anionic, cationic, or nonionic, depending upon their constitution.

Tenderize (Tender)—To lower the fiber strength of fabric by chemical or mechanical means.

Tensile Strength—The measure of the ability of a yarn or fabric to resist breaking.

Tertiary Treatment—A phase of wastewater treatment after 85-95 percent of matter has been removed following the secondary stage. It includes such processes as carbon adsorption, reverse osmosis, ion exchange, and demineralization.

Tetrachloroethylene—See Perchloroethylene.

Textile—Pertaining to the construction of yarns or knitted or woven fabrics.

Thermoplastic—Having the property of becoming soft under application of heat, specifically referring to certain synthetic resins and textile fibers.

Thermosetting—Having the property of hardening or setting with heat as certain plastics or synthetic resins.

Thixotropy—The property of a substance decreasing in viscosity upon agitation and increasing in viscosity on standing after agitation. This term is encountered mostly in soap stock tanks.

Titanium Stripper—A chemical reducing agent containing a compound of titanium used for dye or stain removal.

Titanium Chloride ($TiCl_3$)—A compound of titanium and chloride that is an active reducing agent. It is strong enough to remove many dyes, and is used as a stain remover.

Tolerance—Ability to withstand or endure without ill effects.

Top Dye—To add color to a fabric that has already been dyed to produce a greater depth or a change of shade to match the desired standard.

Total Fatty Acid (T.F.A.)—The total amount of fatty material that is obtained when a sample of fat or fatty acid is completely saponified and after acidulation, or extraction with petroleum ether or ethyl ether.

Translucent—Allowing passage of light, but diffusing it so that objects beyond cannot be clearly seen. In between transparency and opacity.

Two-Bath System—A dry-cleaning system utilizing two distinct cycles in the cleaning process; one with solvent containing detergent, the other with clear rinse solvent.

Vapor—A gas, especially from a substance that is a solid or a liquid at ordinary temperature.

Vat Dye—An extremely light and wash-fast type of dye applied to fibers in a soluble form by reducing action and then permanently set by oxidizing to its original insoluble form. Used primarily on cotton yarns and fabrics.

Verdigris—A greenish or bluish deposit of copper soap or salts formed on copper, brass, or bronze surfaces.

Viscosity—The resistance to flow exhibited by a liquid product. Viscosity in detergent practice is measured in centipoises, with water at room temperature having a viscosity of 1 centipoise. The higher the viscosity, the thicker (less fluid) the product.

Viscous—Possessing or characterized by viscosity.

Volatile—Readily evaporated.

Volatile Matter—That portion of a chemical substance that vaporizes below a specified temperature within a specified length of time.

Warp—The heavy yarns that cross lengthwise (parallel to the selvage) in a fabric and upon which the cross yarns or filling yarns are built.

Wash-and-Wear—Pertaining to fabric or garments treated with a wrinkle-resistant finish allowing them to be washed and used without pressing.

Washing Soda—A form of soda ash containing crystallized water within its molecular structure.

Wash Wheel—An industry term referring to a washing machine.

Water Conditioning—The treatment of water prior to washing to remove undesirables suspended or dissolved matter.

Waterproof—Referring to fabrics that have been treated in such a manner as to make them impervious to penetration by water. Rubber-, oil-, or plastic-coated fabrics are typical.

Weight—To apply a finish to fabric to give it increased weight.

Wet—To cover or saturate with water or solvent.

Wet Clean—To clean by washing by water.

Wet Side—Pertaining to detergents or spotting agents that are soluble and may be rinsed in water.

Wetting Agent/Wetting—A material that increases the spreading of a liquid medium on a surface.

Whiteness Retention—The whiteness reflectance of a laundered or dry cleaned fabric expressed as a percentage of the original reflectance.

Yarn—The continuous thread-like strand resulting from the spinning operation and used for weaving, knitting, or crocheting.

Yarn Count—The number of yarns per inch used in the construction of a fabric.

Zeolite—A hydrous aluminum-sodium silicate that is capable of exchanging sodium for calcium, magnesium, and other metal. It also has the capability of regenerating (reversing) itself when treated with brine (concentrated sodium chloride solution).

Zero Soft Water—Sometimes called "zero hardness." This refers to water that is free from hardness salts.

APPENDIX B

TROUBLESHOOTING GUIDE

This chapter has provided the information necessary to establish an efficient washroom operation. This appendix outlines the factors that are usually at fault when problems develop.

Poor Soil Removal

- Not enough suds baths
- Insufficient suds time
- Temperature too low
- Insufficient alkali/soap/detergent
- Overloaded wash wheel
- Improper water level
- Hard water
- Improper classifying
- Mixing soil loads
- Wrong formula being used

Poor Color (Redeposition)

- Hard water
- Overloaded wash wheel
- Insufficient alkali/soap/detergent
- Poor balance of alkali to soap/surfactant
- Too few rinses
- Cutting rinse times

Poor Color—Whites (other than Redeposition)

- Yellow/Brown
    - Iron
    - Poor rinsing
    - Undersouring
    - Not neutralizing bleach
- Yellow
    - Chlorine retentive resins
- Pink
    - Iron/bleach/brightener complex
    - Bleeding
- Green
    - Metallic salts
    - Bleeding
- Dull
    - Insufficient bleach
    - Bleach is too weak
    - Bleaching time is too short
    - Not enough flushes
    - Not enough rinses
    - Rinses too short
    - Poor soil removal

Poor Color—Colors (other than Redeposition)

- Dull
    - Not enough flushes
    - Not enough rinses
    - Rinses too short
    - Poor soil removal

Poor Stain Removal

- Too little bleach being used
- Bleach solution too weak
- Improper bleach pH
- Temperature too high or too low
- Water level too high in bleach bath
- Overloading
- Too much soil in bleach bath
- Too short a bleaching time
- Improper bleach for stain type

High Tensile Strength Loss

- Bleach too strong
- Too much bleach
- Low bleach pH
- Bleach temperature too high
- Steam on bleach bath
- Excessive mechanical action
    - Underloading
    - Stages are too lengthy
    - Too much time between filling and draining
    - Water levels too low
- Excessive use of highly alkaline builders in presence of steam or very high temperatures
- Improper souring agents

Linting/Pilling

- Excessive mechanical action
  - Underloading
  - Stages are too lengthy
  - Too much time between filling and draining
  - Water levels too low
  - Leaky wash wheel
- Short textile fibers
  - Low twist yarns
  - Rough surfaces in wash wheels, tumblers, or on flatwork ironers
  - Excessive use of bleach, low pH bleaching, or high-temperature bleaching
  - Excessive use of strong alkalies in presence of steam or very high temperatures
  - Improper souring agents

Odor in Textiles

- Hard water reacting with soap
- Fermentation of poorly soured loads
- Excessive use of sour
- Poor soil removal
- Incomplete rinsing
- Resin-treated fabrics

Flatwork Rolling

- Excess sour
- Too short a souring time
- Improper addition of sour
- Wrong type of sour
- Work too damp
- Dirty ironer chests
- Build-up or rust on ironer chests
- Cold chests
  - Improperly sized steam lines
  - Steam pressure not high enough
  - Traps not operating properly
  - Chests bound with air
- Warped chests
- Starch on chests
- Static electricity
- Improper feeding
- Lack of lubrication in fabrics
- Poorly maintained apron covers, padding, ribbons, or guide strings

Adapted from Cohen, H. and Linton, GC. Chemistry and Textiles for the Laundry Industry. *New York: Textile Book Publishers, 1961.*

APPENDIX C

FIBERS AND TEXTILES

A basic understanding of fibers and textiles used in athletic clothing is needed to ensure their proper care. Understanding their properties, uses, and functions helps in learning the dos and don'ts of fabric maintenance.

Athletic wear has changed radically in design and fabric content over the past 25 years, but there are still two basic categories of fibers—natural and man-made. Even with today's advanced technology, the comfort and feel of natural fibers such as cotton, wool, or silk cannot be reproduced exactly. Many man-made fibers, however, have certain advantages over natural fibers. The advent of polyester, nylon, and Spandex has provided lightweight, durable clothing for athletes to wear in competitive play. Further, blending fibers yields a garment offering the advantages of each fiber. Blends are very common in athletic garments and usually consist of a combination of cotton, nylon, polyester, rayon, and/or Spandex.

NATURAL FIBERS

In general terms, natural fibers are derived from nature, usually animals, vegetables, or minerals. The advent of man-made fiber technology has made many natural fibers partially or fully obsolete. With the exception of cotton, all other natural fibers make up only one percent of the total fiber market. Nonetheless, some natural fibers are still used in the athletic clothing industry. (See Table One on page 133 for more information on some common natural and man-made fibers.)

Cotton. Cotton is a member of the cellulosic fiber group. Obtained from the seed hair of the cotton plant, it is the most common natural fiber, accounting for approximately 24 percent of the U.S. fiber market (natural and man-made). It is grown in warm climates and is very plentiful to fabric producers.

Cotton offers many favorable qualities. For example, it is very comfortable to wear, it is very absorbent, and it is easily cleaned. It is also unique in that it gains strength when wet. Cotton accepts chemical treatments (permanent press, mercerization, preshrinking, etc.) and dyes readily. Because of cotton's overall versatility, many athletic garments contain cotton exclusively or to some degree.

Wool. Wool is a member of the protein fiber group. Derived from sheep hair, wool is best known for its warmth. Wool is very rare in today's athletic garments, but it is still commonly used to make letter jackets and sweaters. Wool requires delicate care and is best dry-cleaned. Many man-made fibers have slowly replaced wool, leaving about one percent of the total U.S. fiber market for wool.

Rubber. Natural rubber is derived from rubber trees and is used in the clothing industry for elastic. Technically, rubber is classified as an alastomeric fiber, or one that can be stretched repeatedly without loss of form or function. Spandex has slowly replaced rubber in many areas of the athletic marketplace, but rubber is still used in many elasticized clothing features such as cuffs, strapping, and wristbands.

MAN-MADE FIBERS

Man-made fibers are created by human technology. They account for approximately 70 percent of all fibers manufactured by American textile producers. Man-made fibers are used in a vast array of products, including carpeting, clothing, upholstery, artificial turf, ropes, and parachutes. Nylon, Spandex, polyester, and rayon are the most common fibers used in athletic clothing and equipment.

Most man-made fibers are derived from petroleum products and chemicals. Because these fibers are formed as a result of research and development, it is possible to engineer them to provide the characteristics required for the product.

For example, man-made fibers can be extruded in different thicknesses, or "denier." This is the industry's term for measuring the size of a continuous monofilament, a multifilament yarn, or cut staple fiber. Besides various thicknesses, these fibers are also made in different shapes, lengths, textures, blends, and treatments. It is their versatility and adaptability that make man-made fibers so desirable.

Nylon. The term nylon is a generic name for polyamide fibers. The DuPont Company engineered the development of nylon in the United States in the 1930s and 1940s. Since then, constant refinement and improvement have made nylon a very versatile fiber with a multitude of functional uses.

Nylon's favorable characteristics include its strength, stretch, and weight. It is the strongest common man-made fiber, which helps clothing made with nylon resist wear and tear. Because of the way it is processed, nylon has a certain amount of stretch, which adds to its comfort. Even high-denier nylon is lightweight and durable, two features that make it particularly functional for athletic wear, as well as for many other uses.

Polyester. Polyester research evolved after the discovery of nylon, and it was introduced to the United States in the 1950s. Polyester is manufactured through a system of polymerization, using petroleum derivatives, much like for nylon, but the actual polymers differ from those of nylon.

The features of polyester that make it desirable are its wrinkle resistance, blendability, low abrasive level, and "wicking" qualities. However, it has poor breathability. Polyester blends very well with other fibers. It is commonly blended with cotton and other fibers to form permanent press and easily-cared-for clothing. Polyester, although not a natural fiber, is relatively cool because of a wicking ability that can be built into the fabric. Wicking draws perspiration from the body to the exterior of the fabric, where it evaporates easily. Not all polyester fibers wick automatically, but more and more polyesters are incorporating the treatment that causes wicking.

Although nylon has higher tensile strength than polyester, polyester is more resistant to abrasions than nylon. This quality makes it more practical for certain items such as baseball uniforms. The biggest drawback of polyester is its inability to stretch, which reduces comfort.

Spandex. Spandex was developed as a substitute for rubber. Although rubber is still used regularly, Spandex has replaced rubber in many instances. For example, Spandex has recently become popular for use in many sports that require skin-tight, form-fitting clothing. Swimmers, gymnasts, speed skaters, and track and field competitors wear Spandex clothing in competition, and athletes in other sports now use Spandex girdles for extra muscle support and to prevent leg chafing.

Spandex blends well with other fabrics; it is most commonly paired with nylon and cotton. Without question, Spandex's biggest asset is its "memory," or its ability to return to its original form after being stretched. It offers strong elasticity and comfort and it's lightweight. In addition, it resists perspiration and mildew and sheds water rapidly.

When washing Spandex, always separate by colors, as it will sometimes accept dyes from other fabrics. Spandex should always be washed in warm or cool water and dried in low heat. Bleach should be avoided, because it causes Spandex to slowly decay. Always refer to care labels when cleaning or drying Spandex.

Others. Many other man-made fibers are used in athletic garments. Fibers such as rayon, acrylic, modacrylic, and polypropylene, to name only a few, are used, but not nearly to the extent of those fibers previously mentioned.

Also note that fibers do not differ between men's and women's apparel in sports. Both are generally the same material for the same type of sports. The garments only really vary in the conceptual design afforded to the user or purchaser.

In the industry, the saying goes, if you want it you can have it—just be willing to pay for it. Basically, any manufacturer will allow you the latitude to design or personalize a garment for your school constructed out of any material of your choosing. The only constraint is how much out of budget you wish to go.

APPENDIX C (CONTINUED)

TABLE ONE
USES AND CHARACTERISTICS OF COMMON FIBERS

Fiber	Chief Apparel & Household Uses	Characteristics	Precautions
		– NATURAL FIBERS –	
Cotton	Light- and medium-weight apparel and household textiles	Versatile, durable, can withstand frequent hard laundering; is easily ironed at high temps	Protect stored items against dampness to prevent mildew
Linen	Women's and children's blouses and dresses, summer suiting, handkerchiefs, table linens, and other household fabrics	Beauty and luster endure through frequent hard laundering; does not shed lint; may be more expensive than cotton; wrinkles easily unless treated to resist wrinkling; resistant to dye-type stains	For best wear, do not press in sharp creases; protect stored items against dampness to prevent mildew; for smooth appearance, iron at high temperature
Rubber	Foundation garments and swimwear	High degree of stretch and recovery; damaged by oils and light	Wash frequently with mild soap
		– MAN-MADE FIBERS –	
Silk	Light- and medium-weight apparel, accessory items such as scarves, and some expensive upholstery and drapery fabrics	Has natural luster and strength; is moderately resilient to wrinkles and readily returns to shape; dyes well; is more expensive than man-made silky yarns; some items may be carefully hand laundered	To clean most items, dry clean; protect from prolonged exposure to light; protect against moths and carpet beetles
Wool	Outerwear, light-, medium-, or heavy-weight apparel, blankets, carpets, and upholstery	Springs back into shape; requires little pressing; has great versatility in fabrics and colors	Dry clean most items; never wash woolens in hot water since moist heat and agitation, as in some laundering, will shrink and felt wool
Acetate	Light- and medium-weight apparel, drapery and upholstery fabrics, and fiberfill	Drapes well; dries quickly; is inexpensive; is subject to fume fading; has poor abrasion resistance; loses some strength when wet	Iron or press only at very low temps to prevent melting and fusing of fibers
*Acrylic	Tailored outerwear, knitted wear, pile fabrics, blankets, and carpets	Resists wrinkling and effects of sunlight; has high bulking power and soft hand; some fabrics have silky texture	Remove oily stains before washing; waterborne stains will come out easily
Anidex	Upholstery and other household fabrics; also for wearing apparel	Has high degree of stretch and recovery; stays resilient through repeated washings and dry cleanings; can be chlorine bleached	Precautions, if any, are not currently established
*Modacrylic	Deep pile and fleece fabrics	Resists wrinkling; resists chemicals; is soft, resilient, and nonflammable	Iron at extremely low temps
*Nylon	Hosiery and lingerie, sweaters, wind jackets, dresses, and carpets	Has exceptional strength and excellent elasticity; retains permanent shape; woven fabrics are often hot and uncomfortable to wear	Remove oily stains before laundering; to maintain whiteness, use any of the nylon whiteners on the market; press at low temps
*Olefin	Hosiery, seat covers for autos and outdoor furniture, and carpets	Has no water absorption; has low melting temperature	None at this time
*Polyester	Wash-and-wear apparel, often in combination with other fibers; curtains; fiberfill	Has sharp pleat and crease retention; some fabrics resist pilling; has exceptional wrinkle resistance; needs little ironing or pressing	Remove oily stains before washing; follow directions given on hang tags
Rayon	Light- and medium-weight clothing, drapery and upholstery fabrics, and some blankets, carpets, and table coverings	Absorbent; inexpensive; wrinkles easily	Launder carefully to prevent shrinkage or stretching; rayon does not withstand treatment that can be given to cotton or linen; when in doubt about the washability of garments, dry clean
*Saran	Seat covers for autos and outdoor furniture, screening, awnings, and luggage	Resists soiling and staining; resists weathering; is flame resistant but sensitive to heat	To remove stains, first blot stain, then rinse with water
Spandex	Foundation garments, swimwear, surgical hose, ski pants, sportswear	Has high degree of stretch and recovery; resists abrasion; is resistant to body oils	To machine launder, use warm water; dry on lowest heat with shortest cycle
*Vinyone	Mixed with other fibers for heat bonding	Resistant to chemicals and sunlight; nonflammable	None at this time

** In addition to specific characteristics mentioned, these fibers have the following general properties in common: moderate-to-high strength and resilience; resilience to moths and mildew; sensitivity to heat of pressing iron; dimensional stability; resistance to shrinking or stretching; tendency to accumulate static electricity in cold, dry weather; nonabsorbency; resistance to non-oily stains but retention of body oils that penetrate the fiber and are hard to remove; and pleat retention because of thermoplastic qualities.*

CLOTHING LABELS

IDENTIFICATION LABELS

On March 3, 1960, the federal government passed the Textile Fiber Products Identification Act (TFPIA). It requires, in part, that each textile product carry a label listing the generic names of fibers from which it is made. These generic fiber categories are established by the Federal Trade Commission, which can add new generic categories as needed. At present, there are 21 generic fiber categories for man-made fibers and another 21 types of natural fibers.

"The listing of fibers is made in order of percentage by weight of fiber present in the product, with the largest amount listed first, the next largest second, and so on. Fiber quantities of less than 5% must be labeled as 'other fibers' unless they serve a specific purpose in the product. Fibers that cannot be identified must be listed as x% of undetermined fiber content."[1]

This legislation was enacted to inform the consumer of the make-up of garments, and to prevent any confusion regarding fiber content. Because of the onset of many new fabrics in the 1950s, this act helped clear up the consumer's confusion when purchasing clothing.

The TFPIA includes nearly all garments manufactured for athletics. Tags with fiber content and make-up are included on everything from jocks to jerseys. Besides informing consumers of fabric make-up, these tags also help equipment managers make cleaning decisions based on fabric content; therefore, it is wise to always leave these tags intact, rather than removing them from the garment.

CARE LABELS

"Clothing care labels became mandatory on July 3, 1972. On this date, the Federal Trade Commission ruled that all wearing apparel and fabrics sold by the yard must carry a permanently affixed label giving instructions for the care of the item. The rule specifically details the items that must be labeled, as well as any exceptions. It also mandates that manufacturers follow certain guidelines in the use of these care labels.

"Labels must disclose fully, clearly, and thoroughly the regular care of the garment or fabric; inform how to wash, iron, dry, bleach, dry clean, and use any other procedures that are considered regular care; carry a warning if a usual care method appears to apply but does not; be easy to locate; be in words, not symbols; and apply to all the findings (thread, buttons, zippers, and trim) on the garment."[1]

Labels must also be visible through bagged or sealed items of clothing, or copied where visible, or written on the bag itself. Manufacturers may not include promotional terms or phrases on care labels.

Virtually all items of clothing used in athletics include care labels. With the huge monetary investment in athletic clothing, it is vital to read and understand these care labels to care for this clothing properly.

When reading care labels, remember that certain cleaning practices are considered common knowledge and are therefore not explained on each label. These include the fact that all fabrics are ironable under normal ironing conditions and all washable fabrics may also be dry cleaned, unless the label specifies otherwise. Except for instructions such as these, the label tells exactly how to care for the garment. For example, a care tag might read:

MACHINE WASH, WARM
TUMBLE DRY, LOW
DO NOT BLEACH
DO NOT DRY CLEAN

This tag explains to the consumer that the garment can be washed in a washing machine or by hand; it should be dried in a tumble dryer at a low heat setting or line dried; it cannot be bleached with either a chlorine or oxygen bleach; and it cannot be dry cleaned. Table One on page 135 provides a list of label instructions and what each means.

In addition to using specific, written instructions on care labels, many manufacturers include voluntary symbol labeling in order to avoid language barriers that arise in international trade. In some cases, colors are added to enhance directions. Red means to stop (do not use the symbol in red), amber means special care or caution is necessary, and green represents that it is okay to use the designated symbol. A bold X that appears over a symbol tells the consumer not to use the cleaning method on which it appears. Table Two on page 136 gives a rundown of the most common symbols used on care labels.

[1] Phyllis G. Tortora. *Understanding Textiles.* New York: Macmillan Publishing Co., 1987.

APPENDIX D (CONTINUED)

TABLE ONE

CARE GUIDE

This guide is made available to help you understand and follow the brief care instructions found on permanent labels on garments. Be sure to read all care instructions completely.

MACHINE WASHABLE

When Label Reads:	It Means:
Machine wash	Wash, bleach, dry, and press by any customary method
Home launder only	Same as above
No chlorine bleach	DO NOT use chlorine bleach. Oxygen bleach may be used
No bleach	DO NOT use any type of bleach
Cold wash/cold rinse	Use cold water from tap or washing machine setting
Warm wash/warm rinse	Use warm water or warm setting on washing machine
Hot wash	Use hot water or hot washing machine setting
No spin	Remove wash load before final spin cycle
Delicate/gentle cycle	Use appropriate machine setting; otherwise, wash by hand
Durable press/permanent press cycle	Use appropriate machine setting; if none on machine, use warm wash, cold rinse, and short spin cycle
Hand wash separately	Hand wash alone or with like colors
Hand wash	Launder only by hand in lukewarm water (hand comfortable). May be bleached. May be dry cleaned
Hand wash only	Same as above, but do not dry clean
Hand wash separately	Hand wash alone or with like colors
Damp wipe	Surface clean with damp cloth or sponge

HOME DRYING

Tumble dry	Dry in tumble dryer at specified setting—high, medium, low, or no heat
Tumble dry, remove promptly	Same as above, but in absence of cool-down cycle, remove at once when tumbling stops
Drip dry	Hang wet and allow to dry with hand shaping only
Line dry	Hang damp and allow to dry
No wring	Hang dry, drip dry, or dry flat only
No twist	Handle carefully to prevent wrinkles and distortion
Dry flat	Lay garment on flat surface
Block to dry	Maintain original size and shape while drying

IRONING OR PRESSING

Cool iron	Set iron at lowest setting
Warm iron	Set iron at medium setting
Hot iron	Set iron at hot setting
Do not iron	DO NOT iron or press with heat
Steam iron	Iron or press with steam
Iron damp	Dampen garment before ironing

MISCELLANEOUS

Dry clean only	Garment should be dry cleaned only, including self service
Professionally dry clean only	DO NOT use self service dry cleaning
No dry clean	NO dry cleaning materials to be used; use recommended care instructions

This care guide was produced by the Consumer Affairs Committee of the American Apparel Manufacturer's Association, and is based on the Voluntary Guide of the Textile Industry Advisory Committee for Consumer Interests.

TABLE TWO

SYMBOLS USED ON CARE LABELS

Washtub—Designates laundering or washing instructions.

EXAMPLES:

- *Machine wash in water temp of 30° C (cold)* 30° C
- *Machine wash in water temp of 102° F or 40° C (warm)* 102°F 40°C
- *DO NOT machine wash*

Square—Designates drying instructions

EXAMPLES:

- *Tumble dry; temperature settings (low, medium, high) are normally stated*
- *DO NOT tumble dry*
- *Clothing should be hung on a line to dry*

Triangle—Designates bleach instructions

EXAMPLES:

- *Clothing can be bleached with both oxygen and chlorine bleach*
- *NO chlorine bleach can be used (oxygen bleach is acceptable when needed)* CL
- *Clothing cannot be bleached with chlorine or oxygen bleach*

Hand iron—Designates ironing or pressing instructions

EXAMPLES:

- *Clothing can be ironed according to written instructions*
- *DO NOT iron garment or specified sections of garment (such as printing or embroidery)*

Dry cleaning cylinder—Dry cleaning instructions

EXAMPLE:

- *DO NOT dry clean*

WATER

The importance of water in laundry care cannot be understated. Water constitutes the single most important material used in laundry. The solvent action (ability to dissolve a wide variety of substances) of water makes it a complete and effective cleaning agent for a large percentage of soil. More substances are soluble in water than in any other solvent. Detergents and builders have been developed only to improve the cleansing of water and mechanical action.

FUNCTION

In the washing process, water is essential. Water's primary function is to dissolve all possible stains or soil. Water, however, does not dissolve every stain. In such cases, water carries cleansing agents to the wash load and takes suspended soil away from the garments. Water also provides the weight and properties that make proper mechanical action in the wash cycle possible.

NATURE

The study of water and its importance in the laundry room is largely directed to its chemical state at the time of use. Because of the omnipresence of dust, dirt, minerals, etc., water is never truly pure. Even the water we drink contains invisible matter. These impurities affect washing efficiency.

"Suspended matter can be classified into two categories: A) 'Sediment' consists of large particles that rapidly settle out in calm water. B) 'Turbidity' consists of small particles that may remain suspended for several days even in calm water. Frequently, both types are referred to as turbidity."[1]

Evaluation of the water supply plays an important role in laundry effectiveness. Therefore, each laundry water supply must be assessed and treated accordingly. A laundry representative or a local water specialist can usually improve water quality by removing impurities. The following lists impurities commonly removed from water supplies to enhance cleaning power.

Acidity. Acidity results when industrial or domestic wastes are deposited or seep into water supplies. Acid rain is a prime example of water with high acidity due to acidic vapors being released into the atmosphere. Acidity levels can be controlled by neutralizing them with an alkali, such as soda ash.

Carbon Dioxide. The presence of carbon dioxide in water reduces its alkalinity level, which lends it corrosive traits. Carbon dioxide is easily removed through aeration or degasification.

Chlorine. Even though chlorine is usually added to water because of its antibacterial qualities, it is still technically considered an impurity. Chlorine is sometimes removed to counter its inhibitive effects on softening of water.

Color. "Color is very common in surface water and is usually due to organic compounds extracted from decaying plant and animal matter. Colored water is usually removed by coagulation, setting, and filtering, the normal function of municipal water treatment plants."[1]

Hardness. The amount of magnesium and calcium salts present in water determines its hardness. Hard water is detrimental to effective cleaning because it counteracts the efforts of detergents and soaps. Many geographic areas across the country render naturally soft water; other places possess very hard water. With laundry operations, simply remember that the softer the better. Adding water-softening capabilities may be a necessity to perform cleaning services in your area. Other areas may be fortunate enough to bypass softening stages if water supplies render naturally soft water. The city or state water department can help determine the degree of hardness in a particular water supply. Testing kits for private water supplies are available from chemical supply houses and from some manufacturers of mechanical water softening equipment.

Hydrogen Sulfide. Hydrogen sulfide is a gas that smells like rotten eggs. In addition, it is also corrosive to most metals and should be eliminated before the water is used in the washroom.

Iron. Iron is picked up in water when water passes through lines that are rusty. It maintains a colorless form until it is exposed to air, resulting in a yellowish or reddish deposit on clothing. "Since the allowable level of iron for drinking water is much higher than [what is desirable] for laundry use, it may be necessary to treat for iron in the laundry. Aside from the stains produced by iron, it can accelerate the action of some chemicals such as bleach and cause textile damage."[1]

[1] Charles L. Riggs. *Textile Laundering Technology.* Hallandale, Florida: Linen Supply Association, 1979.

Organic Growths. Exposure to the atmosphere causes organic growths in water supplies. These growths cause bad odors and taste, add color, and can be hazardous to one's health. Treating water with carbon or chlorine, depending on the type of growth, and keeping water supplies covered can prevent the presence of organic growths.

Oxygen. All water contains oxygen. Because it is also active chemically, oxygen is highly corrosive to water lines. Higher temperatures increase the corrosiveness, which causes hot water lines to deteriorate before cold water lines do.

SOFTENING FOR LAUNDERING

As mentioned previously, geographic location will dictate the need for a water softener. If the water supply yields naturally soft water, you probably will not need softening equipment. If you are in an area of naturally hard water, however, being equipped with a water softener is probably a necessity.

Hard water can cause problems even before you get started. "Water hardness is attributable to the salts of calcium and magnesium and other less abundant elements of the alkaline earth group. These are troublesome because they form insoluble compounds with laundry soaps, or reduce the effectiveness of synthetic detergents. This is objectionable both from economic and performance considerations. The insoluble soaps that are formed tend to entrap soil particles in the fabric, giving rise to a condition of grayness."[1]

Quality water is a must for effective cleaning. Therefore, a supply of soft water should be ensured before the first drop is ever pumped into the washer.

There are many techniques for softening water, including lime-soda treatment, phosphate treatment, chelate treatment, demineralization, and base-ion exchange. Base-ion exchange is used by the vast majority of water softening services. It requires a water softening company to install equipment to maintain a constant supply of softening chemicals. Investing in water softening equipment is a wise decision in the long run. Ultimately, a softener will enhance cleaning power, resulting in the use of less detergent, soap, and builders. Softeners also add to the life of the machinery by removing corrosive chemicals that cause plumbing and internal machine parts to deteriorate.

[1] Charles L. Riggs. *Textile Laundering Technology.* Hallandale, Florida: Linen Supply Association, 1979.

APPENDIX F

IN-HOUSE VS. CONTRACTED LAUNDRY

The debate about using contracted laundry services or doing it all in house has gone on for many years. Many factors come into play when making this decision. Usually, the expense of hiring a laundry service is high and, in most cases, is less desirable than an in-house operation. If, however, no facility or space exists to house laundry equipment, or no work force is available to operate it, an outside laundry source may be needed.

When trying to decide whether or not to set up an in-house laundry system, it is important to initiate a feasibility study to establish the costs and advantages and disadvantages of such a system. Normally, decisions such as this are dictated by economics. If an in-house system will pay for itself in an acceptable amount of time, and funds are available for initial setup and operation, it is fiscally wise to establish such a system. This decision should be based on a comparative cost analysis over a certain time period. "A Comparative Cost Analysis: In-House vs. Contracting" on page 140 offers such an analysis of contracting your laundry needs out versus doing it in-house.

Many costs must be considered when conducting a feasibility study for in-house systems. The first expense is the initial investment. Washer-extractors commonly used in athletic laundry rooms cost $7,000 to $12,000. Dryers cost between $2,000 and $5,000, depending on their size and condition. Other expenses include the plumbing, electrical work, and venting necessary to operate the equipment. Accepting competitive bids for this labor will ensure the lowest price for the work.

Besides initial capital costs, there will also be operational costs. The added costs of water, electricity, and gas will be reflected in a higher monthly utility bill. There is also the cost of laundry supplies. Once again, representatives from laundry companies are familiar with these costs and can usually provide estimates on these expenses. Providing personnel to operate the laundry room will also mean labor costs. This can often be kept to a minimum by making laundry duty the responsibility of the coaches or managers, or by hiring student labor at a minimum wage. It is wise to include unexpected repair costs when forecasting operating expenses. Even the best equipment will eventually need minor repairs or adjustments.

The advantages of contracting laundry out includes that it assures that laundry is taken care of by professional people who are well versed in cleaning and stain removal. This can be advantageous when considering the cost of replacing damaged uniforms. Contracting eliminates the need for additional space or facility alterations that accompany in-house laundries. Also, no large monetary investment is necessary; payments can be made monthly, and only for those items that are washed. Distracting noise and humidity levels do not exist, as they do with an in-house system. Furthermore, no time is needed to train laundry personnel, and no downtime occurs because of broken equipment.

In-house laundry systems also have certain advantages. Having laundry equipment on site is very convenient; laundry can be done at any time. This is particularly important when teams are practicing more than once a day, or on weekends when most laundry services are closed. Fewer inventories are needed; because cleaning can be done any time, the clothes never leave the premises. This tends to reduce pilfering and theft. Student labor is usually available, which provides a low-cost work force. Also, items other than clothing, such as protective gear, pads, and bags can be washed with these heavy-duty machines.

Another advantage is that an in-house laundry helps to stop uniforms from being ruined in home washers, which can occur when athletes are responsible for their own cleaning. Also, uniforms can be cleaned immediately after competition, which optimizes the life of the uniform. Because laundry is easily accessible to athletes, they can wash items daily rather than tossing them in their lockers, where odors can permeate. Monetarily, the in-house system usually pays for itself over the long run, because most machines will last from 10 to 20 years with proper maintenance.

There is another basic reason you should keep your uniforms in house whenever possible: if you have a problem you can deal with it immediately rather than the day prior to the game. This will also allow you to have your uniforms set and packed for the next week, whether home or away. Lastly, by having the uniforms on-hand, you can alter and repair them as needed, rather than rushing at the last minute.

When installing an in-house laundry system, the following are some things to consider. Locate the system in a room on the ground level, with extra large doors. This allows the easiest movement of equipment in and out of the laundry room. Try to place the room where ample drainpipes already exist, and next to an outside wall to allow easy venting. Cement floors that slowly slope to a drain are best. Cement is a good anchor for the machines, and cement floor is impervious to water. A non-slip surface treatment of some type is also desirable for flooring. Place the room where noise or humidity will not affect classrooms, offices, or high-security areas. Allow plenty of space between and behind machines for easy servicing and for laundry chemicals. This is particularly pertinent when an automatic injection system is to be used.

Deciding on the size, type, and amount of machinery will require some research. Assess your needs according to the amount of laundry to be done and the time available to complete it. Obviously, less time available will demand more machinery, and vice versa. Having a washroom set up properly makes the equipment manager's job much easier. The replacement of uniforms (a major concern and a facility's biggest repetitive cost) goes down dramatically. When uniforms are treated properly, they will last many years without fading or showing wear and tear. The other area that this set-up serves is the most time consuming and costly part of caring for uniforms: the labor. With the right equipment, the labor involved in cleaning is reduced dramatically and frees up time for more pressing matters.

Wash wheel capacity is determined by its size (diameter and length) (see "Loading Guidelines" on page 105). The recommended washer-extractor for any institution that has a football, baseball, or hockey program is one that can hold no less than 50 pounds and no more than 85 pounds. It is also recommended that you have at least one smaller or "pony" washer (an 18- or 25-pound unit) for those small quick loads or loads that show up unexpectedly or after you've already started a large wash. For institutions without major sports such as those stated above the required washer would be no larger than a 65-pound unit with an additional "pony" washer. It is also recommended that, if and when room permits, you install a back-up washer to the main washer. For programs with many sports, a large washer with a "pony" will never get the job done in adequate time. Therefore, larger programs should have a minimum of three washers.

A basic principle is that for every program, you need three hours to process a load of linen. This includes the towels, personals (jocks, tees, etc.), and uniforms. Therefore, for institutions that have more than three programs on a given day, another washer is required. A prime example would be an institution that has soccer, volleyball (men's and women's), lacrosse, football, baseball, and softball. This facility should ideally have at least one large washer (85 pounds), two medium washers (50 to 65 pounds), and one "pony." Of course, some facilities do not have the area for this type of setup. The job of a good manager is to find the room for the best setup possible.

As far as dryers are concerned, a general rule of thumb is to provide twice as much drying capacity as washing capacity. That is, if a 50-pound washer is used, it is best to have two 50-pound dryers or one 75- to 100-pound dryer. This holds true because drying time per load is usually double that of a heavy wash load.

A Comparative Cost Analysis:

In-House vs. Contracting Laundry

To help illustrate the potential savings that can be recognized with an in-house laundry system, the following information provides a comparative cost analysis of an in-house system versus contracting laundry service to a professional cleaner. These figures are strictly estimated expenses and should not be used when assessing your own particular situation. Remember, everyone's laundry needs are different.

College A has chosen to have its laundry professionally cleaned by the local laundry service at the rate of 58 cents per pound, including pickup and delivery of bulk laundry, game uniforms, and towels. The college averages 450 pounds of laundry every day, for eight months out of the year. If we take an average of 30 days per month, this means that its yearly laundry bill is $62,640. College A's contract with the cleaners is for four years, resulting in a total laundry cost over that time of $250,560.

College B has decided to install an on-premise laundry system. The initial investment includes $34,000 in equipment and $3,000 in facility adaptations. Their projected yearly operational costs include an $8,000 increase in utility payments, $2,000 in labor costs, $5,000 for supplies, and $750 for any equipment repairs. This represents a $37,000 initial cost and $15,750 in yearly operational costs. After four years, college B's total laundry cost is $100,000 which equates to a yearly cost of $25,000. So, in this example, college B has saved $150,560 in laundry expenses over four years. But the equipment and facility adaptations will last far more than four years, so the savings continue to accrue even faster after that.

APPENDIX F (CONTINUED)

Of course, even if you have an in-house laundry, you may want to contract certain things out occasionally. For example, many pro teams send their uniforms out to professional cleaners. There are very few times that this is necessary. Nowadays, most stains can be removed in the wash cycle with the right chemical, programs, and equipment. There are, however, a few times, even today, when a professional cleaner should be utilized. These are when there just is not enough time or people and the equipment is not sufficient to do the job. Basically, when you have a fixed-cycle washer, you will not be able to get the job done as you wish and, thus, will need many stain removers. You will also need to do many washes, which will take up much too much time and labor. Many teams are also worried that they cannot get the job done properly. Yet, with the right chemical and washer, uniforms will and do come out nearly perfect, if not perfect.

Still, you may feel that you cannot get the job done, and that the only way to get your uniforms done properly is to send them out to a professional cleaner. When picking a professional cleaner, one must make sure that the cleaner has the right equipment. By this, I mean that you need to make sure that they have the right size equipment so that your uniforms are done in a timely fashion. You must also make sure that they have some experience in washing uniforms. Once you have selected a company to outsource your uniforms, you must give them as much information about your uniforms as possible. The most important thing you must inform them of is what type of fabric you have and any special washing instructions that the manufacturer may send. The manufacturer's specifications must be followed unless you have their permission to alter them. Without their permission, altering the specifications may void any warranty. This means that if any damage is done due to the cleaner's—or your—negligence, you may have to purchase all new uniforms rather than the manufacturer replacing the uniforms under the implied warranty.

Obviously, the decision concerning whether or not to use an on-premise laundry system varies with each particular case. When deciding, research your situation thoroughly. Assess and weigh all factors and variables. Contact professionals to acquire accurate and pertinent information. And consider all the advantages and disadvantages that accompany each alternative.

AEMA
CERTIFICATION
MANUAL
ATHLETIC
EQUIPMENT
MANAGERS
ASSOCIATION
Reference
Sections
By Dorothy Cutting

Protective Equipment Other Than Helmets and Shoulder Pads

Protective equipment is generally recognized as a viable method of preventing both initial injury and re-injury. It is used to disburse, absorb, and/or slow down the rate of energy, to deflect blows, limit excessive movement, and protect against sharp objects. To be effective, protective devices must be appropriate for the intended use and be fitted properly. They must also be specific for the age group. Equipment managers are critical in fitting, controlling access to, and supervising the usage of protective equipment.

This reference section provides a list of protective equipment other than helmets and shoulder pads, and a brief description of each piece of equipment. For a comprehensive discussion of football helmets and shoulder pads, see Chapter 4, "Fitting."

When purchasing protective equipment, try to find equipment designed to give maximum protection with the least amount of bulk. Buy best possible quality from reputable manufacturers. Always make certain you have the correct equipment for the correct sport. Follow manufacturers' directions "to the letter." Maintain equipment properly and warn participants about dangers of improper use. Routinely inspect and replace defective equipment.

The design and manufacture of protective equipment are overseen by the National Operating Committee on Standards for Athletic Equipment (NOCSAE), a voluntary organization that has developed standards for a variety of sports protective equipment. This reference section describes the primary uses and characteristics of the most commonly used protective equipment. It is not meant to be an exhaustive resource for how to use this equipment. Protective equipment for sports is constantly undergoing modifications and improvements. **Always refer to manufacturers' guidelines for the proper fitting, use, and maintenance of protective equipment.** Manufacturers can be excellent sources for information on the purpose, capabilities, and limitations of the protective equipment they make.

Chest protectors (various sports): Chest pads offer protection to the vital chest and heart areas. Chest pads are generally made of nylon wrapped around layers of foam or harder padding. Chest protectors actually protect most of the upper body and generally include a clavicle protector, extended shoulder caps and bicep muscle floaters in addition to an air-cushioned or foam pad chest protector. Chest protectors may also include a spine protector for the back.

Chin straps (sports with helmets): Chin straps perform two functions. First, they protect the chin area, with a cup that fits snugly underneath and around the chin. Second, the straps snap onto your helmet to hold it firmly on your head. That's why it's crucial to keep it centered and without slack. Helmets come with standard chinstraps, but you can buy different styles and replacement straps.

Collar pads/neck rolls (football): These attach to the back of shoulder pads to further protect the collarbone. Most manufacturers make specific models to fit their pads and offer both youth and adult sizes. You can also purchase a back plate for added protection to the back area and a sternum plate to further protect this area.

Elbow pads (various sports): Elbow pads are necessary to protect against painful bone bruises, and even fractured elbows, from falls or being hit. Elbow pads can cover the muscular part of the arm in addition to the elbow. Most elbow pads are adjustable and are secured with Velcro straps, so sizing is general according to body size. There are also varying numbers of straps available on different pads to help with adjustments. You may want to add a forearm slash pad for further protection in a sensitive, highly vulnerable area.

Facemasks/Shields (hockey and field hockey goalies/lacrosse): There are three main types of facemasks or shields used in lacrosse and by hockey and field hockey goalies:

- Wire cages—A wire cage consists of a metal or composite shield that covers the entire face area. Wire cages provide more protection and do not fog up like face shields.
- Face shields—These are generally made of a high-impact-resistant plastic that covers the front of the face. Some players choose face shields because they offer better overall vision with no wires getting in the way. Face shields tend to fog up during use, but they are often now made with fog-resistant coatings.
- Combination masks—Some manufacturers now offer the best of both designs—a mask that has a plastic face shield to protect the eyes and upper part of the face and a wire mesh to cover the lower jaw while providing some ventilation.

Facemasks/Shields (football): Football helmets come in two basic ways: with and without the mask. There is a wide array of facemasks offered, each designed to protect various parts of the face and to optimize protection for different players while still allowing them the best visibility to play their position. Manufacturers often use letters to designate the protection that a given facemask is designed to give.

- OPO—oral protection only
- JOP—jaw and oral protection
- NOPO—nose and oral protection only
- NJOP—nose, jaw, and oral protection
- EGOP—eye glass and oral protection

In order to protect the carbon steel that is generally used in facemasks, manufacturers may offer different coatings, with a premium paid for more durable coatings. Within each type of football facemask there are also many styles to help maximize needed protection while still allowing players to play their positions. These differences are usually indicated by an abbreviation, as follows:

- R (reinforced)—Refers to the reinforced bar at the top of the facemask. This strengthens the facemask and minimizes the chance of vertical spreading.
- DW (double-wire configuration)—This adds stability and strength. It also decreases the opening in the facemask so hands, fingers, and feet are less likely to strike the player's face. This design minimizes the chance of horizontal spreading, which is important for linemen and other positions where players either block or tackle and end up in the pile.
- SW (single-wire configuration)—This eliminates a bar running in the "east-west" direction. This design suits players in positions where visibility is critical.
- UB (U-bar attached)—This is often called a bull ring. As with a double-wire design, the U-bar also is designed to minimize the chances of fingers, hands, or feet striking the player's face.
- SK (skill position players)—This style of facemask is slightly larger than the others and is angled back to give players better peripheral vision.

Forearm pads (football): A variety of pads are offered to protect the hands and arms of players, usually offensive and defensive linemen who use their arms to block and tackle. These pads can provide crucial protection from the fingertips to just past the elbows.

Gloves (baseball and softball): Like the hands they fit, baseball and softball gloves come in a variety of styles and sizes. They also are geared to fit both the position and the level of play. Softball gloves are similar to baseball gloves except that they are generally larger both in the pocket and length to help players handle the larger ball.

Gloves (hockey and field hockey goalies): Hockey gloves protect the hand and wrist without loss of flexibility or comfort. Traditional gloves have all-leather construction, but modern versions incorporate Kevlar and nylon for increased strength, durability, and comfort. It is okay for gloves to be a little large, as long as the padding covers all areas of the hand and wrist.

Gloves (football): Different positions require different types of gloves. Linemen should look for gloves that are heavily padded on the top of the hand and wrist. Receivers, running backs, and defensive backs should be outfitted in flexible, soft gloves that have some tackiness (stickiness) to them.

Gloves (lacrosse): Lacrosse gloves have heavy padding on the tops of the fingers and around the wrist to protect against being hit by a stick. The palm is made of leather or a leather substrate for comfort and handling, with thick pads around it for protection. It is okay for gloves to be a little large, as long as the padding covers all areas of the hand and wrist.

Goggles (various sports): Goggles are used for eye protection. Some are shaded for protection from the sun.

Hip and tailbone pads (football): Hip pads are a must for nearly every player, but certainly those who take punishment from tackles such as running backs, receivers, and quarterbacks. Tailbone pads help protect the sensitive tailbone area of running backs and receivers, who often get hit here. Since these often extend outside the pant, you can buy them in colors to closely match your team's uniform colors. Hip and tail pads are usually sold as three-piece sets. Football pants do not have pockets for hip and tail pads, so you will have to purchase a "girdle" as well.

Knee pads (football): All football players benefit from kneepads. Most knee pads are made of vinyl-dipped foam which is lightweight, flexible, and molds to the body.

Knee pads (various sports): Kneepads are designed to prevent knee injuries and scrapes. Pads can be soft or hard shell. Pads need to be fastened securely around the leg. Pads are usually sized small, medium, or large according to body size.

Leg/Shin guards (hockey): These are mandatory to protect against hits by a puck or an opponent's stick. Shin pads range from 7 to 17 inches in length and are designed to fit over the kneecap to just above the skate top. They are sized according to the player's height. Forwards usually prefer lighter pads with less protection that allow them to skate faster. Defensemen should look for a heavier shin guard that helps protect against pucks and opponent's sticks.

Leg/Shin guards (soccer and other sports): Shin guards are made to either deflect or absorb the impact of a blow. At the same time, they should be comfortable and not interfere with a player's game. Shin guards are made from a variety of materials: fiberglass, foam rubber, polyurethane, plastic, and EVA foam.

- fiberglass is lightweight and stiff and offers excellent protection
- foam rubber is light and moldable but offers less protection
- polyurethane is slightly heavier and less moldable but offers optimal protection
- plastic is generally used in less expensive shin guards
- EVA foam or Lycra backing is commonly found on the backside of all guards for comfort

Mouth guards (various sports): protect teeth, help prevent concussions by absorbing blows to the chin, minimize lacerations to lips and cheeks, and minimize mandible fractures. Mouth guards should be flexible.

Pad sets (football): Many manufacturers offer protection systems, complete with hip, tail, thigh, and kneepads. These sets generally will save you money compared to buying the pads individually. Seven-piece sets generally include two hip pads, one tail pad, two thigh pads, and two knee pads. Three-piece sets generally include two hip pads and one tail pad combination.

Pelvic protectors/Cups and jocks (various sports): Pelvic protectors for women and cup and jocks for men protect the pelvic area from impact.

Rib pads (various sports): Several styles of rib protection are offered. They are recommended for players with sore ribs or those who take constant pounding. Many shoulder pad manufacturers sell a rib protector that extends from the bottom of their pads. These are bought by the size that corresponds to the shoulder pad size as specified by the manufacturer.

Also available are vests that use hook-and-loop closures to secure the vest, which has padding built-in to the vest to protect players' ribs. Vests are fitted by chest size, according to each manufacturer's specifications. Some models come with suspenders that then have rib protection padding at the bottom. Rib pads can be attached to shoulder pads or worn separately with suspenders; the latter are typically used when pads aren't worn but you still want to protect sensitive ribs.

Thigh pads (football): Thigh pads give protection to players who are often tackled. These pads slide into pockets in the football pants. Most thigh pads are made of molded plastic inserts, covered with foam and then vinyl-dipped.

Researched at http://www.thesportsauthority.com

What is Athletic Equipment?

Equipment is not unlike equipment managers—it varies from organization to organization, from level to level, and from team to team. Some organizations have practically unlimited budgets, where others have very stringent budgets. This reference section provides a list of possible equipment needs, including general equipment and sport-specific equipment for some of the major sports.

This list is to be used only as a guideline. Do not make any equipment purchases without first checking all current rules of the organization you are purchasing for. Coaches and athletes can be excellent sources of information when selecting styles and brands of equipment.

Most, if not all, sports have a men's and a women's team; in this Manual we are giving only a generalized list by sport. Many of the items listed below are optional. Not all items that could be requested by a coach are listed. Most items are needed for both men and women. Many of the sports listed below also have additional field or court equipment needs. Always check with coaches and/or grounds personnel for specific needs.

Most teams require home and away uniforms. Color will usually dictate which uniform will be worn at home and which one is reserved for away contests.

STANDARDIZED EQUIPMENT FOR MEN AND WOMEN

Practice Gear

- Pin and bag and/or laundry loop
- Towels
- T-shirts
- Socks
- Shorts
- Athletic supporters (cups)/sports bras
- Sweats (usually fleece)
- Rain gear
- Running shoes
- Cross-training shoes
- Sport-specific shoes
- Practice jerseys, scrimmage vests, or reversibles
- Wrist/head bands

Game Gear

- Game sweats (fleece)
- Warmup suit
- Travel suit
- Duffle(s)
- Jacket
- Hat/cap/visor

Cold-Weather Climates

- Coat and/or cape
- Boots

SPORT-SPECIFIC EQUIPMENT AND UNIFORMS FOR MEN AND WOMEN

Baseball

UNIFORM

- Jersey
- Under jersey (sleeves)
- Socks and/or stirrups
- Under socks (sanitary)
- Belt
- Pants
- Batting gloves
- Baseball shoes (cleats)

ACCESSORIES

- Whiffle balls
- Jugs™ balls
- Batting tees
- Chest protector hardware and elastic
- Pine tar
- Resin bag
- Eye black
- Bat weights
- Bat
- Bat bag
- Ball bag
- Plates
- Baseballs

PROTECTIVE GEAR

- Catcher's mask
- Catcher's helmet
- Throat guard
- Batting helmet
- Batting facemask
- Sliding shorts
- Chest protector
- Leg guards

Basketball

UNIFORM

- Shorts
- Jersey
- Shooting shirt
- Socks
- Basketball shoes
- Accessories
- Basketballs (different sizes by gender)
- Slip Nott

Cheerleading

UNIFORM

- Skirt (female)
- Pant (male)
- Sweater
- Vest/shirt

ACCESSORIES

- Pom poms
- Megaphones

Field Hockey

UNIFORM

- Jersey
- Shorts/briefs
- Kilt
- Socks
- Turf and grass shoes

ACCESSORIES

- Sticks
- Stick accessories (tape, grips)
- Balls
- Gloves
- Stick bag

PROTECTIVE GEAR

- Shin guards
- Helmet/face mask/throat protector
- Mouth guard
- Chest protector
- Leg guard/kickers
- Goalkeeper pants/girdle

Football

UNIFORM

- Home and away jerseys
- Football pants
- Game socks
- Game shoes (turf, grass, running, cross training, kickers)
- Under jersey

ACCESSORIES

- Gloves (lineman, receiving, winter)
- Girdle
- Compression shorts
- Football belt
- Hand warmers
- Kicking tees
- Helmet decals
- Helmet and shoulder pad hardware and accessories (see manufacturers' specifications)
- Replacement cleats
- Air pump for air helmets
- Wrist coaches
- Eye black
- Footballs

PROTECTIVE GEAR

- Helmet
- Shoulder pads
- Spider pads
- Girdle pads (high-rise, hip pads)
- Thigh pads
- Knee pads
- Arm pads
- Elbow pads
- Face mask
- Chin strap
- Neck rolls
- Flack jacket
- Mouth guard

Golf

UNIFORM
- Shirts
- Shorts/pants
- Socks
- Shoes

ACCESSORIES
- Gloves
- Clubs
- Bag
- Balls
- Tees

Gymnastics

UNIFORM
- Leotard
- Shoes

ACCESSORIES
- Hand grips

Hockey

UNIFORM
- Jersey
- Pants (padded, or shell with underpads [girdle])
- Socks
- Skates

ACCESSORIES
- Sticks
- Pucks
- Tape

PROTECTIVE GEAR
- Helmet
- Shield or mask
- Gloves
- Shin guards
- Neck/throat protector
- Mouth guard
- Cup and jock (men)
- Pelvic protector (women)
- Shoulder pads
- Chest protector
- Elbow pads
- Rib pads

Note: Some shoulder pads are combinations of pads called upper-body protectors

Lacrosse

UNIFORM
- Jersey
- Shorts/kilt (depending on gender)
- Socks
- Turf and grass shoes

ACCESSORIES
- Sticks
- Replacement parts for sticks (heads, handles, strings, leathers, mesh kits, handle tape, end caps, pocket nylon)
- Replacement helmet hardware and accessories
- Stick bags
- Air horns
- Lacrosse balls
- Goal nets and cages
- Clock

PROTECTIVE GEAR
- Gloves
- Arm pads
- Shoulder pads
- Rib pads
- Throat guard
- Helmet/goggles/wire eye cages
- Shin guards
- Chest protector
- Mouth guard

Soccer

UNIFORM
- Jersey
- Shorts
- Socks
- Soccer shoes

ACCESSORIES
- Soccer balls
- Captains bands

PROTECTIVE GEAR
- Shin guards
- Gloves
- Helmet
- Knee pads

Softball

UNIFORM
- Jersey
- Under jersey (sleeves)
- Socks and/or stirrups
- Under socks (sanitary)
- Belt
- Pants
- Batting gloves
- Softball shoes (cleats)

ACCESSORIES
- Replacement cleats (if not molded)
- Chest protector hardware and elastic
- Pine tar
- Resin bag
- Eye black
- Bat weights
- Bat
- Bat bag
- Ball bag
- Plates
- Softballs
- Whiffle balls
- Jugs™ balls
- Batting tees

PROTECTIVE GEAR
- Catcher's mask
- Catcher's helmet
- Throat guard
- Batting helmet
- Batting facemask
- Sliding shorts
- Chest protector
- Leg guards

Tennis

UNIFORM
- Shirt
- Shorts/skirts
- Socks
- Briefs
- Shoes

ACCESSORIES
- Racquets
- Grips
- String
- Balls

Track and Field

UNIFORM

- Tank tops
- Shorts
- Socks
- Track shoes (different for each event)

ACCESSORIES

- Hurdles
- High jump standards
- Vaulting poles
- "Pits" or padding
- Shot
- Discus
- Hammer
- Hammer gloves
- Starting blocks
- Replacement spikes
- Measuring bars
- Stop watches
- Starter's gun with blank ammunition
- Javelin

Volleyball

UNIFORM

- Jersey
- Shorts, briefs
- Socks
- Volleyball shoes

ACCESSORIES

- Volleyballs
- Nets
- Floor tape

PROTECTIVE GEAR

- Knee pads

Wrestling

UNIFORM

- Singlet
- Wrestling shoes
- Briefs
- Socks

PROTECTIVE GEAR

- Knee pads
- Head guard
- Chin strap
- Face guard

Water Sports

UNIFORM

- Swimsuit

ACCESSORIES
(DEPENDING ON SPORT)

- Buoys
- Life vests
- Water polo balls
- Wet suit
- Goggles
- Swim mask
- Paddles
- Swim cap
- Swim fins
- Pull buoys

INDEX

Made in the USA
San Bernardino, CA
06 July 2014